A Descriptive Catalogue with Checklists of the
Letters and Related Documents in the

Delius Collection
of the
Grainger Museum
University of Melbourne, Australia

Rachel Lowe

Delius Trust: London 1981

CONTENTS

APPENDICES:-

LIST OF ILLUSTRATIONS

PERCY GRAINGER AND FREDERICK DELIUS IN 1923

Photograph by Alfred Krauth, Frankfurt am Main.
Reproduced by courtesy of the Grainger Museum Board,
University of Melbourne.

concerning the friendship of Frederick Delius (1862-1934) and
Percy Grainger (1882-1961)

> You know by all the papers I have sent you, with
> Percy's 'interviews' & 'Articles' from time to
> time, how he has always spoken of you as the
> greatest living composer ...

wrote Percy Grainger's mother Rose in her letter to Frederick
Delius dated 'Dec. 13th 1918'.

That this was a true estimate of Grainger's feelings for his friend
is borne out by the letters which passed between the two men from
1907 until the older composer's death. Then, a glance at the
newsclippings Rose Grainger sent to Jelka and Frederick Delius from
1915 onwards, and with which Percy continued to keep them abreast of
events after her tragic death in 1922, shows how hard he worked to
make his friend's music known in the New World to which he had
emigrated at the outbreak of the 1914-1918 War.

In America Grainger played Delius's Piano Concerto frequently and
encouraged conductors to read and perform the more accessible scores
such as the two *Dance Rhapsodies*, the 'mood pictures' for small
orchestra and the tone poems with most audience appeal such as
Brigg Fair (An English Rhapsody) and *Appalachia (Variations on an
Old Slave Song)*. After his mother's death Grainger himself
introduced *The Song of the High Hills* to American audiences in
memorial concerts (which he also financed) in Bridgeport and New
York in 1924 and at Los Angeles in 1926.

He was well fitted to conduct *The Song of the High Hills* by then,
having rehearsed it, at Delius's request, with the choir which
performed it at the Frankfurt celebrations for the older composer's
birthday in 1923. On the other hand, his claim on several occasions,
that his own *Hill Songs* had inspired Delius to write this work, which
he completed in 1912, can hardly be substantiated, as sketches for
The Song of the High Hills date from before the turn of the century.
However, among the related documents of Appendix II is the curious
open letter of 1924 headed 'To My Fellow Composers', in which
Grainger confesses the belief that *The Song of the High Hills* is
'one of the few great works of all time'. Writing to Balfour Gardiner
twenty-one years later, on 21 October 1949 from Boston, he was to
quote the same work as an example of 'flawlessness' in music.

If Grainger's claims to have inspired *The Song of the High Hills*
are a little extravagant, it is true to say that he introduced
Delius to the Lincolnshire folk song upon which the popular
orchestral work *Brigg Fair (An English Rhapsody)* is based. Later
he introduced Delius to Grieg's piano arrangement of 'I Ola Dalom'
which inspired *On Hearing the First Cuckoo in Spring*. Again, that
this last piece (along with *Summer Night on the River*) was scored
for small orchestra and thus became the most widely known of
Delius's works was, as we see from his letter dated '5.3.1913'
(No. 93-7) also due to Grainger and his practical business sense.

1

In that same letter which urged Delius to write for small orchestra we find Grainger, who had heard (in 1912) Beecham's concert version of the Entr'acte from the opera *A Village Romeo and Juliet*, suggesting that it should be published separately from the opera; and, in following this advice, Delius produced another concert favourite, *The Walk to the Paradise Garden*.

In working so hard to promote his friend's music, Grainger may have felt himself to be, in part, repaying a debt; for, in the years before the First World War, after their first meeting in London in 1907, Delius had taken every opportunity to bring the younger composer's works to the notice of German conductors who were already sympathetic to his own music. Again, it was Delius who had secured the first hearing of Grainger's setting of the *Irish Tune from County Derry* and the Lincolnshire folk song *Brigg Fair* at the 1909 Liverpool Festival of the Musical League which, with Elgar, he had founded for the promotion of music by British composers. Then, in 1923, as Grainger tells us in his essay 'About Delius' contributed to the 1950 Bodley Head reprint of *Delius* by Peter Warlock (Philip Heseltine), it was due to the older composer that two Grainger works were published in Vienna in 1923. Despite increasing infirmity, Delius also attended all six of Grainger's own rehearsals at Frankfurt in the spring of 1923, knowing that his re-introduction to Europe after the war years was vital if Grainger the composer was ever to equal Grainger the pianist. Summing up his obligation to Delius in that same essay, Grainger estimates that a composer 'never had truer colleague' and that on Delius's death he felt his music 'had lost its best friend'.

In 1907 Grainger had many good friends within the English group of composers who that year first came into contact with Delius when his *Appalachia* was given its first London performance. Few of these friendships survived the years completely unimpaired as did his friendship with the Deliuses. They, with their cosmopolitan background, their home in France, and Frederick's knowledge of America and Scandinavia (not to mention his friendship with Grainger's friend Edvard Grieg), were able to view tolerantly the obsessive relationship between Rose and Percy Grainger and to understand the complex motivation behind their flight to America at the start of the War.

It was natural then that, after his mother's death, the Deliuses should offer Percy their home as his European base whenever he should need it. As far as we know from available evidence, Grainger did not visit Grez-sur-Loing until 1925; but 1923, a crucial year for both of them, brought the two composers together, first in Germany and then in Norway. Unfortunately, as will be seen from the complete chronological list of extant correspondence, that whole year is missing from the collection at the Grainger Museum, and only represented by letters from Delius to Grainger housed in America and copies for the Delius Trust, London.

After spending the early part of 1923 in Frankfurt with the Deliuses, Grainger went on his planned way, but was summoned to Delius again in the summer, this time in Norway at his mountain holiday home. The new need was for assistance with additional music which had to be supplied to Delius's 1920 score of the incidental music for Elroy

Flecker's play *Hassan* which had been given its world première in German in Darmstadt. Basil Dean, who was preparing for the London première in September on a much more lavish scale, found that he needed the extra music for ballets and scene shifting.

Extensive copying was impossible for Delius, for at this stage of increasing paralysis the pencil often had to be tied to his hand. It was an equally difficult task for Jelka to work over his lightly pencilled scrawl. Both were thankful to leave the completion of the extra ballet to Grainger, who supplied fifty-seven bars following the composer's opening, to make a middle section and a reprise, the latter effected by a favourite method of Delius, that of counterpointing the opening ideas against the new material. Grainger also introduced into the texture the typical Delius effect of wordless voices. The Grainger touch can be seen in the instruction to be 'very nasal' and the loud shout at the end.

After the amazing opening night in London the Deliuses wrote to describe everything in detail to Grainger, including the success of the movement tactfully referred to by Frederick as 'our dance', although Grainger's name has never yet appeared upon it. In retrospect, however, perhaps the biggest gift made by Grainger to Delius that year was the famous hill climb carrying the invalid to see his last Norwegian sunset 'from the heights'.

Winter by the Mediterranean, followed by an attempted cure at the Cassel Sanatorium, was made possible by the success of the London *Hassan* production, but only two of the 1924 letters are at the Grainger Museum. A temporary recovery enabled Delius to attempt at least his own signature in a May 1924 letter and then, in October, a whole letter in his own hand announced that he had sent his latest scores to Grainger's home. This [20/10/1924 - copy DT/LC] is probably the last holograph Delius ever wrote, for, in 1925 came a total collapse.

Thereafter, Grainger and Balfour Gardiner visited Grez at least once a year until the last two years of the composer's life when Grainger was busy with Australian visits. In Jelka's long letters we find a full picture of other visitors, welcome and unwelcome, but have to rely on the Grainger Museum photograph collection, supported by anecdotes in Eric Fenby's book *Delius As I Knew Him* for glimpses of the tonic effect of Grainger's visit.

With the appearance of the blind composer at the 1929 Queen's Hall Delius Festival (perpetuated by both the James Gunn portrait of that time and Eric Fenby's poignant book first produced in 1936), a legend of a grim and egotistical old man was built up. We know from his essay quoted above that Grainger detested this view of Delius and felt it to be unjust to the essential Delius within the diseased body. For him Delius would always be the man he knew in his prime and so it is only appropriate that the overwhelming impression gained by a study of the Delius holding at the Grainger Museum is of the composer in his happiest years, his rich middle period, with his youth still fresh in his memory, still a source of inspiration. This is so whether one considers the music collection already described by Robert Threlfall for *Studies in Music* (University of Western Australia), No. 7, 1973, or the large

number of letters which passed between Delius and his wife beginning with the days of their first friendship in Paris in 1896,
the notebooks preserved with the letters in the small, blue
attaché case, or the photograph collection. Finally, setting the
seal on the whole image of vitality is the portrait of Delius
painted by his wife, Jelka Rosen, as he was before the stressful
years of the First World War.

Grainger made great claims for Delius and would appear to have
allotted him a key position in the musical cosmos of which the
Grainger Museum is a reflection. The exact nature of this position
will only emerge when all the Museum's extensive archival holdings
have been analysed. Meanwhile, even a cursory inspection reveals
Grainger's constantly maintained admiration for Delius as man and
artist, both as an historical phenomenon and as a unique composer,
expressed equally in letters to others and in jottings and anecdotes.
Allowing for the ebullience of language in which words such as
'darling' and 'adorable' are common currency, applicable to male
and female alike, we find that while Grainger's viewpoint is seldom
orthodox and his conclusions often argued from mutually exclusive
premises, his musical instinct is frequently correct. It is
possible, therefore, that the current re-appraisal of Delius's
music may endorse some of Grainger's claims for his friend. To
assist in the evaluation of those claims must be the justification
for this publication of a descriptive catalogue of the Delius holding
of the Grainger Museum Board, Melbourne.

RACHEL LOWE

Perth, W.A., 1977 - London, April 1980

A preliminary inventory of the letters and related documents in the
Delius holding of the Grainger Museum, University of Melbourne,
Australia, was made during visits to Melbourne in 1974 and 1975
financed by the generosity of the University of Western Australia and
the Grainger Museum Board of the University of Melbourne, assisted by
the Music Board of the Australia Council.

The task of dating the many undated items and re-organising the
material chronologically has taken place in England during 1978 and
1979, with the aid of the microfilm effected at the time of the
inventory and xerox copies of more recently discovered documents
supplied by the Grainger Museum Archivist; while reference has been
made to material in other archives, more especially the Delius Trust,
London, and the British Library, Department of Manuscripts.

The decision to 'calendar', or describe, the material for publication
and so produce a readable narrative with source references in addition
to checklists was taken jointly with Dr Kay Dreyfus, the Grainger
Museum Archivist. This decision has set a nice problem of balance
between the need to standardise entries for cataloguing purposes,
ease of reference, and economy of space, and the need to represent
the style and substance of the documents with reasonable accuracy.

The Delius/Grainger correspondence has been more fully described than
the letters which passed between Delius and his wife because much of
the latter correspondence is domestic, particularly the very long
letters of Jelka Delius, née Rosen. The policy has been one of
recording anything of musical and biographical value and of simply
indicating the range of the remaining topics.

As far as possible, apart from an occasional 'sic', editorial
interference in quotations has been avoided. Readers will soon realise
that the four main letter-writers are cosmopolitans who mix their
languages; and, in the case of Percy Grainger, we have one who
invented his own 'blue-eyed' English.

Much use of obliques has been made in the description of the documents
to indicate line endings in the quotations from letters and in letter-
heads and addresses, because the writers, especially Frederick Delius,
are erratic in their use of punctuation and the use of obliques avoids
unnecessary editing.

Obliques are never used in the description of postmarks unless they
appear in the stamp itself, but every effort has been made to trans-
cribe the various postmark styles as well as such information as is
visible, except for *times* of posting which, unless quoted for a
special purpose, have been omitted. In the few cases where the name
of a town or district in an address is represented in the original
document with an oblique to indicate abbreviation, I have edited by
substituting a stop so that there is no confusion with the use of the
oblique for a line ending. For example, 'S./Aurdal' becomes simply
'S. Aurdal'. The many pencilled datings found on the Delius items,
often in the hand of Jelka Delius (possibly always in her hand), have
also been recorded. These often appear to have been an attempt to

edit the correspondence at a much later date, perhaps between the death of Frederick in June 1934 and Jelka's own demise in May 1935, and as such are sometimes misleading.

Percy Grainger's own classification and numbering system have been employed to identify the documents for permanent storage and a system of double numbering has been used in the case of the letters between Frederick Delius and his wife. In this group the position of each letter in the exchange of correspondence between the two writers is indicated with a number in round brackets which appears after the Grainger Museum number.

Opening sentences have been quoted for identification purposes in all the Delius letters, but not quite so uniformly in the case of Grainger and his mother, where the Grainger Museum Archivist preferred that, in the main part, salient sentences should be quoted for this purpose, regardless of their position in the text. Endings have only been quoted where they serve to show the progress of the friendship or indicate the character and style of the author in some way. For all other editing practices adopted in this catalogue the reader is referred to the list of abbreviations and symbols which follows.

It remains for me to thank those who have helped me with this project: firstly, those who have prepared the script - Mrs Ford in Perth, Western Australia, who typed the first partial draft in 1976; and, in England in 1979 and 1980, the invaluable typing and editorial assistance of Jean Callaghan. Secondly, since space prevents my naming all the librarians who have generously assisted with information and/or facilities, I must simply list the staff of the libraries of the Universities of Western Australia, Melbourne, Southampton, Exeter and London; the British Museum, the Royal Academy of Music, and the Royal Northern College of Music.

Mr Wayne Shirley of the Library of Congress and Dr Lionel K. Carley, Archivist to the Delius Trust, London, have helped greatly in the correlation and dating of specific items; while Dr Carley has also given up valuable time to reading my penultimate draft and has shared his own readings of the microfilm.

I thank Professor Frank Callaway of the Department of Music, University of Western Australia, for his constant encouragement and practical help; Mr Frank Strahan, Archivist to the University of Melbourne, for his courteous advice, together with Dr Kay Dreyfus and her assistants at the Grainger Museum, especially Elaine Counsell, Anthony Prescott and Wendy Nixon.

In addition to the financial assistance already mentioned, I must also record the generosity of the Grainger Museum Board of the University of Melbourne for the provision of photographic material for reproduction in this volume. For permission to quote and summarise from the letters I am grateful to: the Delius Trust, London; the Grainger Museum Board, University of Melbourne; Mr James Holden of New York, attorney in settlement of the Estate of Percy Grainger; and Mr Stewart Manville of White Plains, New York.

In conclusion I must record my great debt to the Delius Trustees for their generous funding of this publication.

RACHEL LOWE (Rachel Lowe-Dugmore)
London, 1980.

ABBREVIATIONS AND SYMBOLS

The Writers of the Letters

PG   Percy Grainger

RG   Rose Grainger [née Aldridge, mother of Percy Aldridge Grainger]

EG   Ella Grainger [née Ström, m. Percy Grainger 1928]

FD   Frederick Delius [known as Fritz until his marriage 1903]

JD   Jelka Delius [née Rosen, m. Frederick Delius 1903]

Archives

GM   Grainger Museum, Melbourne

DT   Delius Trust, London

EG est.   Estate of Ella Grainger

LC   Library of Congress

BL   British Library

Copy - DT/LC   Copy (whether in type or by photography) from
                        the Grainger collection at the Library of
                        Congress effected for the Delius Trust
                        archives by Dr Lionel K. Carley

Copy - DT/LKC   Copy in the archives of the Delius Trust:
                        information from the archivist, Dr Lionel
                        K. Carley

Terms used in the Description of the Documents

AL   Autograph letter [a holograph, i.e. wholly
                        in the hand of the writer stated, unless
                        otherwise indicated]

ALS   Autograph letter signed

PC   Postcard

PCS   Postcard signed

PPCS   Picture postcard signed

T   Percy Grainger's symbol for a typed copy of
                        an original letter, whether the original
                        was a holograph or typed letter

TL   Typed letter

TLS	Typed letter signed
PG/FN	Percy Grainger's footnote made as autograph marginalia to Ella Grainger's typed copies
n.d.	No date
<date>	A conjectural dating made by the editor
[date]	A conjectural dating made by Percy Grainger or a former custodian of the letters and found to be correct by the editor, or an acceptable postmark date
<place name>	A conjectural address or partial address where writer gives none
[place name]	An address or partial address supplied on internal evidence or on the evidence of a postmark
pmk(s)	Postmark(s)
[ ]	Editorial comment
/	The end of a line in a quotation or a letter-head
. ...	The end of a sentence in a quotation followed by further material which is omitted by the editor
...	Material omitted by the editor
Grez	Short for Grez-sur-Loing. [Note: Delius usually writes Grez sur Loing with no hyphen, but the Deliuses' letterhead hyphenates the word.]

Books and References Abbreviated

Other literary references have had their titles quoted in full.

RL Cat.	Rachel Lowe, *Frederick Delius 1862-1934. A Catalogue of the Music Archive of the Delius Trust, London* (London: Delius Trust, 1974).
RT Cat.	Robert Threlfall, *A Catalogue of the Compositions of Frederick Delius. Sources and References* (London: Delius Trust, 1977).
RLD/*SIM* 12	Rachel Lowe-Dugmore, 'Documenting Delius (Part One: The Years 1913-1915', *Studies in Music* (University of Western Australia), No. 12, 1978, pp. 114-129.

8

RLD/*SIM* 13   Rachel Lowe-Dugmore, 'Documenting Delius
                                (Part Two: The Years 1916-1919), *Studies
                                in Music* (University of Western Australia),
                                No. 13, 1979.

L(K)C/*The Paris Years*   Lionel Carley, *Delius.   The Paris Years*
                                (London: Triad Press, 1975).

L(K)C & RT/*DALP*   Lionel Carley and Robert Threlfall, *Delius.
                                A Life in Pictures* (London: Oxford
                                University Press, 1977).

D. Redwood   Dawn Redwood, *Flecker and Delius - the
                                making of 'Hassan'* (London: Thames
                                Publishing, 1978).

Slattery   Thomas C. Slattery, *Percy Grainger
                                The Inveterate Innovator* (Evanston: The
                                Instrumentalist Co., 1974).

Bird   John Bird, *Percy Grainger* (London: Paul
                                Elek, 1976).

Measurements: The letters of Jelka and Frederick Delius have been
                measured, in centimetres, length x breadth, in
                accordance with the usual practice of the Delius
                Archive in London.   These measurements must be
                considered approximate.

Both Frederick and Jelka Delius vary in their
presentation of titles, sometimes using German
quotation marks, and at other times the various
English methods, or no punctuation at all. For
the sake of illustration, Delius's treatment of
the names of his works is retained exactly in
quotations from the first seven letters to
Grainger, series 95-1 to 95-7. Thereafter, while
retaining the writers' idiosyncrasies of spelling,
usage of articles, numbering and capital letters
in all quotations, titles of works will be
presented uniformly in Italics (except for sonatas,
concertos and songs, which will appear in Roman
type).

To preserve the uniform appearance of this catalogue,
the same treatment will be accorded to quotations
from all other correspondence. It is hoped in this
way to make all titles stand out clearly from the
surrounding text, so aiding quick reference.

Introductory Item

GRAINGER, PERCY
From Bennett, W.R. & Co./Solicitors/P. Emanuel
16 July 1936
74 Great Russell Street, Bloomsbury Square, WC 1.
TLS   One single leaf

 The trustees of the estate of Mrs Jelka Delius
 deceased authorise the return of the letters
 of Percy and Rose Grainger to Percy Grainger.

CHECKLIST AND INDEX of the letters of Percy and Rose Grainger
to Frederick and Jelka Delius

DATE	CORRESPONDENTS	TYPE OF COMMUNI-CATION	GRAINGER MUSEUM NUMBER REVISED	PAGE
Introductory item: 16/7/1936	Bennett, W.R. & Co./Soli-citors/P. Emanuel			11
[27/4/1907]	RG/FD [signed portrait of PG]	PPCS	91-1	21
6/7/1910	PG/FD	ALS	93-1	28
26/1/1911	PG/FD	ALS	93-2	29
<1 or 2/1/1912>	PG/FD	ALS	93-3	29
[15/2/1912]	PG/FD	PCS	93-4	30
18/2/1912	PG/FD	ALS	93-5	30
18/9/1912	PG/FD	ALS	93-6	30-31
23/9/[1912]	RG/FD	ALS	91-2	21
18/10/[1912]	RG/JD	PCS	91-3	21-22
3/1/1913	RG/JD	ALS	91-4	22
5/3/1913	PG/FD	ALS	93-7	31
6/3/1913	RG/FD	ALS	91-5	22-23
19/3/1913	RG & PG/FD	PPCS	91-6 & 93-8	23,31
12/11/1913	PG/FD	ALS	93-9	32
<Jan. 1914>	PG/FD	ALS	93-10	32
25/1/1914	PG/FD	ALS	93-11	32-33
<25 or 26/2/ 1914>	PG/FD	ALS	93-12	33
11/3/1914	PG/JD	ALS	93-13	33-34
26/4/1914	PG/FD	ALS	93-14	34
[6/5/1914]	PG/FD	PCS	93-15	34
[12/6/1914]	PG/FD	PCS	93-16	35

DATE	CORRESPONDENTS	TYPE OF COMMUNI-CATION	GRAINGER MUSEUM NUMBER REVISED	PAGE
Wed. <24/6/1914>	RG/FD	ALS	91-7	23
10/8/1914	PG/FD	PCS	93-17	35
30/8/1914	PG/FD	PCS	93-18	36
[16/10/1914]	RG/JD	PCS	91-8	23-24
11/11/1914	PG/FD	ALS	93-19	36
18/4/1915	PG/FD	ALS	93-20	36-37
28/4/1915	RG/FD	ALS	91-9	24
19/6/1915	PG/FD	ALS	93-21	37
18/8/1915	PG/FD	ALS	93-22	38
20/8/[1915]	RG/FD & JD	ALS	91-10	24
2/12/1915	PG/FD	PPCS	93-23	38-39
7/12/1915	PG/FD	PPCS (2)	93-24	39
14/9/1916	PG/FD	ALS	93-25	39-40
[14/9/1916]	PG/FD	PCS (3)	93-26	40
4/6/1917	PG/FD	ALS	93-27	41
29/7/1917	RG/FD	ALS	91-11	24-25
19/6/1918	RG/FD	ALS	91-12	25
14/9/1918	PG/FD	ALS	93-28	41
13/12/1918	RG/FD	ALS	91-13	25-26
15/12/1918	PG/FD	TLS	93-29	41-42
22/1/1921	RG/JD	ALS	91-14	26
3/11/1921	PG/FD	TLS	93-30	43
28/3/1922	PG/FD	TL (copy)	93-31	43

DATE	CORRESPONDENTS	TYPE OF COMMUNI-CATION	GRAINGER MUSEUM NUMBER REVISED	PAGE
Aug. or Sept. 1922	PG/JD	ALS	93-32	44
29/1/1932	PG/JD	TL (Copy)	93-33	44
14/7/1934	PG & EG/ JD	TM	93-34	45
Additional item (1916-17)	RG/FD & JD	Flower & greet-ing with PG's com-ments	91-[15]	26-27

CHRONOLOGY OF THE CORRESPONDENCE

OF PERCY AND ROSE GRAINGER WITH FREDERICK AND JELKA DELIUS

held in the custody of the Grainger Museum, Melbourne
and the Delius Trust, London, at date of publication

*This must be considered as an interim list subject to
alteration at any time as documents from other archives
are received.*

*Addresses and dates have been standardised and/or
abbreviated.*

<1907 - prior to 22/4/1907>	PG/FD	[London]	DT
22/4/1907	FD/PG	90 Oakley St, Chelsea SW	GM
[27/4/1907]	RG/FD	pmk S. Kensington [London]	GM
12/5/1907	FD/PG	Grez-sur-Loing	GM
20/5/1907	PG/FD	5 Harrington Rd, London SW	DT
[31/5/1907]	FD/PG	Grez	GM
8/6/1907	PG/FD	5 Harrington Rd	DT
10/6/1907	FD/PG	Grez	copy DT[EG (LKC)]
[6/7/1907]	FD/PG	Grez	GM
[5/9/1907]	FD/PG	Grez	GM
<6/9/1907>	FD/PG	Grez	GM
9/9/1907	PG/FD	Svinkløv, Jutland	DT
31/12/1907	PG/FD	Changing address that day to 31A King's Rd, Sloane Sq. SW [London]	DT
[26/<3>/1908]	FD/PG	Grez	GM
28/3/1908	PG/FD	Royal Hotel, Crewe [on tour]	DT
13/9/1908	PG/FD	RMS Orontes	DT
31/1/1909	PG/FD	Auckland, N.Z.	DT
17/8/1909	PG/FD	pmk London	DT
19/9/1909	PG/FD	31A King's Rd	DT

6/7/1910	PG/FD	31A King's Rd	GM
[31/12/1910]	FD/PG	Dresden	GM
26/1/1911	PG/FD	Veendam	GM
23/5/1911	FD/PG	Grez	GM
11/7/1911	FD/PG	Grez	GM
<1 or 2/1/ 1912>	PG/FD	31A King's Rd	GM
[14/2/1912]	FD/PG	Grez	GM
[15/2/1912]	PG/FD	pmk London	GM
18/2/1912	PG/FD	[London]	GM
[21/2/1912]	FD/PG	Grez	GM
18/9/1912	PG/FD	31A King's Rd	GM
23/9/[1912]	RG/FD	31A King's Rd	GM
18/10/[1912]	RG/JD	31A King's Rd	GM
3/1/1913	RG/JD	31A King's Rd	GM
5/3/1913	PG/FD	31A King's Rd	GM
6/3/[1913]	RG/FD	31A King's Rd	GM
19/3/1913	PG & RG/ FD	pmk London	GM
12/11/1913	PG/FD	Helsingfors	GM
18/11/1913	FD/PG	Grez	GM
<January 1914>	FD/PG	Grez	GM
<early January 1914>	PG/FD	American Hotel, Amsterdam	GM
25/1/1914	PG/FD	American Hotel, Amsterdam	GM
<25 or 26/2/1914>	PG/FD	19 Cheniston Gdns, Kensington	GM
11/3/1914	PG/JD	19 Cheniston Gdns	GM
<9/4/1914>	FD/PG	Grez	GM
26/4/1914	PG/FD	7 Pembroke Villas	GM
29/4/1914	FD/PG	Grez	GM
[6/5/1914]	PG/FD	7 Pembroke Villas	GM

[12/6/1914]	PG/FD	31A King's Rd	GM
Wed. <24/6/1914>	RG/FD	31A King's Rd	GM
10/8/1914	PG/FD	31A King's Rd	GM
30/8/1914	PG/FD	c/o Miss I. Du Cane, Ballards, Goudhurst, Kent	GM
[16/10/1914]	RG/JD	pmk New York	GM
11/11/1914	PG/FD	Hotel Calumet, 340 West 57th St, N.Y. City	GM
18/4/1915	PG/FD	c/o Antonia Sawyer [Concert Direction], 1425 Broadway, N.Y. City	GM
28/4/1915	RG/FD	Hotel Calumet, N.Y. City	GM
19/6/1915	PG/FD	c/o Antonia Sawyer, Aeolian Hall, W.42 St., N.Y. City	GM
18/8/1915	PG/FD	c/o Antonia Sawyer, Aeolian Hall, W.42 St., N.Y. City	GM
20/8/[1915]	RG/FD & JD	New York	GM
26/9/1915	FD/PG	Gjeilo, Hallingdal [Norway]	GM
22/10/1915	JD/RG	Juelsminde	GM
[n.d. early Nov. 1915]	FD/PG	Published *The Musical Leader* 18/11/1915. See Appendix III and illustration facing p. 225.	GM
[25/11/1915]	FD/PG	Grez	GM
2/12/1915	PG/FD	The Southern, 680 Madison Av., N.Y. City	GM
7/12/1915	PG/FD	The Southern, 680 Madison Av., N.Y. City	GM
21/12/1915	FD/PG	Grez	GM
11/1/1916	FD/PG	Grez	GM
23/7/1916	FD/PG	Grez	GM
14/9/1916	PG/FD	The Southern, 680 Madison Av., N.Y. City	GM
[14/9/1916]	PG/FD	pmk New York	GM
5/10/1916	FD/PG	Grez	GM

15/11/1916	FD/PG	Grez	GM
4/6/1917	PG/FD	680 Madison Av., N.Y. City	GM
23/6/1917	FD/PG	Grez	GM
29/7/1917	RG/FD	680 Madison Av., N.Y. City	GM
19/6/1918	RG/FD	680 Madison Av., N.Y. City	GM
20/7/1918	FD/PG	Biarritz	copy DT/LC
14/9/1918	PG/FD	309 W.92nd St, N.Y. City	GM
13/12/1918	RG/FD	309 W.92nd St, N.Y. City	GM
15/12/1918	PG/FD	309 W.92nd St, N.Y. City	GM
14/1/1919 cont. 16/1/1919	JD/RG	44 Belsize Pk Gdns, London NW3	GM
16/1/1919	FD/PG	44 Belsize Pk Gdns, London NW3	GM
14/2/1919 [?]		A dried geranium flower with a holograph greeting may possibly have been intended as a 'Valentine' for 14/2/1919. See additional item: Rose Grainger's letters.	GM
18/2/1919	JD/RG	44 Belsize Pk Gdns	GM
17/12/1919	FD/PG	Grez	GM
22/1/1921	RG/JD	680 Madison Av., N.Y. City	GM
3/11/1921	PG/FD	7 Cromwell Place, White Plains, N.Y.	GM
28/3/1922	PG/FD	Bellingham, Washington	GM
[Aug. or Sept.] 1922	PG/JD	Grand Hotel, Carl Johans Gate, Kristiania [Oslo]	GM
16/12/1922	FD/PG	Domplatz 12, Frankfurt [dictated but signed]	copy DT/LC
28/3/1923	FD/PG	Domplatz 12, Frankfurt [dictated but signed]	copy DT/LC
29/4/1923	JD/PG	Hotel Rose, Bad Oeynhausen	copy DT/LC
17/8/1923	JD/PG	s/s Paris/Fred Olsen's linie Between Kristiania and Antwerp	copy DT/LC

23/9/1923	JD/PG	Cox's Hotel, Jermyn St, St James's, SW1	copy DT/LC
29/9/1923	FD/PG	Grez [dictated]	copy DT/LC
14/10/1923	JD/PG	Grez	copy DT/LC
29/11/1923	JD/PG	Grez	copy DT/LC
23/1/1924))))))	FD/PG	Rapallo [dictated] Extensively quoted in *Musical Courier* 17/4/1924 and *The Musical Leader* 18/4/1924. See Appendix III and illustration facing p. 225.	copy DT/LC
23/1/1924))	JD/PG	Rapallo [misdated 1923 by JD but pmk legible]	copy DT/LC
[24/2/1924]	JD/PG	pmk Rapallo	copy DT/LC
21/3/1924	JD/PG	La Napoule [Alpes Maritimes]	copy DT/LC
4/4/1924 cont. 6/4/1924	JD/PG	[La Napoule, Alpes Maritimes]	copy DT/LC
13/4/1924	FD/PG	<Mandelieu, Alpes Maritimes> [dictated]	GM
<13 or 14/4/ 1924>	JD/PG	<Mandelieu>	GM
26/5/1924)))	JD/PG	Cassel	copy DT/LC
26/5/1924))	FD/PG	Cassel [dictated but signed F.D.]	copy DT/LC
20/10/1924)))	FD/PG	Grez [his last holograph in the series]	copy DT/LC
20/10/1924))	JD/PG	Grez	copy DT/LC
n.d. [late November 1924]	JD/PG	Hotel zur Post, Cassel	copy DT/LC
28/3/1925	JD/PG	Schlosshotel, Wilhelmshöhe bei Cassel	copy DT/LC
[3/5/1925]	JD/PG	Schlosshotel, Wilhelmshöhe bei Cassel	copy DT/LC

12/9/1925	JD/PG	Grez	copy DT/LC
25/10/1925	JD/PG	Grez	GM
8/12/1925	JD/PG	Grez	copy DT/LC
20/5/1926	FD/PG	Grez [dictated]	GM
20/5/1926	JD/PG	Grez	GM
30/3/1927	JD/PG	Grez	GM
26/4/1927	JD/PG	Grez	GM
2/7/1927	JD/PG	Grez	GM
27/12/1927	JD/PG	Grez	GM
11/5/1928	JD/PG	Grez	copy DT/LC
Xmas Day 1928	JD/PG	Grez	copy DT/LC
28/5/1929	JD/PG	Grez	copy DT/LC
12/6/1929	PG/FD	Lilla Vrån, Pevensey Bay, Sussex	EG's holograph copy
27/8/1929	JD/PG	Grez	copy DT/LC
27/12/1929	JD/EG	Grez	GM
23/4/1930	JD/PG	Grez	copy DT/(LKC)
4/11/1930	JD/PG	Grez	copy DT/LC
n.d. [2?/6 or 7/1931]	JD/PG	Grez 'My dear Percy, What a surprise!'	copy DT/LC
20/12/1931	JD/PG	Grez	copy DT/LC
29/1/1932	PG/JD	In the train	copy GM
17/3/1932	JD/PG	Grez	copy DT/LC
18/8/1934	JD/PG & EG	Grez	GM

GRAINGER, ROSE (with PERCY)   91-1
To Frederick Delius
n.d. [27 April 1907]
PPCS   pmk S. Kensington [London] Ap 27 07
        addressed: F. Delius Esq./90 Oakley St/Chelsea./S.W.
        photograph portrait of 'MR PERCY GRAINGER' signed
        'Yrs heartily Percy Grainger'.
        Message in Rose Grainger's hand, also signed.

        When you next are/coming to London, do let/us
        know - & send a p.c. to Percy c/o E.L. Robinson/
        Concert Direction/7 Wigmore St. W ...

        Do send Percy a photo ...

        We enjoyed meeting you so much ...

GRAINGER, ROSE   91-2
To Frederick Delius
Sept 23$\underline{rd}$ [1912]
31A King's Road/Sloane Square/S W [letterhead]
ALS   One leaf folded
[PG's number GM91-5(T)]   PG/FN2, 3 & 4

        Dear Mr Delius, What a pity we/are just going
        away from/London as you come & that we/cannot
        hear your lovely/work - We leave either Sunday
        30/or Monday Oct 1$\underline{st}$. ... [Rose's error:
        1 October was Tuesday in 1912.]

Rose gives information about hotels and Percy's professional
engagements:- returning to London 13 October, conducting *Green
Bushes* at Queen's Hall 19 October, leaving again, for Holland, 20
October.

Rose also implies that Delius has been ill, as she is glad he is
'well now'.

GRAINGER, ROSE   91-3
To Jelka Delius
Oct 18. [1912]
31A King's Road/Sloane Square/S W [letterhead]
PCS   pmk illegible
        addressed: Mrs. F. Delius/Grez sur Loing/Seine et Marne/
                    France
[PG's number GM91-6(T)]   PG/FN5

This postcard is written to assure the Deliuses that Percy is
better after a rest in the country and will be fit to conduct
Green Bushes 'to-morrow'.

... We heard/Delius's lovely "Dance Rhap."[*] a
few nights ago &/loved it. We regret not to
have seen y^r husband, but look forward to doing
so in winter, &/you too; & to hear his work. ...

so glad to hear/that Mr. Delius is well & strong/
again. ...

*A Dance Rhapsody (no. 1)

GRAINGER, ROSE   91-4
To Jelka Delius
January 3rd 1913.
31A King's Road/Sloane Square/S W [letterhead]
ALS   One leaf folded
        Envelope addressed: Grez
        pmk illegible except for the time, 11.15 a.m.,
        but addressee is 'Frederick Delius Esq.' - see below
[PG's number GM91-1(T)]

        Dear Mrs Delius,/Just a few words to/wish you,
        & Mr Delius, much/happiness, health, & luck/in
        this New Year, from Percy/& me. We have both
        been very/happy to-day with your/dear husband's
        Piano/Concerto, which I am/glad to say, Percy
        adores, & is now going/to learn it. ...

        Dear little Beecham/was here last night ...

        looking forward to/the Mass of Life in/Feb. ...

Rose also refers to the success of a Beecham concert in Berlin, the
appreciation of Delius's 'music', 'Percy's Mock Morris' and his
recent continental tour.

GRAINGER, ROSE   91-5
To Frederick Delius
March 6. [1913]
31A King's Road/Sloane Square/S W [letterhead]
ALS   One leaf folded
        [The envelope of 91-4, originally numbered GM91-1(T)
        by Grainger, addressed to Delius, should probably
        belong here.]
[PG's number GM91-2(T)]

        Dear M^r. Delius,/We got a card from/Mrs Delius
        with the glad/news that you w^{ld} be here/Thursday
        night, & that both of/you would be in London/for
        the Mass of Life ...

Rose invites Frederick and Jelka Delius to tea on 'Friday at 4.30'
or Saturday 'at (5 o'cl.?' and asks them to bring 'Mrs Stoop'.
Percy will shortly be in Switzerland on a concert tour and so
unable to attend the Mass of Life, but will, apparently, be able to
attend the tea party, as Rose says that his pupils will have to be

re-arranged to allow of their meeting him that day. She wishes he
'could/earn money quicker, so that he could/live quietly - & only
compose - ...'

[A conjectural dating 1913-1914 has been added, but the occasion to
which Rose refers, the second performance in England of Delius's
Mass of Life, took place on Monday, 10 March 1913, at Covent
Garden. The previous English performance occurred 7 June 1909 and
there were no further performances until after the 1914-18 War.]

GRAINGER, ROSE (with PERCY)   91-6 [93-8]
To Frederick Delius
19.3.13
no address [London]
PPCS   pmk London 20 Mar [13]
         pmk Grez 21-3 13
         addressed: Grez (in Rose Grainger's hand), with the message:

         ... Percy has now/sent the Choruses to Prof.
         Schwicke-/rath, [in Munich] ...   We/enjoyed y$\underline{r}$
         concerto last night - ...

         verso: photograph of Percy signed 'fondly Percy 19.3.13'
         with a similar message beginning 'A thousand thanks ...'.

[PG's number GM91-3(T)
and GM93-6(T)]   PG/FN1

GRAINGER, ROSE   91-7
To Frederick Delius
Wed. <24 June 1914>
31A King's Road/Sloane Square/S W [letterhead]
ALS   One single leaf of which the verso is blank
[PG's number GM91-4(T)]

         Our dear Friend/I enclose you the/2 tickets for
         Percy's/Recital on Tuesday next/June 30$\underline{th}$
         afternoon ...   We were so glad to see you
         yesterday/looking so well - & look forward to/
         being with you at dear Balfour's/week-end -
         July 4$\underline{th}$.   With our love/also to y$\underline{r}$ wife,
         when writing ...

[A conjectural date of 1913 is incorrect, as the recital mentioned
took place at the Aeolian Hall on Tuesday, 30 June - see *The Times*,
July 1, 1914, p. 10.]

GRAINGER, ROSE   91-8
To Jelka Delius
n.d.
no address [New York]
PCS   pmk New York Oct 16 1914
        pmk Grez 22-10 14
        addressed: Grez
[PG's number GM91-7(T)]

Letters addressed to us/c/o Miss Isabel Du Cane/
"Ballards"/Goudhurst/Kent. England./will reach us. ...

[On the recto Delius (?) has written in pencil 'Marshall Hall'.]

GRAINGER, ROSE   91-9
To Frederick Delius
Ap[ril] 28th [1915] [year date added in red pencil is confirmed
        by the address and contents]
Hotel Calumet/340 West 57th Street/New York [letterhead]
ALS   One single leaf
[PG's number GM91-8(T)]

        Dear Friend,/By this post/I am posting you some of/
        Percy's critiques, press cuttings,/etc. - showing
        you what a/really sensational success he/has been
        this season ...

It has been an expensive year with American living costs and start-
ing Percy's performing career again in this new continent. Rose
requests the necessary information for publicity and contract
purposes concerning Delius's Piano Concerto, so that Percy may play
it in the coming season and begin to sponsor Delius's work in America
[see Appendix III].

GRAINGER, ROSE   91-10
To Frederick and Jelka Delius
Aug 20th [1915] [year date added in red pencil on verso]
New York
ALS   One single leaf
[PG's number GM91-9(T)]

        So glad you are both in dear/Norway ...

        Percy is fighting like [deleted] hard to/make his
        beloved Delius music/known in America ...
        [Several works are to be heard this season]

        We love America, but it is a/frightfully
        expensive place to/live in ...

She sends love to Fru Grieg and her sister, the Hals and Halvorsens;
and enquires after 'poor little Miss Gerhardi', where and how she is.

GRAINGER, ROSE   91-11
To Frederick Delius
July 29th 1917
The Southern/680 Madison Avenue/N. York City. [letterhead: 'N. York
                                    City' added in Rose's hand]
ALS   Two leaves folded
        Envelope addressed: Grez
        pmk New York Jul 30 1917
        verso: From Mrs John Grainger, 680 Madison Avenue
                N.Y. City
[PG's number GM91-10(T)]   PG/FN6

My dear Friend,/I want to tell you about/Percy, ...

Rose goes on to explain that Percy has enlisted in the US Army

> ... about/∅ [deleted] 7 weeks ago, 2 weeks after
> hearing/of his father's death. As long as he/
> lived Percy had to support him, &/the poor fellow
> being paralysed,/needing a nurse always with him,/
> & doctor's attention, needed much/money ...

Percy's present pay since recent promotion to '2nd Class Musician'
is 36 dollars a week. Rose is staying at Fort Hamilton where
Percy is stationed. She describes his duties in detail: he plays
oboe, conducts in the leader's absence, does gardening duties and
gives fund-raising concerts for the Red Cross. Before duty, from
5.00 a.m., he works in Rose's room at composition and arrangements
for military band.

GRAINGER, ROSE   91-12
To Frederick Delius
June 19th 1918.
The Southern/Madison Avenue and Sixty-Second Street/New York City,
    N.Y./Evan H. Patrick/Proprietor [letterhead: 'Telephone
    Plaza 4867' given in the top margin, and Rose has added
    'City, N.Y.' in the address]
ALS   One single leaf
[PG's number GM91-11(T)]

> My dear Friend,/Percy asked me to/write you a few
> words, & enclose the/letter of introduction to
> Damrosch,/the Conductor of the N.Y. Symph.
> Concerts,/to whom Percy gave some of your works,/
> wh. Damrosch performed so splendidly./ ...
>
> I/wrote to you, & to Mrs Delius when/I was living
> at Fort Hamilton, but/got no reply from either of
> you. We/were overjoyed to get your last little/
> letter to Percy, & to know you were/both well,
> & safe. ...

Damrosch is now in Paris with an orchestra of fifty. Percy was to
have gone to Europe, but was transferred to Governor's Island as
'Assistant Instructor' in the Music Training School.

GRAINGER, ROSE   91-13
To Frederick Delius
Dec 13th 1918.
Tel. Riverside 6280/309 West 92nd St., N.Y. City, N. York
    [the whole address in Rose Grainger's holograph]
ALS   Two leaves folded
    Envelope addressed: Frederic Delius Esq. Composer-/
                         Grez-/sur Loing Seine et/Marne/
                         France
    Re-addressed: 44 Belsize Park Gardens/Londres
    pmk New York 14 Dec 1918 [A pencil note which reads
                      '(Feb?) 14, 1919' is incorrect.]

verso: from Mrs John Grainger/309 West 92nd St. N. York
            City; New York
[PG's number GM91-12(T)]   PG/FN7, 8 & 9

My dear Friend/I must write you a few/hasty words to
tell you how happy/Percy & I are about the great/
success of your *Life's Dance*/at last night's Philh.
Concert. ...

Stransky conducted splendidly. ...

She describes Grainger's tireless propaganda for Delius 'as the
greatest living composer'. Grainger has given Damrosch a copy of
A Dance Rhapsody (no. 1) and has 'convinced Henry T. Finck' [critic
of the *New York Evening Post*] of Delius's genius by playing the
Piano Concerto. Grainger is still at Governor's Island with no
time for composition or piano practice but learning 'a great deal'
about instruments.

GRAINGER, ROSE   91-14
To Jelka Delius
Jan. 22nd 1921
Telephone Plaza 4867/680 Madison Avenue/New York City [letterhead:
                          see 91-12]
ALS   One single leaf
       [The recto and three and a half lines of the verso
       appear to be in another hand]
[PG's number 91-13(T)]

A letter of New Year's greetings which concludes with:-

        Frederick/Delius has no greater admirer in this/
        world than Percy Grainger -

Rose gives a synopsis of their news:- They have just toured Cuba
and Grainger is in the South now; in July they intend sailing for
Denmark to collect folk songs and folk-lore with Evald Tang
Kristensen; Rose's 'At Home' in New York for Gervase and Lady
Winefride Elwes was only five days before Gervase's 'terribly tragic'
death; Cyril Scott, now touring Canada before his second New York
recital on 4 February, has stayed six weeks with them; USA is now
swamped with 'musicians from Everywhere' and she thanks God that
Percy arrived ahead of them. She signs herself 'Yrs affectionately/
Rose Grainger'.

GRAINGER, ROSE   91-[15]
Additional item. An envelope inscribed by Percy Grainger:-

        Rose ['& Percy' - deleted] Grainger's/Letters,
        postcards, etc./to Fred & Jelka Delius/Dried
        geranium with words from/Rose Grainger to Deliuses/
        clipping from musical paper (1916-17) & postcards
        with PG's/press cuttings on.

The dried geranium flower, threaded into a piece of paper, inscribed by two different hands, was found with another piece of paper carrying a pencilled explanation in Percy Grainger's hand to the effect that the words 'Martha Washington Geranium' are in Mrs Edith Simond's writing and the message:-

> Carrying our love to you both -/Yrs affectionately:/
> Rose Grainger -

is in Rose Grainger's holograph.
PG dates this '(1916-1921?)'.

Also found with the above: A press cutting 'Percy Grainger on Tour' (n.d.) captions a photograph entitled 'PERCY GRAINGER AND HIS MOTHER'.

[Found with this item was the empty envelope of the letter 91-13 (PG's number GM91-12(T)) whose postmark Grainger misconstrued as 'Feb 14, 1919' instead of 14 Dec 1918. It would, perhaps, be not too fanciful to suggest he read this date wrongly because in his mind he thought of the flower as having been sent for Valentine's Day 1919.]

ROSE GRAINGER, AGED 49

Photograph by Rude og Olfing, Kristiania, Norway, September 1910.
Reproduced by courtesy of the Grainger Museum Board,
University of Melbourne.

In the Archive of the Delius Trust, London, there are ten original letters and postcards from Percy Grainger to Frederick Delius which pre-date the following list from the Grainger Museum.

> *(i)*   n.d. [*prior to 95-1, FD to PG*
>   *22/4/07*]
> *(ii)*   20.5.07
> *(iii)* 8.6.07
> *(iv)*   9.9.07
> *(v)*   31.12.07
> *(vi)*   28.3.08
> *(vii)* 13.9.08
> *(viii)* 31.1.09
> *(ix)*   17.8.09
> *(x)*   19.9.09

GRAINGER, PERCY   93-1
To Frederick Delius
6.7.10
31A King's Road/Sloane Square/S W [letterhead]
ALS   One leaf folded
[PG's number GM93-1(T)]

> My dear friend Delius/I was so/overdelighted to
> get your lines/& we both <u>rejoice</u> to hear that/
> you are better. It was so sad/to see you so seedy
> when here.[*] ...

Delius is introducing Grainger to the conductor, Hermann Suter. The
English Dance is mentioned as not yet copied out in full, but
Grainger is beginning to compose seriously. He lists his engage-
ments of the last six months and forecasts the future, summing up:-

> The last 6 months/has [sic] made an indescribable/
> difference in my hopes/& chances. ...

He concludes:

> Ever yours/Percy Grainger

A postscript asks:

> Is adorable *Brigg Fair* printed yet?

*See 178B-209 et seq. in this volume and 178A-JD/Leni(i) -
4 January 1911.

GRAINGER, PERCY   93-2
To Frederick Delius
26.1.1911
Veendam
ALS   One single ruled leaf, written recto only
          Envelope addressed: Hotel Juisisana, Wiesbaden, Duitschland.
          pmk Veendam 26.1.11
[PG's number GM93-2(T)]

          My dear Friend/I cant say how/grieved I am to hear
          you are seedy* ...

          ... deep delight at & thankfulness/for your
          dedication of *Brigg Fair* to me. ...

He has shown it to Mengelberg who, however, knew it already.

Grainger concludes:

          God bedring is the heartfelt wish of your/fond Friend/
          Percy

*See 178A-JD/Leni(i) - 4 January 1911.

GRAINGER, PERCY   93-3
To Frederick Delius
n.d. <1 or 2 January 1912>
31A King's Road/Sloane Square/S W [letterhead]
ALS   One leaf folded
[PG's number 93-7(T)]

          My dear friend/I loved to/hear from you. ...

In answer to a request he sends Fru Grieg's Copenhagen address:
p.adr: Hr Wilhelm Hansen/Gothersgade 11.

          We saw a lot of her & her/sister (Tony Hagerup)
          in the/fall when we were in Norway & had jolly
          times . ...

Grainger embarks 'to-morrow' on a concert tour (30 concerts)
and wonders if they might meet in Dresden where he plays on 1 February
after a recital on 31 January in Leipzig. The enthusiasm for
Delius's works in Frankfurt following a recent performance of
Sea Drift has gladdened him. He concludes:

          Ever your fond & admiring/friend Percy

[Grainger's day book shows that he was in The Hague on 3 January
1912 (GM).]

```
GRAINGER, PERCY                          93-4
To Frederick Delius
n.d. [15 February 1912]
no address [London]
PCS      pmk London 15 Feb 1912
         pmk Grez 16-2 12
         addressed:  Grez
[PG's number GM93-3(T)                   PG/FN10
```

Conveys thanks for Delius's card.

> ... Beecham ... is a <u>genius</u> ... in my *English Dance* ...

```
GRAINGER, PERCY                          93-5
To Frederick Delius
18.2.12
no address [London]
ALS      One single leaf
[PG's number GM93-4(T)]
```

> My dear Delius/Beecham did/your entr'acte music/to
> "Romeo & J" today/just before my piece./I never loved
> anything/more in my life ...

> <u>perfect</u> in every/deepest sense. ...

Grainger concludes:-

> Your loving & thank-/ful friend/Percy

```
GRAINGER, PERCY                          93-6
To Frederick Delius
18.9.12
31A King's Road/Sloane Square/S W [letterhead]
ALS      One single leaf
[PG's number GM93-5(T)]
```

Enclosures: Two printed programmes   (i) 7 Okt. 1912 Berlin
                                      (ii) 11 Okt. 1912 Hamburg
            including PG's arrangement of the *Irish Tune from
            County Londonderry* and Grieg's folk song arrangement
            Opus 66, no. 14, 'Im Ola Tal'.

> My dear friend/We rejoice to hear/from dear Miss
> Gerhardi that you/will soon be in London ...

On 30 September Rose and Percy leave for Berlin and return from
Hamburg about 30 October, so they will be unable to hear Delius's
'work' at Birmingham.

> ... longing to hear your/adorable *Dance Rhap*. again
> on/Oct 15 at Woods "Prom" concert. ...

Wood recently did Grainger's *Mock Morris* 'perfectly'. Grainger conducts his own *Green Bushes* on 19 October at Queen's Hall [see Appendix III newsclipping 23/12/1912 from *The Standard*].

[Page 2 of this letter has not been filmed.]

GRAINGER, PERCY   93-7
To Frederick Delius
5.3.13
31A King's Road/Sloane Square/S W [letterhead]
ALS   Two leaves folded of which pages 3 and 6 are written across
         the fold.
[PG's number GM93-8(T)]   PG/FN11

>   My dear friend/I rejoice to see that/Beecham is
>   giving your *Mass of/Life* on March 10, but at the
>   same/time gnash my teeth, as I/am in Switzerland
>   that date/playing. .../It is a great joy to follow
>   the/progress of your works in this/country
>   within the last year./You are written of & spoken
>   of/in quite another tone now, &/tower above the
>   other British/composers more & more in/all sorts
>   of people's minds. ...

He emphasises the part Beecham and Balfour Gardiner have played in
this and outlines his own remarkable success as composer this year.

This letter shows both Grainger's good business sense and genuine
concern for the older composer's success. He suggests that Delius
should confirm his present pre-eminence in the rank of British
composers by writing works for small orchestra and publishing the
'Entr'acte' from *A Village Romeo and Juliet* as a separate work in
order to reach a wider audience.

Grainger concludes:

>   Very much love from your/fond admirer/Percy.

GRAINGER, PERCY (with ROSE)   93-8 [91-6]
To Frederick Delius
19.3.13
no address [London]
PPCS   pmk London 20 Mar [13]
         pmk Grez 21.3.13
         addressed: Grez (in Rose Grainger's hand), with the message:

>   ... Percy has/now sent the Choruses to Prof.
>   Schwicke-/rath [in Munich] ... We/enjoyed y^{r}
>   concerto last night - ...

>   verso: photograph of Percy signed 'fondly Percy 19.3.13'
>   with a similar message beginning 'A thousand thanks ...'.

[PG's number GM91-3(T)
and GM93-6(T)]

GRAINGER, PERCY   93-9
To Frederick Delius
12.11.1913
Grand Hôtel/Fennia/Helsingfors/Finland [letterhead]
ALS   One single ruled leaf
[PG's number GM93-9(T)]

       Darling Delius./We rejoiced unspeakably/to
       hear your *Lebenstanz*/<u>gloriously</u> performed by
       Schneevoigt/here two nights ago. I love it
       more/each time. ...

Schneevoigt has also performed it in Sweden and 'is doing it in Riga
to-night'. Grainger has just completed 'a wonderfully successful/
tour of 60 concerts in Norway Russia & Finland'.

He concludes: 'Yrs ever/Percy'.

GRAINGER, PERCY   93-10
To Frederick Delius
n.d. <early January 1914> [1913-14? added in pencil]
American Hotel / Amsterdam [letterhead]
ALS   One single ruled leaf
[PG's number GM93-11(T)]

       My dear Delius/Lovely to hear from you. ...

Grainger regrets he is touring in Holland 'all this month' and so
will not hear Mengelberg perform Delius's Two Pieces for Small
Orchestra in London [21 January 1914]. Mengelberg conducted
Grainger's *Mock Morris* at 'a London Philharmonic before Xmas' ...
'with great success'.

Grainger wonders whether the Vienna Philharmonic's decision to give
his *Father and Daughter* under Schrecker is due to Delius and whether
they can meet in London 10 March for the latter's *Sea Drift*
performed by the Oriana Society. This performance in its turn owes
something to the backing of both Balfour Gardiner and Grainger. He
concludes:

       Am happ[y] to hear of your Wiesbaden performance
       Feb. 15./Love from/<u>Percy</u>.

GRAINGER, PERCY   93-11
To Frederick Delius
25.1.1914
American Hotel / Amsterdam [letterhead]
ALS   One single ruled leaf
[PG's number GM93-10(T)]   PG/FN12 & 13

       Darling Delius./I hear Mengelberg/did your 2
       new pieces for small orch/here about 14 nights
       ago. ... He told me he <u>loved</u> them ...

He notes that he finds Delius 'steadily more and more appreciated
in all the countries' where he goes. He gives Mengelberg's Amsterdam
address. The Manager of the Concertgebouw wants FD's biographical
details.

> ... I see your & my pieces were done together in
> Chicago/with much success the other day./Love from
> us both. Fondly/Percy G

GRAINGER, PERCY   93-12
To Frederick Delius
n.d. <25 or 26 February 1914>
19 Cheniston Gardens / Kensington [letterhead]
ALS   One leaf folded
[PG's number GM93-16(T)]

> My dear Delius/A thousand/thanks for the 2
> lovely/little scores. I rejoice/in them &
> long to hear/them. Have already told [Dan]
> Godfrey (Bournemouth)/of them. ...

Grainger is concerned to hear of the high performance fee of five
pounds required by the publishers for Delius's piano concerto which
Grainger is booked to play at Torquay on 16 April. He asks
whether this is true because, if so, it will 'almost kill' the
Concerto in England ...

> Met Schuricht to-day at/Lady Speyers. What a
> darling! ...

Grainger, about to tour Germany and Holland, is 'just off to
Saarbrucken'.

He concludes:

> With love, & warm/thanks for the lovely scores/
> Yrs ever/Percy

[This letter was probably written during a brief stop in London
between Sheffield, where Grainger played on Tuesday 24 February,
and Ostend where he arrived before 8.00 p.m. on Thursday, 26
February. He reached Saarbrucken on Friday 27 February 1914 (GM).]

GRAINGER, PERCY   93-13
To Jelka Delius
11.3.14
19 Cheniston Gardens/Kensington [letterhead]
ALS   One leaf folded of which two sides are blank
[PG's number GM93-13(T), but internal evidence shows it should
precede his GM93-12(T).]

> Dear Mrs Delius/A thousand/thanks for your kind
> letter & for your inter-/vention with Univ[ersal]
> Ed[ition]. ...

He has written to accept the 'special Bedingungen [terms] so kindly conferred'. He is 'now busy getting up the lovely work ...' [the Piano Concerto].

He enthuses over 'last night's performance of *Seadrift*[*] and the *First Cuckoo in Spring*'. 'I almost love Seadrift the best ...'.

A red ink postscript enquires whether the 1907 [Harmonie] Edition of the Piano Concerto (which he is using) is quite correct.

*See 93-10 above.

GRAINGER, PERCY   93-14
To Frederick Delius
26.4.14
7 Pembroke Villas,/Kensington, W.   [Balfour Gardiner's letterhead]
ALS   Two single leaves
[PG's number GM93-14(T)]   PG/FN14

        My dear Frederick/Torquay was/delicious ...

The success of the Concerto ...

        ... really effective & rather easy,/thanks to
        its excellent Klaviersatz. ...

[Torquay Festival of 16 April 1914, directed by Basil Cameron, with Beecham as guest conductor for the Delius items and Grainger conducting his own *Colonial Song*.]

Grainger has also heard both the 'Impressions' [*On Hearing the First Cuckoo in Spring* and *Summer Night on the River*] at Bristol, New Philharmonic Society, well done by Barter, and he expands at some length an interesting fact that some of Delius's works, more especially these two pieces and *A Dance Rhapsody* (no. 1), are closer to his heart, and more exactly what he himself would like to express in music, than his own works.

He concludes:

        With much love/Ever fondly/Percy.

GRAINGER, PERCY   93-15
To Frederick Delius
n.d. [6 May 1914]
7 Pembroke Villas,/Kensington, W. [letterhead]
PCS   pmk London 6 May 14
        pmk Grez illegible
        addressed: Grez
[PG's number GM93-15(T)]   PG/FN15

        Dear friend. How very sweet of you to put/me on
        for Bradford, Nov 27. I have already/signed for it. ...

GRAINGER, PERCY   93-16
To Frederick Delius
n.d. [12 June 1914]
31A King's Road/Sloane Square/S W [letterhead: the word 'permanently'
                                        in red ink beside it]
PCS   pmk London 12 Jun 14
          pmk Grez 14-6 14
          addressed: Grez
[PG's number GM93-12(T)]

          Dear friend/I am very happy to tell you/that I shall
          be playing the Concerto at Helsingfors/(with
          Schneevoigt) on October 19, & at Manchester with (Sir
          H./Wood) at Brand Lane's Concerts* on January 23. [1915] ...

Grainger also hopes to play the Concerto at 'Luzern'.

He concludes:

          Fondly yrs. Percy

[By October Percy and Rose had emigrated to USA.]

*Grainger means 'Brands Lane' concerts in Manchester.

GRAINGER, PERCY   93-17
To Frederick Delius
Aug. 10-1914.
31A King's Road/Sloane Square/S W [letterhead]
PCS   pmk London 10 Aug 14
          pmk Grez 13-8 14
          addressed: Grez
[PG's number GM93-17(T)]   PG/FN16

          Dear friends./How are you both ...

Grainger wonders how the War is affecting Grez and says there are
no ill effects of war so far in England. He intends to play the
Concerto with the LSO on 8 February 1915 but has put off his Autumn
tour [to the Continent]. He is conducting 'at Wood's Proms' on 18
August.

He concludes:-

          Much love from us both to you both/Percy
          Grainger

In his copy file Grainger has annotated this last point:-

          First London performance of *Shepherd's Hey*
          for full orchestra; also *Colonial Song*.

GRAINGER, PERCY   93-18
To Frederick Delius
30 Aug. 1914.
C/o Miss Isobel Du Cane, "Ballards", Goudhurst, Kent.
PCS   pmk Goudhurst 30 Au 14
          pmk Grez illegible
          addressed: Grez
[PG's number was not supplied for this as he did not make a copy
of it.]

> Enchanted at your card./Am taking mother for a
> short trip to America on Tuesday/(1st Sept) as
> she is sleeping so/badly .../Take my advice, dont
> remain/in Grez. You two dears are/too percious [sic]
> to the future./ Dont wait for a panic near/you.
> Leave now for/England & from here to U.S.A. ...

GRAINGER, PERCY   93-19
To Frederick Delius
Nov. 11. 1914.
Hotel Calumet/340 West 57th Street/New York City. N.Y. [letterhead]
ALS   Two single leaves
[PG's number GM93-18(T)]   PG/FN17

> Darling Delius,/We were overjoyed to/hear from
> you, & such an interesting &/you-ish letter too,
> & beside ourselves with/joy at the thought of
> your/coming over here! ...

Advice about hotels and prices and the possibility of Schirmer as
a publisher for Delius. Agents he still does not know.
Damrosch, who is 'doing 3' of Grainger's 'orchestral works' in
December and January, is looking forward to meeting Delius. In
his hurry to leave England Grainger forgot the score and band
parts of the Piano Concerto and he would like Delius to send them.

GRAINGER, PERCY   93-20
To Frederick Delius
April 18. 1915
C/o Antonia Sawyer/1425 Broadway/New York City. N.Y./U.S.A.
ALS   Five single leaves
[PG's number GM93-19(T)]

> My dear friend,/We are both so happy to know
> that/you & your dear wife are safe in England./
> It was lovely to hear from you. My pianistic
> success/here has been simply tremendous, & next
> winter/I will be having almost more to do than
> I can manage. ...

Having established the Grieg Concerto with US audiences, Grainger will
do the same for Delius, beginning with a booking for Friday, 26
November 1915, now that the full score and parts have arrived from
England. He wonders how to transmit performing rights money to

Universal Editions [his contract was 100 marks a year for as many performances as he liked, each music society to pay 30 marks in addition - April 1915-16] - possibly via Switzerland? He gives advice about publicity in USA. Schirmers tell him that the high performing rights on Delius's works have caused his scores to be unobtainable in USA and his name unknown except to the top rank conductors. American audiences, he insists, are still 'star-worshippers' rather than 'compositionally interested'.

> ... Even *Tipperary* which was played everywhere
> suddenly/became silent in restaurants, etc. when
> they clapped/on a performing fee. ...

Grainger suggests Delius's publishers should make some initial concessions to establish his name in USA and he should spend some money on advertisement in two musical papers. In the meantime he would like a eulogistic letter from Delius to himself for advance publicity* with regard to his playing of the Concerto and quotes at length, with many deletions, a model for Delius to follow 'laying the jam on pretty thick, as I have, as USA needs this'. The letter ends on page 6 'Lovingly yrs/Percy Grainger/' but then continues for four more pages concerning publicity.

*See *The Musical Leader* 18/11/15, Appendix III.

GRAINGER, PERCY   93-21
To Frederick Delius
June 19, 1915.
'N.B. permanent' c/o Concert Direction/Antonia Sawyer/
        Aeolian Hall. W42 St./New York City. U.S.A.
ALS   One leaf folded
[PG's number GM93-20(T)]   PG/FN18

    My dear friend/Lovely to hear from you ...

Delius has assisted in the renewal of Grainger's 1915-16 contract with Universal Editions*. Grainger agrees to be careful in future not to speak of Delius as Anglo-German [but only as English] and Damrosch is delighted with the scores of the two works for small orchestra.

He concludes:

        Ever fondly/Percy

A postscript eulogises *A Dance Rhapsody* (no. 1).

*See 93-20 above and Related Documents, Appendix II.

GRAINGER, PERCY   93-22
To Frederick Delius
Aug 18. 1915.
c/o Concert Direction Antonia Sawyer/Aeolian Hall. W42 St/
        N. York City. U.S.A.
ALS   Two single leaves
[PG's number GM93-21(T)]   PG/FN19

        My dear Frederick/I am so rejoiced at/having
        got a letter this morning from/Stokowski (to
        whom I sent the *Dance Rhaps*) beginning:/"I have
        arranged to do/Delius' *Dance Rhapsody* on Oct
        29-30." ...

        That is jolly: Philadelphia Orchestra doing/
        the "Dance R", Damrosch (N York Symphony)/giving
        your "Stimmungsbilder", & the N.York/Philharmonic
        & I doing the Concerto./Now I shall write Stock
        (Chicago Symphony)/& enthuse to him about "Dance R"
        &/"Stimmungsbilder" & send him scores, too. ...

        ... Muck (Boston Symphony) ... is said to be
        violently anti-British. ...

        I enclose a few stray newspaper notices/in which
        your name (even under the form of/Delino!) appears ...

The misprint is, he observes, the result of small newspapers
copying from the *Musical Quarterly* and the *Musician*, in which
Grainger has written 'a few words', and also an article by the
New York critic Finck [see Appendix III]. Grainger plans a full
article 'specially about your music ...'. He concludes by urging
Delius to stay on in Norway lest he be pressured into war work less
valuable than composing.

        ... we love to think of you safely in/adorable
        Norway. ...

He concludes:

        Ever devotedly/<u>Percy</u>

A postscript refers to his article 'Impress of Personality' already
sent to Delius.

GRAINGER, PERCY   93-23
To Frederick Delius
Dec. 2. 1915.
The Southern./680 Madison Ave./New York City. U.S.A.
PPCS   pmk New York Dec 2 1915
         pmk Grez omitted
         addressed: Grez
A portrait photograph
[PG's number GM93-22(T)]

Dear friend/Your Piano Concerto/went <u>magnificently</u>, ...

This announces the success of the Delius Piano Concerto with
Stransky conducting and also of the Two Pieces for Small Orchestra
'last Sunday' under Damrosch. Many advance notices and Grainger's
article in the *Musical Courier* paved the way. Schirmer would now
like to publish something by Delius.

[See Appendix III.]

GRAINGER, PERCY   93-24
To Frederick Delius
Dec 7. 1915
The Southern/680 Madison Ave/New York City.
PPCS (2)
            Two cards with similar portraits as above, having on
            the reverse side advertisement reprints concerning
            Grainger and the Tchaikovsky Concerto.
            Presumably sent in an envelope which has not survived.
[PG's number GM93-23(T)]   PG/FN20

The short holograph message beginning

            Darling Delius/Mother & I are/<u>so</u> overjoyed that
            you are both back/in Grez safe<u>ly</u> & are so happy
            there. ...

shows that these two cards accompanied a cutting of Grainger's
article on Delius from the *Musical Courier*[*], three criticisms and
some 'printed matter' which goes out to '5000 people in which your
works are mentioned'. Grainger has enjoyed meeting the Osbournes
with their recent news of Frederick and Jelka.

*See Percy Grainger, 'The Genius of Frederick Delius', *Musical
Courier* 1915, Appendix III.

GRAINGER, PERCY   93-25
To Frederick Delius
Sept 14. 1916.
The Southern, 680 Madison Avenue, New York City
ALS   Two folded leaves of which pages 3 and 6 have been written
        across the fold
[PG's number GM93-24(T)]   PG/FN21

            My dear Frederick./You will think my silence/
            very long; but you would forgive me if you/
            knew how overworked I am. ...

He advises Delius not to come to USA until after the war when his
pieces are in stock again and by which time Grainger's efforts to
popularise a few works will have borne fruit. Oberhoffer at
Minneapolis has given *A Dance Rhapsody* and, on Grainger's
advice, is going to do the '2 Mood pictures' [*On Hearing the*

First Cuckoo in Spring and *Summer Night on the River*] on the day
of Grainger's new Suite and the Grieg Concerto. Tandler in Los
Angeles '(who produced the *D. Rhap.* in this country)' is 'going
to give the 2 M.Ps'. Grainger is 'bringing out' his own *In a
Nutshell Suite* for orchestra, '10 new piano pieces, 4 pieces for
2 pianos''and 2 other trifles'. He is designing all his own
covers for these publications and has 'a vast pianistic winter
ahead'. He is also now at work on the composition of *The Warriors*.
He advises Stoeckel of Norfolk [Connecticut] as a good man to 'bring
out' new material in the USA. Grainger has spoken to him and has
also given Delius's credentials to Mr G.S. White of Schirmer and
[Mr] Heinecke of Breitkopf & Haertel, New York.

He concludes:

> With lots of love/to you both from us both/Yrs
> ever/Percy

GRAINGER, PERCY   93-26
To Frederick Delius
n.d. [14 September 1916]
no address [New York]
PCS (3) pmk New York Sep 14 1916
        pmk Grez 4-10 [1916]
        addressed: Grez

On the reverse side are printed excerpts from newspapers.

The card now labelled (a) displays excerpts from the *New York
Evening Post, Tribune, Press* and *The New York Evening Sun* all
dated 'Nov. 27, 1915' [the last erroneously 1916] headed:-

> Grainger plays Delius Concerto (First Performance
> in America)*

A second copy of (a), possibly enclosed in an earlier letter, has
no address and instead a message in blue pencil:

> Do you want more of these, could you use them?

*See newsclippings concerning 26 November and 28 November 1915 -
Appendix III.

The card now labelled (b) is headed:-

> Grainger's *In a Nutshell Suite* for orchestra,
> Piano and Deagan Percussion Instruments.

This is followed by printed excerpts from *The New York Times* and
the *New York Tribune* of 11 June 1916, *The Sun* (N.Y. City) and the
Boston Evening Transcript of 10 June 1916, and H.O. Osgood in the
Musical Courier of 15 June 1916.

These have not been numbered by PG.

GRAINGER, PERCY   93-27
To Frederick Delius
June 4 1917.
680 Madison Ave. New York City, USA.
ALS   One leaf folded
         Envelope addressed: Grez
         pmk New York June 4 6.30 pm 1917 Grand Central Sta.
         Opened by the French military censor.
         Found empty at time of original inventory, the envelope
         is presumed to have contained PG's item GM93-25(T), now
         numbered 93-27.
[PG's number GM93-25(T)]

         Darling Frederick/This is to tell you/that I
         have now heard 2 rehearsals/of my latest
         orchestral piece *The/Warriors* (which I am
         conducting at the Norfolk, Conn., Festival on
         June 7)/& that, altho I do not consider it a/
         perfect work in many ways, I look/upon it as
         my best orchestral work/in large form, & feel
         it is trully [sic]/emotional & also trully
         orchestral/in feeling./Therefore I am dedicating/
         it to you, ...

The rest of the letter describes his emotional response to Delius
and his music and notes the things they have in common. It is clear
he feels uncertain of his future in the 'tragic times' they live in
and he concludes:

         Reverently & lovingly yrs/Percy Grainger

A postscript indicates he is overworked and concludes 'Goodbye'.

GRAINGER, PERCY   93-28
To Frederick Delius
Sept 14, 1918.
309 West Ninety-second Street/New York City. U.S.A.
ALS   A single leaf of which one side is blank
[PG's number GM93-26(T)]

         Beloved friend/Above is our new/permanent
         address. ...

He introduces two gifted Americans who wish to visit Delius when
in Europe:- Miss Mary Cameron who plays Delius's Piano Concerto,
and Lieut. Leo Sowerby (band leader), 'gifted composer'.

GRAINGER, PERCY   93-29
To Frederick Delius
Dec. 15, 1918
'New address 309 West 92 Street, New York City, U.S.A.'
TLS   Two leaves, typed recto only, with PG's holograph emendations
[PG's number GM93-27(T)]   PG/FN22

Beloved friend,/Stransky and the New York Philomonic
[sic]/gave your *Life's/Dance* last Thursday and mother
and I were there. It was an insp/ired performance
and had a great and genuine success. The whole/
press treated it big and liked and admired it and
acclaimed you as/a genius, as you will see from
the enclosed clippings, which represent/the entire
press, so far. ...

Grainger outlines his present work as an assistant band leader and
its value to him in orchestration:

I have ceased to be a guesser and amateur/as
regards wind instruments ...

The War, with its emphasis on life's brevity, has made him want to
earn money as quickly as possible to realize some of his ambitions
both for himself and his friends:

to give occasional big concerts

of works he personally liked with no feeling of 'duty'.

Your works, Cyril Scott's/and my own are
the compositions I am most interested in. ...

With this in view, he is beginning to plan and requests a list of
the works Delius wants performed. He suggests Delius should visit
USA in the winter of 1920, as

Americans love the presence of the/man ...

He encloses an article from the *Metronome* in which he alludes to
Delius.

It was exquisite to hear *Life's Dance* again ...

What sadistic passion, what agony of bliss;
and what a glory in the horn/theme smashed
out near the end! ...

I became a full American citizen last June ...

USA is, in composition

where England was some 10 or 12 years ago;/
coming out of its shell and realizing what
itself signifies musically./In 5 or 10 years
time it will be in full blast compositionally. ...

He foretells fame for John Alden Carpenter, and Howard Brockway,
and '3 negro composers, W.M. Cook, Dett and Diton'.

He concludes:

Ever worshippingly/Percy

GRAINGER, PERCY   93-30
To Frederick Delius
Nov. 3, 1921
Seven Cromwell Place White Plains. New York, U.S.A. [letterhead]
TLS   One leaf, typed recto only
[PG's number GM93-28(T)]   PG/FN23

        My dear Frederick,/I enclose an interview with me,
        in the "ETUDE" (the musical news-/paper with the largest
        circulation), in which your music is dealt with. ...

Grainger is playing the Piano Concerto in Brooklyn 7 January, and
N.Y. City 8 January [1922]. He notes he still holds the material
[score and parts] of the Piano Concerto and requests information as
to whom at Universal Edition he should write. He suggests they
exchange lists of new works as they come out. His *Two Hillsongs*
(1901-1907) come out with Schirmer in February 1922, *Green Bushes*
(1909) appears soon with Schott - both for two pianos first and
later for 'Room Music'. *The Warriors* will be published as soon
as he has made some amendments. He asks permission to arrange
(without payment) *A Dance Rhapsody* (no. 1) for two pianos*

        ... which I regard as a good study-medium for/
        modern works. ...

The White Plains house is a saving towards his ultimate, though
(owing to inflationary conditions) postponed, goal of giving his
own concerts of Anglo-Saxon music.

Grainger concludes:

        Ever fondly,/Percy

*See Philip Heseltine to PG November 18th, 1923, Appendix II.

GRAINGER, PERCY   93-31 [copy]
To Frederick Delius
March 28, 1922
Bellingham, Wash.
TL   One leaf [a copy]

        Darling Frederick:/Most deeply distressed to
        hear from Balfour/Gardiner that you are having
        such a bad time, trouble/with lameness etc. ...

        ... You recovered/so well from your last trouble
        in 1912 or 1912 [1913?], have/been so prolific
        since ... that I am hoping that you will/soon
        have this trouble behind you also. Nervouse [sic]
        troubles/are terrible while they last.* ...

Grainger begs Delius to cheer himself with the thought of the 'many
souls ' he has 'touched to the core', especially his inspiration to
fellow artists. He concludes 'Your loving and admiring friend'.

*See 93-1 and 93-2 above; also FD to JD from Mammern July 1910,
178B-209 et seq.; and 178A-JD/Leni(i) - 4 January 1911.

GRAINGER, PERCY   93-32
To Jelka Delius
n.d. [Aug. or Sept. 1922 - written in Grainger's hand]
Grand Hotel/Carl Johans Gate/Kristiania [letterhead]
ALS   One leaf folded
[PG's number GM93-29(T)]

>   My dear Mrs Delius/Thanks for your kind letter.
>   I/am longing to see you both. But the 8th
>   (Friday)/is my Kristiania Recital ...

This recital is Grainger's first in several months and the first
in Europe for several years.

Grainger proposes Thursday, the day of the Deliuses' arrival, or
Saturday before they leave, 'if not bad for Frederick', and concludes:

>   Love to you both/Percy

[The recital took place on 8 September 1922 (GM).]

---

*PG to FD 12.6.29 - handwritten copy by Ella Grainger in
Library of Congress.*

*[Grainger writes from Pevensey Bay, Sussex, to describe
his special journey to London to hear Delius's Double
Concerto which 'Beecham conducted like a God.'|*

GRAINGER, PERCY   93-33 [copy] *
To Jelka Delius
Jan. 29th 1932 [Delius's 70th birthday]
'In the train'
Two copies were received by the Grainger Museum in 1975 from the
collection of typed copies deposited by Grainger in Adelaide.

>   Dear Jelka,/Thanks so much for your last lovely
>   letter. I wish to come back to something we have
>   discussed before: the desirability of having
>   Fred's sayings and opinions noted down by someone
>   who masters shorthand & can therefore take down
>   all he says without having to ask Fred to repeat.
>   A rare goldmine of wisdom, originality & fun will
>   be lost to the world if this is not done ...

He develops the point at some length, suggesting that Balfour Gardiner
or Fenby might ask provocative questions with a shorthand writer at
hand and provide material for an illuminative book. He concludes:

>   Please talk it over with Balfour & other Fred-
>   worshippers, as occasion arises, will you, dear
>   Jelka?/With our fond love and admiration always/
>   lovingly/Percy.

*This item is not on the microfilm.

GRAINGER, PERCY   93-34
To Jelka Delius
[14 July, 1934]
Draft telegram [not on the microfilm]

        July 14, 1934 Delius, Grez s.L., S et M, France
        We deeply mourn your beloved genius husband and
        sweet companion Ella Percy Grainger.

ELLA GRAINGER

Photograph by S.P. Andrew, U.S.A. [n.d.] [after 1927]
Reproduced by courtesy of the Grainger Museum Board,
University of Melbourne.

CHECKLIST AND INDEX of the letters of Frederick and Jelka Delius
to Percy and Rose Grainger

DATE	CORRESPONDENTS	TYPE OF COMMUNI-CATION	GRAINGER MUSEUM	PAGE
22/4/1907	FD/PG	ALS	95-1	51
12/5/1907	FD/PG	ALS	95-2	51
[31/5/1907]	FD/PG	PPCS	95-3	52
[6/7/1907]	FD/PG	PPCS	95-4	52
[5/9/1907]	FD/PG	PPCS	95-5	52
<6/9/1907>	FD/PG	PPCS	95-6	53
<26/3/1908>	FD/PG	PPCS	95-7	53
[31/12/1910]	FD/PG	PPCS	95-8	53-54
23/5/1911	FD/PG	ALS	95-9	54
11/7/1911	FD/PG	ALS	95-10	54
[14/2/1912]	FD/PG	PCS	95-11	55
[21/2/1912]	FD/PG	PCS	95-12	55
18/11/1913	FD/PG	ALS	95-13	55-56
<January 1914>	FD/PG	PPCS	95-14	56
<9/4/1914>	FD/PG	PPCS	95-15	56-57
29/4/1914	FD/PG	ALS	95-16	57
26/9/1915	FD/PG	ALS	95-17	57-59
22/10/1915	JD/RG	PPCS	97-1	59
[25/11/1915]	FD/PG	PCS	95-18	59-60
21/12/1915	FD/PG	PCS	95-19	60
11/1/1916	FD/PG	ALS	95-20	60-61
23/7/1916	FD/PG	ALS	95-21	61
5/10/1916	FD/PG	ALS	95-22	62

DATE	CORRESPONDENTS	TYPE OF COMMUNI-CATION	GRAINGER MUSEUM NUMBER	PAGE
15/11/1916	FD/PG	ALS	95-23	62-63
23/6/1917	FD/PG	ALS	95-24	63
14/1/1919) cont.) 16/1/1919)	JD/RG	ALS	97-2	64-65
16/1/1919	FD/PG	ALS	95-25	65-66
18/2/1919	JD/RG	ALS [Enclosure: *The Times* 31/1/19 re Violin Concerto]	97-3	66-67
17/12/1919	FD/PG	ALS [Enclosure: *Frankfurter Zeitung* re *Fennimore and Gerda*]	95-26	67-68
13/4/1924	FD/PG dictated [JD's hand]	ALS	95-27	68-69
<13 or 14/4/ 1924>	JD/PG	ALS	99-1	69
25/10/1925	JD/PG	ALS	99-2	70
20/5/1926	FD/PG dictated [JD's hand]	ALS	95-28	70-71
20/5/1926	JD/PG	ALS	99-3	71-73
30/3/1927	JD/PG	ALS	99-4	73-74
26/4/1927	JD/PG	ALS	99-5	74-75
2/7/1927	JD/PG	ALS	99-6	75-76
27/12/1927	JD/PG	ALS	99-7	76
27/12/1929	JD/Ella Grainger	ALS	99-8/EG	77

FREDERICK DELIUS DIED 10 JUNE 1934

DATE	CORRESPONDENTS	TYPE OF COMMUNI-CATION	GRAINGER MUSEUM NUMBER	PAGE
18/8/1934	JD/Percy & Ella Grainger	ALS	99-9/ PG & EG	78

CHECKLIST AND INDEX of the letters of Jelka Delius to Rose Grainger
(Percy Grainger's mother, Mrs John Aldridge
Grainger)

DATE	CORRESPONDENTS	TYPE OF COMMUNI-CATION	GRAINGER MUSEUM NUMBER	PAGE
22/10/1915	JD/RG	PPCS	97-1	59
14/1/1919 cont. 16/1/1919	JD/RG	ALS	97-2	64-65
18/2/1919	JD/RG	ALS [Enclosure: *The Times*]	97-3	66-67

CHECKLIST AND INDEX of the letters of Jelka Delius to Percy Grainger
and/or his wife, Ella Grainger, née Ström

DATE	CORRESPONDENTS	TYPE OF COMMUNI-CATION	GRAINGER MUSEUM NUMBER	PAGE
<13 or 14/4/ 1924>	JD/PG	ALS	99-1	69
25/10/1925	JD/PG	ALS	99-2	70
20/5/1926	JD/PG	ALS	99-3	71-73
30/3/1927	JD/PG	ALS	99-4	73-74
26/4/1927	JD/PG	ALS	99-5	74-75
2/7/1927	JD/PG	ALS	99-6	75-76
27/12/1927	JD/PG	ALS	99-7	76
27/12/1929	JD/EG	ALS	99-8/EG	77

FREDERICK DELIUS DIED 10 JUNE 1934

18/8/1934	JD/PG & EG	ALS	99-9/ PG & EG	78

DELIUS, FREDERICK   95-1
To Percy Grainger
22/4/07
90 Oakley Str/Chelsea SW [London]
ALS   One blue linen leaf folded of which one side is blank
         17.5 x 11 cms.

         Dear Grainger!/Thank you so/much for your/kind
         words about/"Appalachia" which pleased/me
         exceedingly/I hope you will/hear it once in/
         London as it/sounds better/on the Orckestra [sic]/
         than on the piano/I will bring the/piano score
         on/Thursday & also/the Concerto & am/looking forward
         to meeting/you again./Sincerely yours/Frederick
         Delius

[Found in Rose Grainger's sewing table.]

DELIUS, FREDERICK   95-2
To Percy Grainger
12/May 1907 [sic]
Grez sur Loing/Seine & Marne
ALS   One blue linen leaf folded
         17.5 x 11 cms.
         Envelope addressed: Percy Grainger Esqr/5 Harrington R^d/
                              South Kensington/Londres S W
         pmk Grez 12-[5 07]
         pmk London on verso illegible

         Dear Grainger!/Here I am again!/It is summer and/
         lovely & warm & I/hope you will come/and pay me a
         visit/before long. ...

He describes the old house and garden leading down to the 'clean
river' and a stag which swam across that morning to graze by the
pond (pièce d'eau') in their garden.

         ... I like your work/more than I can/tell you ...

Delius asks for a score of 'green bushes' and promises to send a full
score of *Appalachia* as soon as it arrives from Germany. He has
'several works/to arrange for pianoforte (2 hands)' and will send
'one of them/shortly to look at'. He is hard at work again, sends
a photograph with regards to Rose, and signs himself 'Your friend/
Frederick Delius'.

[Found in Rose Grainger's sewing table.]

DELIUS, FREDERICK   95-3
To Percy Grainger
n.d. [31 May 1907]
[Grez-sur-Loing]
PPCS   pmk Grez 31-5 07
          pmk London omitted
          addressed: 5 Harrington Rd.
          photograph: old bridge and ruined tower at Grez-sur-Loing

          Dear Grainger!/I sent you "Appalachia" which
          please take with you/to Grieg when you go as/
          he knows nothing of/my music & it will put/us
          in touch again as I/really like him so much. ...

He stresses that the score is for Grainger to keep and 'only shew
it/to Grieg'. He is in no hurry to receive *Green Bushes* as he is
working 'at something/new'.

_____

FD to PG 10/6/1907 - [Estate of Ella Grainger]

_____

DELIUS, FREDERICK   95-4
To Percy Grainger
n.d. [6 July 1907]
[Grez]
PPCS   pmk Grez 6-7 07
          pmk London omitted
          addressed: 5 Harrington Rd.
          photograph: 'Le pont et la rivière' at Grez-sur-Loing

          Dear Grainger/I suppose you will/be on the point
          of/starting for Norway ...

He wishes him well for his tour and adds:-

          ... My editor writes/me that "Paris" will only/
          be brought out this winter/I will bring you the
          score/when I come in September ...

DELIUS, FREDERICK   95-5
To Percy Grainger
n.d. [5 September 1907]
[Grez]
PPCS   pmk Grez 5-9 07
          pmk London Sep 6 07
          addressed: 'Percy Grainger' c/o Robinson/Concert
                      Direction/7 Wigmore Str/Londres W.
          re-addressed: Svinkløv Plantørbolig/Svinkløv
                      pr. Fjerritslev, Jylland, Denmark
          photograph: 'Le Loing, vu du moulin de la Fosse' at Grez

          Dear Grainger,/I suppose you/are back again/
          in London. I shall/arrive on Oct 1. and/shall
          bring my newest/Work a "Brigg fair", English
          Rhapsody. ...

DELIUS, FREDERICK   95-6
To Percy Grainger
<6 September 1907>
[Grez]
PPCS   pmk Grez illegible
         pmk Kensington Sp 7 07
         addressed: 5 Harrington Rd.
         re-addressed: (1) c/o E.L. Robinson/7 Wigmore St
                        (2) Svinkløv/Jytland
         photograph: 'Le pont et la rivière' at Grez-sur-Loing

         Dear Grainger/I just saw/in the papers/the
         announcement of/Grieg's death. I am very/very
         sorry. Have you/any particulars/Please write me/
         all you know./Warmly your friend/Frederick Delius

DELIUS, FREDERICK   95-7
To Percy Grainger
<26 March 1908>
PPCS   pmk Grez 26 ... 08 month obscure
         pmk London 27 ... 08 month obscure
         photograph: portrait of Delius
         addressed: 31a Kings Rd/Chelsea/Londres SW/Angleterre

         I send you some tickets/for a lute recital by an
         old/friend of mine - She sings/some folk songs. ...

He hopes to be in London for *Appalachia* and ends:

         With love to you both/your friend/Frederick Delius

Editorial Note: From this point names of works will be uniformly
         treated in italics both in quotations and in editorial
         synopses.

         See p. 1 Editorial Note Concerning Names of Works.

DELIUS, FREDERICK   95-8
To Percy Grainger
n.d. [31 December 1910]   *
Villa Hohenzollern./Weisser Hirsch. Dresden
PPCS   pmk [Weisser Hirsch] 31.12.10
         pmk London omitted
         addressed: 31a King's Rd.
         picture: 'Dresden. Freitreppe der Brühl'schen Terrasse'

         Hearty good wishes to you/& your mother for a
         happy/new year - We are staying here/until End of
         Feb. Send me/Mrs Grieg's address if you/know it. ...

*See 178A-JD/Leni(i) - 4 January 1911.

He concludes:

    Yrs affectionately/Frederick Delius

[Found in Grainger's 'bead box' sent from White Plains to the
Grainger Museum in May 1977, and so not on microfilm]

DELIUS, FREDERICK   95-9
To Percy Grainger
23 May 11
Grez sur Loing/(S & M)
ALS   One single leaf
        26.9 x 20.7 cms.
        Envelope addressed: 31a King's Road
        pmk Grez 23-5 11 12.55
        pmk London My 24 11 7.45 a.m.*

    Dear Percy -/I am coming to London on the/12th
    of June for a fortnight & hope/to see a lot of
    you - Beecham/gives a Concert of my works on/
    June 16$\underline{th}$ We shall live at 9/Hans Place - ...

He regrets he cannot come for Grainger's concert on 29 May, notes
that Dr Haym has engaged Percy for Elberfeld and Suter 'will of
course' also engage him.

*[These very clear postmarks have been quoted in full to illustrate
the excellent postal service in those days of steam train and sea
transport.]

DELIUS, FREDERICK   95-10
To Percy Grainger
11 July 1911
Grez sur Loing/S & M
ALS   One single leaf
        26.9 x 20.8 cms.
        Envelope addressed: 31a King's Rd
        pmk Grez 12-7 11
        pmk London omitted

    Dear Percy -/I was so pleased to receive your/warm
    & sympathetic letter & am/already looking forward
    to the performance/of your English dance by Beecham./
    You can depend on him doing justice/to it - & you can
    also always depend/upon me doing my utmost for/your
    work, which I love & admire ...

They are leaving for Norway on 15 July, returning via Thisted in Denmark
where Jelka will make sketches for 'the scenery/of Niels Lyhne'
[*Fennimore and Gerda*]. He is finding Grez 'heavenly' after his
'London social exertions'.

Delius concludes:

    With best love I am/always y$\underline{r}$ affectionate/
    Frederick Delius

DELIUS, FREDERICK   95-11
To Percy Grainger
n.d. [14 February 1912]
[Grez]
PCS   pmk Grez 14-2 12
         pmk London omitted
         addressed: 31a King's Road

         Ever so many/thanks dear friend/for all the
         music/which greeted me/this morning - The/
         2 songs are lovely/especially "Dedication"/
         The dances are/unique & I must hear them - ...

He will be going to Germany in March and will take the dances with
him.

DELIUS, FREDERICK   95-12
To Percy Grainger
n.d. [21 February 1912]
[Grez]
PCS   pmk Grez 21-2 12
         pmk London omitted
         addressed: 31a King's Road

         Dear Percy - Your loving & sympathetic/note just
         arrived & gave me/so much pleasure. I am so/
         awfully glad your dance went off/so well & that
         you are so pleased with/it - I have a splendid
         man for/it [in] Germany - a 2nd Beecham/Kapellmeister
         Langs - ...

Delius is writing to Langs about Grainger's work so that when he
goes to Elberfeld he can call on him at Hagen and Langs may attend
his concert.

DELIUS, FREDERICK   95-13
To Percy Grainger
18 Nov 13
Grez sur Loing/S & M
ALS   One leaf folded
         15.2 x 11.2 cms.
         Envelope addressed: 31a Kings Rd
         re-addressed: 24 Cheniston Gds
         pmk Grez obscure
         pmk Paddington Nov 19 13

         My dear Percy,/It was so awfully/sweet of you
         to write/& tell me all about/*Lebenstanz* in
         Helsing-/fors ...

Delius has just returned from Leipzig where, he says

... Nikisch did most/beautifully 2 small/
Orchestra pieces of/mine in the Gewand/-haus -
They are the/2 pieces for small/Orchestra which
I spoke/to you about when I/was in London a
couple/of years ago - quite/small orchestra -/
1) *on first hearing/the Cuckoo in Spring/2) Summer
night on/the river.* ...

On 20 November he will

leave for/Vienna to attend the/first performance
of/a quite new work -/*An Arabesk* for Baritone
Solo, Chorus/& Orchester [sic]. Words by/J.P.
Jacobsen ...

which 'comes off on the 26th'. On 1 December there will be a
recital of his songs in Vienna and he hopes to be in London early
in 1914.

Delius concludes:

your affectionate friend/Frederick Delius/My
wife sends her best love to you/both

DELIUS, FREDERICK   95-14
To Percy Grainger
<January 1914>
[Grez]
PPCS   pmk Grez illegible
        addressed: 31a Kings Rd
        photograph: Grez-sur-Loing 'Le pont vu des Jardins de
                                    1'Hôtel Chevillon'

        Dear Percy. If you are in London/go & hear my
        2 pieces for small/Orchestra at the Philharmonic/
        I hear Mengelberg is doing them/on the 20th or
        21st? I have in-/troduced "I ola Dalom"* in the/
        1st one - Spring always means/for me a longing
        for Norway./Tell me your plans as I do not/want
        to miss you when I come/over to London - With love/
        Fr. Delius.

*Norwegian folk-song arranged by Grieg as Opus 66, no. 14, for piano
solo. Percy Grainger first brought this volume to the notice of
Delius. See also PG to FD 93-6.

DELIUS, FREDERICK   95-15
To Percy Grainger
<9 April 1914>
[Grez]
PPCS   pmk Grez illegible
        pmk Kensington. W. 10 Ap 14
        addressed: 19 Cheniston Gardens/Kensington
        re-addressed: 7 Pembroke Villas/Kensington
        photograph: Grez-sur-Loing, 'La Tour et 1'Eglise vues du
                                     Moulin de la Fosse'

Dear Percy. I am so sorry I/cannot come to Torquay
& hear/you play the Concerto. ... I shall be over/
for a fortnight in June &/hope to see a good deal
of/you - ...

DELIUS, FREDERICK   95-16
To Percy Grainger
29 April 14
Grez-sur-Loing/Seine et Marne [letterhead]
ALS   One single leaf
       29 x 22.5 cms.
[stored by Percy Grainger in a special piece of transparent
paper with 'Happy Xmas' design]
       Envelope addressed: 19 Cheniston Gardens
       re-addressed: 7 Pembroke Villas
       pmk Grez illegible
       pmk Kensington 1 My 14

       What pleasure your letter gave/me, dear friend!
       You are always/the one who sends me good/news
       from England - I love your/impulsive letters -
       they are so/entirely yourself & just like your/
       music which you know I love so much./I feel we
       have an enormous lot in/common & that you under-
       stand better/than anyone what I am trying to/do -
       I was so happy to hear of/your success in Torquay. ...

Delius asks whether Grainger might play his Piano Concerto again
at Bradford on 27 November in a concert devoted to his works.
[He makes an important statement about the piano part, which
should be compared with the Delius/Szanto correspondence (Delius
Trust Archive), indicating that at the time Theodor Szanto played
the Concerto in 1907 there was a measure of disagreement between
them. Here he says: 'Szanto arranged the Klaviersatz/most
beautifully - & made it much/more effective - ...']

He suggests that Percy and his mother should visit Grez either
before or after his June visit to London. He describes the 'Lilacs
& Laburnums in full/bloom'.

Delius concludes:

       Ever so much love to you & to your/mother -
       your loving friend/Frederick Delius

DELIUS, FREDERICK   95-17
To Percy Grainger
Sept 26th 1915
Gjeilo/Hallingdal [Norway]
ALS   Two single leaves of ruled paper
       29 x 22.3 cms.
       Envelope addressed: Percy Grainger Esqr/c/o Concert
                            Direction/Antonia Sawyer/Aeolian Hall/
                            W 42 Street/New York City/N.Y./U.S.A.
       re-addressed: The Southern/Mad. Ave. & 62 St
       pmk Gjeilo 26 [I]X 15
       pmk New York Oct 8 1915

57

          Dear Percy/Your letter, newspaper cuttings/&
          'Impress of Personality' arrived here/safely
          & gave me immense pleasure./What a devoted
          friend you are to boom/me & my music in America &
          get me/all those performances - ...

Delius expects the proofs of his 'Sonata for Violin and Piano' any
day and promises a copy as soon as it is published. He describes
the wonderful Autumn colours of the 'Højfjeld. 3000 ft', their
first snowfall that morning, and encloses some flowers picked
'on the Fjeld'. Of Norway he adds 'The/country agrees with me
like no other'. They plan to move in a few days time via Kristiania
[Oslo] to Denmark for a month, staying with the Schous [mutual
friends] at Palsgaard-Juelsminde and in Copenhagen. All the same
they long for Grez, as he cannot work in 'Hotels & private houses'
and, as he is sure the 'Germans will/never get to Paris or anywhere
near/it anymore', they may 'risk the North Sea in November'.

Delius comments on Percy's article, 'Impress of Personality':-

          ... it is quite excellent &/the most lucid
          thing I have read since/years on the subject - ...

He develops at some length the theme that art, 'especially music',
in which instinct outweighs intellect, is 'right & rare', but
he considers that once intellect outweighs instinct 'the trouble
begins'. He gives as example the 'wonderful' discordant sound
of primitive music which when 'intellect gets hold of the idea
& systematises/it - it sounds wrong & is wrong/& is not rare -
since it runs/around like the measles ▬▬▬▬▬▬▬
&/one finds every Tom, Dick, Harry/& Louisa doing it - ...'*

In this letter Delius also shows his distrust of schools of
composition in any art, giving Cubism as an example:-

          ... I admit that one/man can come along & see
          everything/in Cubes - He may have something the/
          matter with the lense of his eyes, but/I dont
          admit that several thousand at/once see everything
          in Cubes - otherwise/than thro their intellect
          which has less/to do with art than one likes to
          think. ...

*Delius was to take up this theme of commercial exploitation in
an article 'At the Cross-Roads' published in the *Sackbut*
September 1920 and in an interview for *The Daily Telegraph*
5 October 1929 with special reference to commercialised jazz:
e.g. 'Jazz is an invention of so-called Americans who have taken
rag-time and pretend that it is negro music.'

He remarks that 'Conscription/is coming on apace in England', but being '52* already' he is unlikely to be called up. He would love to come to America again, but feels Grainger's advice as to the correct time to visit will be essential. He might try to have his 'Drama, *Fennimore & Gerda*' staged in New York, feeling that America must have 'a lot of good unformed/stuff ... & less prejudice; ...' and that 'the war will/last at least another year - ...'.

*'52 already' - Delius was, in fact, 53 on 29 January 1915, but until some time after 29 January 1923 (his 60th birthday celebrations in Frankfurt) believed himself to have been born in 1863. Philip Heseltine was the first to look up the birth certificate.

DELIUS, JELKA   97-1
To Rose Grainger
22.10.1915
[Denmark]
PPCS   pmk Juelsminde [Denmark] 2[2] 10.[1]5.
         pmk New York. N.Y. Times Sq. Sta. Nov 9 1915
         addressed: c/o Concert Direction/Antonia Sawyer/W 42 St/
                     New York City/U.S.A.
         re-addressed: The Southern/680 Madison Ave.
         photograph: 'Palsgaard Slot'

         Dear Mrs Grainger, I want to/send you a 'hilsen'
         from love-/ly old Palsgaard! ...

         We shall/stay here till End of the month, then
         14 days/Copenhagen and then back to France/via
         Bergen - Newcastle - London ...**

The message ends and is signed on the recto, written round the photograph, with the postscript 'Please address to Grez-sur-Loing Seine et Marne/France'.

**See Rachel Lowe-Dugmore, 'Documenting Delius (Part One)', *Studies in Music* (University of Western Australia), No. 12, 1978.

See *The Musical Leader* 18 November 1915, Appendix III. This quotes a letter from Delius to Grainger (n.d.) authorising Grainger to introduce his Piano Concerto to America. See also PG to FD 18/4/15, 93-20 above.

DELIUS, FREDERICK   95-18
To Percy Grainger
n.d. [25 November 1915]
[Grez]
PPCS   pmk Grez 25-11 15
         pmk New York. N.Y. Times Sq. Sta. Dec 18 1915
         addressed: Concert Direction Antonia Sawyer, as above
         re-addressed: 680 Madison Avenue

Dear Percy - Here we/are again in Grez-/sur-
Loing (S & M) We/risked mines & sub/marines in
order to/get back in to our/home - travelling/
nowadays is insupport/able - France is the
country/to live in & we shall not/budge from
here until/the war is over. How are/you both.
I am just/longing to get news from/you. I am
working now/in the garden which has been/
frightfully neglected./Y^rs lovingly Fr. Delius.

DELIUS, FREDERICK   95-19
To Percy Grainger
21/12/15
PCS   pmk Grez partially obscured: 21 ... 15
         pmk New York omitted
         addressed: 680 Madison Ave/New York City/N.Y.

The message, fully headed, begins

         Grez-sur-Loing/(Seine & Marne) 21/12/15
         Dear Percy. I was delighted/to get your
         card with such/good news - ...

Delius repeats the gist of his PCS above, pmk 25-11-15 [95-18],
and emphasises:-

         Don't/neglect your composition work/au fond
         that is the only thing/that counts in the
         end. ...

concluding:-

         Ever your affect^te/Friend Fr. Delius

DELIUS, FREDERICK   95-20
To Percy Grainger
Jan 11 1916
Grez-sur-Loing/Seine et Marne [letterhead]
ALS   Two single leaves, the verso of the first leaf blank
         29 x 22.4 cms.
         Envelope addressed: The Southern/680 Madison Ave./New York
                                      City/NY

         pmk illegible

         Dearest friend - All your cards & the wonder/ful
         criticisms* arrived safely & we were both/overjoyed
         with your marvellous success - I/am also so glad
         you met the Osbournes -/they wrote me a long letter,
         full of en-/thusiasm & admiration for you - They/also
         sent me criticisms - Both your letters/arrived on
         the same day - so it was/a "jour de fête"
         with us - I have been/working at the *Requiem*
         & have now/completed it ...

He muses on the possibility of taking up the Osbournes' invitation
to stay on their ranch in California and is thinking of the possibility of having some USA first performances.

> ... I have the *Song of the/high Hills* the
> *Arabesk* & the/*Requiem* & also 'N̶i̶e̶l̶s̶-̶L̶y̶h̶n̶e̶'
> *Fennimore*/which have never been performed ...

He longs for "Sea-drift" [*Sea Drift*] to be performed in America.
He is worried about the effect of conscription on his English
musician friends, especially Balfour Gardiner, and praises Percy's
perspicacity in moving to America. The only reminder of the war
in Grez is their inability to find a gardener and so they are
working hard in the garden every afternoon. They enjoyed Norway
'immensely' and found the Norwegians 'violently pro allies - Such
a/contrast with the Danes - who avoid/the subject most carefully ...'
and he feels 'that they are all/doing splendid business selling
their/margarine & pigs to Germany - ...'

He is reading the Norse sagas again and names 'Grettir' and 'Howard
the Halt'.

*See newsclippings for 1915, Appendix III.

DELIUS, FREDERICK   95-21
To Percy Grainger
July 23rd 1916
Grez-sur-Loing/Seine et Marne [letterhead]
ALS   One single leaf
         29 x 22.4 cms.
         Envelope addressed: "The Southern"/680 Madison Avenue,/
                               New York City/N.Y.

         pmk illegible

> My dear Percy - If I came to New/York in the
> Autumn or winter would/it be possible to have
> some of my works/produced? My new String
> quartett [sic] -/the *Arabesque* [sic] - Published
> by <u>Uni/versal Edition</u>. My double Concerto -/My
> new *Dance Rhapsody* No. 2/My *Requiem* - Chorus -
> Baritone/Soprano & Orchestra -/Perhaps Schirmer
> would like to publish/some of these - ...

He asks advice as to whom to approach in America. He gives news of
Balfour Gardiner, who has been conscripted and, after weeks of
training in dreadful conditions (graphically and amusingly
described by Delius), is working in the censor's office in Calais.
Delius himself has 'been working splendidly' since his return to
Grez. He concludes:-

> Write soon/dear friend, with love to you both -/
> devotedly yours/Frederick Delius

DELIUS, FREDERICK   95-22
To Percy Grainger
October 5th. 1916
Grez-sur-Loing/Seine et Marne [letterhead]
ALS   One single leaf
         29 x 22.4 cms.
         Envelope addressed: 'The Southern'/680 Madison Avenue,
                               New York City.

         My dear Percy -/I was overjoyed to receive your/
         wonderful letter & printed cards & hasten to/reply -
         Firstly let me tell you how glad I am/to learn
         that,in spite of tremendous practical/work, you
         have composed such a lot of new/things - & let me
         thank you, dear friend for/the dedication of your
         new orchestral work *The/Warriors* - ...

The rest of the letter discusses at greater length the suggestions
of the previous one. Should the War be over by 'next summer' he
intends to stay with the Osbournes in California and be in
America for the 1917-18 season.

He has written to Schirmer and Breitkopf and Härtel about possible
publication in America of the Double Concerto, the String Quartet,
A Dance Rhapsody (no. 1), *In a Summer Garden* and *Appalachia*.

He makes the important statement that he is now writing a 'Violin
Concerto' and would like Grainger to negotiate with Kreisler to
play it in America, if possible, when he himself comes over.

DELIUS, FREDERICK   95-23
To Percy Grainger
15th Nov 1916
Grez-sur-Loing/Seine et Marne [letterhead]
ALS   One single leaf
         29 x 22.5 cms.
         Envelope addressed: The Southern/680 Madison Avenue
                               New York City
         pmk illegible

         My dear Percy -/In re-reading your letter it
         occurred to me/that I had not, perhaps, expressed
         myself/quite clearly enough in my reply - ...

He now thinks the war will go on for another two years and so he
would like Percy's assistance to have performed in America all
those works which have not yet had a hearing.

He is considering the possibility of American publication for the
Violin Concerto, the Double Concerto, the String Quartet and
A Dance Rhapsody (no. 2) and is still hoping to arrive for the
1917-18 season. Concerning the Violin Concerto, he asks for
Kreisler's address and proposes to dedicate it to him.

By travelling in the early summer he would hope to be in time to
'make a/few arrangements to conduct for 1917-18 - if possible' ...
'to gain some/money - at least enough to pay travelling expenses.'

In an added note at the top of the first page he observes:

> P.S. Indirectly I hear Stokowsky has the piano
> score of the/*Mass of Life* & likes it very much -
> I am sending him/the full score -

DELIUS, FREDERICK   95-24
To Percy Grainger
23 June 1917
Grez-sur-Loing/Seine et Marne [letterhead]
ALS   One single leaf
         29 x 22.4 cms.

> Your letter caused me/indescribable emotion, dear
> old/friend; I was just wrapping up a copy of/my
> Violin Sonata to send to you - the mere/idea that
> <u>you</u> should have to go to the war/with a hundred
> thousand others & be shot at/brings thoughts &
> feelings to me which I dare/not <u>describe</u> - As I
> have so often told my/wife & others, I feel that you
> are the only/real individual, with an original &
> daring/line of thought & conduct, who I have ever
> met -/& the only musician of genius - bar Grieg -/
> who I ever came in contact with. ...

Delius emphasises his conviction that they have 'an enormous lot in
common' and stresses his gratitude for Grainger's 'loving tribute'
to his music together with the dedication of *The Warriors*. The
submarine war prevents his coming to America but he goes on -

> ... 'I have a feeling that/we shall meet again
> & perhaps before/very long - Something tells
> me the war/will be over before the winter &
> then I/should join you in New York - ...

He signs himself

> your/loving friend/Frederick Delius

[Received at the Grainger Museum from White Plains in May 1977 and
so not on the original microfilm.]

FD to PG 20/7/1918 - copy DT/LC

To Rose Grainger
14.1.1919 continued on 16.1.19[19]
44 Belsize Park Gardens/London N.W.3
ALS   Four single leaves [8 pp.]
          25.3 x 20.3 cms.
          Envelope addressed in Jelka's hand: Percy Grainger Esq/
                          309 West 92 Street/New York City./U.S.A.
          pmk Hampstead 16 Jan 19
          pmk New York omitted
95-25 below was enclosed with 97-2.

          Dearest Mrs Grainger,/We were both perfect-/ly
          delighted with your letter from/Dec 13th
          received this morning -/It was such good news
          that *Life's/Dance* was performed with such/
          success. ...

          We came/to London beginning of Sept./as we
          were thoroughly tired/of our 3 years exile
          in France/entirely away from music! ...

Grez had been in the war-zone since the big German push of Spring
1918. They left Grez for Biarritz taking only the new manuscripts
and their 'Gauguin pictures' [Jelka writes the plural quite firmly
on 'pictures', but might mean the original 'Nevermore' and her own
copy]. They find no-one in England appreciates the importance of
the American intervention which alone had enabled them to return
to Grez so soon.

While in Biarritz their home was commandeered by the French
military as an officers' mess. They returned briefly to lock
up everything they could and then went to a furnished flat in
London taking with them, by special permission, their French maid.
Fearful of mines when crossing the Channel, Jelka had worn a bathing
costume under her outer garment and had placed all the manuscripts
'in watertight bags' ready to fix to a lifebelt and swim with them
if necessary.

The London concert scene is described vividly:- Beecham (with
Pitt and Goosens) only concerned with opera schemes, leaving
Wood the sole concert conductor of stature; Norman O'Neill
valiantly reconstructing the Philharmonic with Balfour Gardiner's
financial assistance and as conductors Toye, Ronald and Boult - the
latter directing Delius's Violin Concerto, with Sammons as soloist,
on 30 January. Wood gave Delius's new work *Eventyr* 'a few days ago'
... 'a spirited performance' ... 'an enormous audience' ... 'the
piece was awfully well received ...'. Beatrice Harrison has
already played the Cello Sonata at two recitals and with her sister
May is studying the Double Concerto for a probable performance in
March.

          Fred would like/and probably will found a/new
          Concert-Society - appeal/ing to a more democratic/
          public, as they certainly seem/to appreciate music
          more than/the Society people; they are/deadly ...

She gives news of Percy's old friends:- Balfour Gardiner is still
in the Army and in Wales guarding a prisoners' camp. He has visited
them twice ... 'so sincere and real'. Cyril Scott they have met
once at Lady Cunard's looking 'rather tired'. The O'Neills are
busy 'bringing up their new baby'. Austin is in the Beecham Opera
while Bax and Toye have come into substantial legacies.

They have escaped from the war but have not escaped all sorrow.
Delius's nephew, aged 19, was killed at the very end of the war,
and the bulk of their money being either in a German bank, or
invested in America through that bank, cannot be made available
for them[*].

[*]See Rachel Lowe-Dugmore, 'Documenting Delius (Part Two)', *Studies
in Music* (University of Western Australia), No. 13, 1979.

DELIUS, FREDERICK   95-25
To Percy Grainger
16th Jan 1919
44 Belsize Park Gardens N.W.3
ALS   Three single leaves, each leaf blank verso
          25.3 x 20.3 cms.
Enclosed with 97-2 above.

          Your letter, dear old pal, arrived here/like
          a flash of sunshine ...

          I was delighted to/hear that *Life's Dance* was
          so well performed/by Stransky & his Orchestra &
          also so well/received. Wood gave the first
          performance/of my new Orchestral Ballad -
          Eventyr (Once/upon a time) after Asbjørnsen -
          He gave/a ripping good performance & took
          no end/of trouble with it - I have a wild
          shout/in it (20 men behind) which came off
          very/well. ...

He still hopes to come to America, possibly for the season 1919-20
'say in October or November' - and lists his new manuscript works as:-

          1) Requiem .../
          2) Concerto for Violin, Violoncello &/orchestra/
          3) Violin Concerto/
          4) Eventyr (once upon a time)/after Asbjørnsen)/
          5) Sonata for Violoncello/
          6) Dance Rhapsody No 2/
          7) Poem of Life & Love/Orchestra/ ...
          8) Song before Sunrise/for small Orchestra ...

He also notes as 'works published, but awaiting a first performance':-
The Song of the High Hills, and *An Arabesk*; and works which
Grainger will not have heard but which might do well in America -
the Violin Sonata (published Forsyth 1917), the '4 Elizabethan Songs'
[*Four Old English Lyrics*] 'published by Winthrop Rogers', and
'2 à capella Chorus's'.

[He omits *North Country Sketches*, at that time still in MS, presumably because it had had a first hearing in 1915.]

He is finding his fellow countrymen dull and looks forward to 'a bit of American alertness and vivacity'.

He concludes:

> What a time we shall have - Ill[*] conduct/the
> Concerto & you play it - Hurrah!!/Ever your
> loving friend/Frederick Delius

*I'll

DELIUS, JELKA   97-3
To Rose Grainger
18.2.19
44 Belsize Park Gardens/London N.W.3.
ALS   One leaf folded and one single leaf
         22.8 x 18 cms.
         Envelope addressed: Mrs Rose Grainger/309 West 92nd Str./
                              New York City/New York/U.S.A.
         pmk Hampstead 18 Feb 19
         pmk New York omitted
         Enclosure: cutting from *The Times*, Friday, January 31,
                     1919 headed: THE PHILHARMONIC SOCIETY/
                     DELIUS'S VIOLIN CONCERTO

> Dear Mrs. Grainger,/We have been think-/ing so
> much of you/and Percy since/your recent letters/
> that I feel I must/write and tell/you once more/
> what great pleas-/ure they gave Fred. ...

The letter describes the successful first performance of the Violin Concerto at the Philharmonic Concert on Thursday night, 30 January, with Sammons playing and Boult conducting. Characteristically Jelka says:

> ... Sammons/played beautifully./But, oh, how <u>could</u>/
> he do otherwise/It is the most lov-/able work, ...
> one great/ceaseless flow and so won-/derfully
> orchestrated - that/the instrument is always/
> heard perfectly; yet the/orchestra is <u>not</u> an
> accom-/paniment, ...

> Augeners/immediately undertook to/publish the
> work ...

> Of course there are none/of those fillings and
> sense-/less runs and other beastly/things that
> make most Concerto's [sic] so hateful.
> Winthrop Rogers is bringing/out Freds Cello.
> Sonata and/4 Elizabethan Songs. ...

Percy's works *Shepherds Hey* and *Molly on the Shore* are frequently
played - 'most popular here'. A French music critic, Raymond
Duval, recently met by 'Fred', wants to introduce Percy's work in
Paris. Balfour Gardiner is still awaiting demobilisation.

They long for the peace conferences to end and to feel 'quite free
again'. Jelka records jubilantly that 'Fred's' music is being
received in Britain to such an extent that the Philharmonic Concert
described was the only well attended concert of the season. Even
so, she finds Anglo-Saxon behaviour lacking in liveliness and
emotional warmth. She wishes she could have sat between Rose and
Percy at the Concert and finds Percy's enthusiasm and many schemes
most invigorating - commenting 'Here they are all too slow, too
slow!!'

[Jelka's single-minded devotion to her husband's music blinds her
to the many reasons, including the War (!) for the slow pace of
London's artistic recovery.]

Note: The paragraph concerning 'Percy's' music has been outlined
      in ink [by Rose?]

DELIUS, FREDERICK   95-26
To Percy Grainger
17 Dec 1919
Grez-sur-Loing/(S & M)
ALS   One single leaf of cross-ruled paper headed '95 -
                          Frederick Delius to PG' [Grainger's hand]
         27 x 21.3 cms.
         Envelope addressed: 309 West 92nd Street, New York City
         pmk Grez 18-12 19
         pmk New York omitted
         Enclosure: a cutting from the *Frankfurter Zeitung* headed
                          FREDERICK DELIUS: "FENNIMORE UND GERDA"

My dear Percy/We have just returned here from London/
where Jelka received a letter from your mother/
asking me to write a work for piano & orchestra/for
you. If I can only get to work again/in peace I
would try & do so: We have been/rushing about
for the last 4 months - First/to Norway for 6 weeks -
then we read in the Danish/papers that my last music
drama *Fennimore/& Gerda* (Niels Lyhne) was going to be
given/in Francfort [sic] on the 18th October - so
after/much difficulty, what with passes etc, we/
went to Francfort for the rehearsals &/first performance & were there a month - It/was all wonderfully
interesting & they gave/themselves endless trouble. -
All the scenery/entirely new for the occasion & the
performance/was excellent & came off on October
21st -/I was called 8 or 9 times - ...

He remarks on the complete absence of anti-English or anti-American
feeling in Germany and thinks that the German defeat in the War
has stimulated interest in music and the arts generally.

In February we go to London again for/the first
performance of *The Song of the high/hills*. The
double Concerto & the *Pagan/Requiem*. ...

Balfour Gardiner came to Grez with them for a few days on their
return from London. 'he is now in Ashampstead/again and very
contented - ...'.

----

*FD to PG (dictated, but signed) 16/12/1922 and 28/3/1923;
FD to PG (dictated) 29/9/1923;
JD to PG 29/4/1923, 17/8/1923, 23/9/1923, 14/10/1923 and
        29/11/1923
FD to PG (dictated) 23/1/1924 quoted as concert publicity
        in the Musical Courier 17 April 1924 and
        The Musical Leader 18 April 1924 (see Appendix III)
JD to PG 23/1/1923 [i.e. 1924], 24/2/1924, 21/3/1924 and
        4-6/4/1924*

        - copy DT/LC

DELIUS, FREDERICK (dictated)   95-27
To Percy Grainger
13.4.1924
<Mandelieu> headed 'address Grez-sur-Loing/Seine et Marne/France'
ALS   One single leaf in Jelka Delius's holograph headed
       'Fred dictates'
       26.8 x 21 cms.
       Envelope addressed: 7 Cromwell Place/White Plains/
                            New York/U.S.A.[1]
       pmk Mandelieu 14-4 24 [Alpes Maritimes[1]]

       Dear Percy/I cannot tell you how sorry/and
       disappointed I am in not being/able to come
       to America to attend/your two concerts[2].

Delius's new doctor from Cassel has advised against the journey and
suggests that he should begin a course of treatment at the Cassel
sanatorium on 1 May. They expect to leave the South of France on
25 April. A postscript adds that initial treatment has been
beneficial and Delius hopes to be able to write next in his own
hand. Percy is conducting *The Song of the High Hills* and *North
Country Sketches* as well as his own *Marching Song of Democracy*.
Delius, deeply grateful, is anxious that Percy should thank the
Chorus and Orchestra in his name and convey his regrets for absence.

1. The Delius/Clews correspondence and Delius/Grainger 1924
    items in other archives confirm that Jelka and Frederick
    Delius had wintered in Rapallo and in March moved near
    to Mr and Mrs Henry Clews' home in La Napoule.

2. 28 April, Bridgeport, and 30 April, Carnegie Hall, New York,
    the second anniversary of Rose Grainger's death.

PERCY GRAINGER WITH JELKA AND FREDERICK DELIUS IN 1923

Photograph by Alfred Krauth, Frankfurt am Main.
Reproduced by courtesy of the Grainger Museum Board,
University of Melbourne.

He promises to send from Grez the newly published *Eventyr* and
A Dance Rhapsody (no. 2). A second postscript* reminds Percy that
'the 3 drummers in the *S. of H.H.*' are essential to the 'real
effect'.

*This refers back to a postcard dated 4.4.1924, DT/LC, which
contains the following statement:-

> Fred wants me to tell you - the score of
> *S. of H.H.* only <u>two</u> drummers are marked -
> But that is a mistake, there ought to be <u>3</u> ...

DELIUS, JELKA   99-1
To Percy Grainger
n.d. <13 or 14 April 1924>
<Mandelieu>
ALS   One half leaf
         21 x 13.4 cms.
Enclosed with 95-27 above.

> Dear Percy, only a hasty/word in addition to/
> Fred's. I think he is/progressing just a little/
> all the time, he is much/freer and less cramped/
> in his walking! ...

Jelka has written to Dr Simon [*Frankfurter Zeitung*] to send his
New York critic to Grainger's Delius concert and has heard that
'Walther Jaeger' will attend.

She has been very busy translating Henry Clews' play *Mumbo-Jumbo*
and has now to write a preface preparatory to his marketing it in
Germany.

[See newsclippings, Appendix III: *Musical Courier* 17 April 1924,
The Musical Leader 2 May 1924; items for 28 and 30 April 1924.
See also Appendix II, item II, 'To My Fellow-Composers', May
1924.]

JD to PG 26/5/1924;
FD to PG 26/5/1924 (dictated but signed 'F.D.');
FD to PG 20/10/1924 (Delius's own hand)
JD to PG 20/10/1924, n.d. [late November 1924?],
28/3/1925, [3/5/1925] and 12/9/1925

- copy DT/LC

DELIUS, JELKA   99-2
To Percy Grainger
25.10.1925
Grez
ALS   Two leaves [4 pp.] violet paper, written in green ink
          27 x 21 cms.
          Envelope (matching) addressed: 7 Cromwell Place/White Plains/
                              New York/U.S.A.
          pmk Grez 2[5 or 6?]-10 25
          pmk New York omitted
          overwritten by PG: 'HOME/Sonneck' [Sonneck was an employee
                              of Schirmer: see below]

          Dear Percy,/I am sending you 2 photos/which I hope
          you will like. How/are your own? And did the films/   *
          arrive alright? I sent them off/the day after your departure ...

Jelka's letter insists that Delius's health is improving and he 'seems
to see just/a little'. Details of their diet and routine are
followed by a list of forthcoming performances of Delius's works and
a suggestion that perhaps Grainger should approach the firm Schirmer
in New York informally to see if they might be interested in taking
over the works published by Augener who seem anxious to 'cede the
works to another/firm ...'.

*All evidence currently available suggests 1925 as the year of
Grainger's first visit to Grez-sur-Loing, despite repeated
invitations, many London meetings before the War, and considerable
time together in Frankfurt and Norway in 1923.

Five photographs were found with the letter: two of Jelka with the
cellist, Barjansky; three of the house and garden with Delius at
the right in a chair; one of Jelka Delius and Percy Grainger;
one of Delius in a wheelchair with a male attendant, presumably
the 'Brüder' mentioned in this letter as being required to return
to his 'Brother house'.

[Received at Grainger Museum from White Plains in May 1977 and so
not on original microfilm.]

JD to PG 8/12/1925 - copy DT/LC

DELIUS, FREDERICK (dictated)   95-28
To Percy Grainger
20.5.26
Grez
ALS   One leaf folded, of which two sides are blank, in Jelka
          Delius's holograph headed 'Fred dictates'
          18 x 14 cms.
          Envelope addressed: 7 Cromwell Place/White Plains/
                              New York/U.S.A.
          [overscored in pencil   keep DELIUS]
          pmk illegible
99-3 below was enclosed with 95-28.

My dear and devoted friend,/Your letter of
May 2d and/your 2 former letters arrived/
safely - the last this morn-/ing. The news about
the con-/cert was indeed very grati-/fying; and
I shall never/be able to thank you enough/for
all you do and have/done for my work. We thought/
of your dear mother on/the 30th so intensely and/
we were with you during/the concert with our hearts ...

[The concert was that of the Los Angeles Oratorio Society on 30
April 1926 at which Grainger directed, as guest conductor, his own
Marching Song of Democracy in revised version, the *Irish Tune* for
unaccompanied chorus, using 'nonsense syllables' and his arrangement for male voice quintet, double mixed chorus and orchestra of
the Faroe Island folk dance song *Fadir og Dotir* (Father and
Daughter), which was encored. Commenting on the success of this
last item which he 'had heard in London', Delius says 'It is a
splendid-/ly original work'. See newsclippings, Appendix III.]

Grainger has sent the Deliuses some gramophone records he has made.
Delius finds his Chopin (B minor Sonata) 'splen-/did - <u>awfully good</u>'
and the *Strathspey Reel* 'delightful, tho/<u>not quite</u> successful/as
a record - the orchestra/never comes out quite so well'.

Delius is 'greatly looking forward' to Grainger's visit to Grez
'next/year' and adds 'Please regard/our place as your home,/your
head-quarters, and/be with us as much as/you can!!'

[Grainger is about to visit his native Australia with four Steinway
grand pianos especially made for the tour: see Slattery, p. 117 et
seq., and Bird, p. 193 et seq.]

DELIUS, JELKA   99-3
To Percy Grainger
20.5.1926
Address stamped Frederick Delius/Grez-sur-Loing/S & M
ALS   Two leaves folded and written in the order recto, verso,
        and across the inside fold to give three pages to a folded
        leaf, six pages in all
        18 x 14 cms.
Enclosed with 95-28 above.

        Dearest Percy,/It is a wonderful/living joy,
        all this / splendid news about/your Los Angeles
        Concert ...

Jelka thanks him for the gramophone records [see 95-28 above dated
20.5.1926] and especially the *Strathspey Reel* about which she
adds 'The brother/[Delius's male nurse, a member of a Protestant
Brotherhood] was quite scared at/all that liveliness'.

She insists that Delius's health is 'ever so much better' and
continues:-

He eats quite normally/and is so much more/
lively and sits up longer/at night, sleeps less
in/the day. ...

Only his eyes do not seem/much changed. ...

She outlines their efforts to obtain a good wireless set. The
present one

... works very well for the/big english [sic]
Station Daventry/but we fail to obtain the/
short wave towns in the/north and on the
continent./Germany has generally beastly/
programmes. But the smaller/English towns
excellent/ones.

She lists recent English programmes they have enjoyed:-

... frequent perform-/ances of Grieg - ...
Yesterday/the whole 2nd act of *Götterdäm-/
merung* from Covent Garden/which was absolutely/
perfect and just as if one/were in the theatre,
singers/and orchestra equally audible./We had
Molly on the Shore/several times and often
madri-/gals (old engl) and Folk/Songs - ...

They have had a number of visitors:-

Fred protests/beforehand every time/and then
enjoys it tho-/ro'ly and is often quite/amusing. ...

The 'Howard Jones's' and 'Barjansky' have been to play the Double
Concerto to Delius and 'the Cassirers ... (the man who con-/
ducted Fred's opera's [sic] in Berlin and Elberfeld' have just
visited.

Later she says that the 'Simons/from Francfort [sic] are coming/
to-morrow' for Whitsuntide.

Jelka blames the General Strike [4-12 May 26] for preventing Beecham's
plan for an English festival in Paris, and now Beecham's lawsuits
have caused him to disappear from their musical world, otherwise
Delius's *Song of the High Hills* would have been included in the
programme with the Philharmonic Choir under Kennedy Scott and the
London Symphony Orchestra.

A similar project to perform *A Mass of Life* in Paris with Klenau
conducting a Paris orchestra has foundered because of the cost of
transporting the Philharmonic Choir. Delius is very disappointed
and Jelka says picturesquely 'I have/emptied my inkbottle in vain
over all this' (despite having so little time to write), and she
wishes she had Percy's 'faculty of doing 2 or 3 things at a
time ...'. She began this letter 'at dawn' and, she continues,
'now the Sun has risen/and I must to work ...'. Her 'work' is
outlined as managing the household, assisting and superintending
the care of the invalid Delius, including long sessions of reading
aloud, a current 'nice book' being *Inland Far* by Clifford Bax.

Good wishes are sent for Percy's Australian tour, a postscript
thanks him for interesting himself on their behalf with Schirmers
(though Jelka is 'afraid it is no good!'), and there is mention of
an 'enthusiastic letter' from their mutual friend Robert
Nichols about the Los Angeles Concert.

DELIUS, JELKA   99-4
To Percy Grainger
30.3.1927
Grez-sur-Loing (S & M) [Station] Bourron [blue letterhead
        with picture of a train before 'Bourron']
ALS   Three single leaves
        27 x 21 cms.
        Envelope addressed: 7 Cromwell Place/White Plains/N.Y./
                             U.S.A.

        pmks illegible

        Dearest Percy,/Both your letters, March 11th/
        and 14th have arrived -

        I am so happy that you have/found this wonderful
        swedish/girl*

Jelka shows in this letter their concern for Percy's welfare since
his mother's death. She says:

        Your life/was becoming too strained,/...
        these/deadly, lonely Concert-jour-/neys -
        all those gushing faces/of people, who, after
        all, give/you nothing - ...

She gives her normal report on her husband's health, insisting he
is 'ever improving tho very little. ...'. During the winter
months they have had several visits from Beecham, who 'also
brought a/London doctor over to see/Fred and he advised a Paris/
Doctor ...'. The latter 'seemed very thoughtful and wise' and
told Jelka that 'it was/rare to see a man with Fred's/illness, so
calm, reposed-/looking and especially so/entirely clear
headed ...'. On his advice they decided not to risk any drastic
treatment. The London doctor had frightened her by suggesting a
Sanatorium.

She gives the latest musical news:-

1) BBC Concert in the London Studio 'for Fred's birthday'
    [29 January] - *Brigg Fair*, Violin Concerto, *In a Summer
    Garden*, *A Dance Rhapsody* (no. 1), conducted by Geoffrey Toye
    with Albert Sammons violinist with 'a little speech'
    addressed 'to Fred,/which seemed so personal and/extra-
    ordinary; he enjoyed/it all.'

*Ella Ström, whom he met on shipboard when returning from
Australia to America.

73

2) '...on the other/hand', she says, 'it is shameful, that
    they/have given 11 big broadcast/Concerts in the Albert Hall,
    with-/out giving a note of Delius - ... Beecham/does not
    hate them [the BBC] for nothing.'

3) The Harrison sisters have been over to play to Delius.
    Beatrice now plays the Cello Concerto 'splendidly ... and
    the youn-/ger sister Margaret the Violin Con-/certo with
    great Style and purity'. A slightly ambiguous but intriguing
    comment follows: 'Fred was delighted with their/playing
    (That little Russian in Franc-/fort quite travestied the
    Concerto)/Beatrice is going to America/in October - ...'
    [and would have liked introductions].

4) The 'useful devotion' of the Harrisons [May (violin),
    Beatrice (cello), Margaret (violin and piano) and their
    parents] was the moving force behind the BBC birthday concert
    and [the BBC's? and/or HMV?] gift of an 'excellent Loud
    speaker and/a first rate H.M.V. Gramophone ...'.

5) '... a friend, Kenneth/Spence, who has been much/to the
    Hebrides and has been/humming to Fred their beauti-/ful
    songs, shearing - milking,/reaping etc. all doing something/
    songs. ...'.

6) 'The Barjansky's are on their way to/Sweden, after an
    exhib in Brussels,/where Mrs B. made the portrait of/the
    Queen of Belgium.'

7) They have not heard from Lippay 'for ages' and wonder if
    Percy has news.

The postscript is almost a page and a half and includes the last
three points above as well as a lengthy commentary on Jelka's
now completed task of translating Henry Clews' play *Mumbo-Jumbo*
into idiomatic German and comments:- 'These intellectual gymnastics/
are most agreable and exhilarat/ing'. Her only regret is that Clews
'repeats/himself so much'. She also adds that 'Fred' approves
Percy's new plans and urges him 'to store some money,/and not
give it all away.' A 'P.P.S.' adds the sly comment concerning
Ella - '"She" had to be a Scandina-/vian of course!'

DELIUS, JELKA   99-5
To Percy Grainger
26.4.1927
Grez-sur-Loing (S & M) [Station] Bourron [blue letterhead as above]
ALS   Two single leaves
         27 x 21 cms.

         Beloved Percy,/It was nice of you to/send cutting
         about Fred. I think/too, crude and exaggerated as/
         these statements are, they give/the romantic
         personal interest/that people want. And of course/
         I never read it all to Fred. Any-/how, Fred is - if
         anything, a wee/bit better, and I think walks/better
         since he takes this new treat-/ment. ...

She explains that, propped between the male nurse and herself,
Delius walks '20 yards' then rests and retraces the distance.
Delius also gave 'a most wonderful lesson during/2 hours' to
[unnamed] unexpected visitors, an 'elderly female' pianist and
'a young girl/singer' at whose performance he had at first raged
and then, after two days feeling remorse, had received them again
and corrected their faults. They 'went away most/eager to go on
studying', while Jelka 'was enchanted that/Fred could make so
sustained/an effort!'. Jelka wonders if Grainger could persuade
Steinway to supply Delius with a grand piano, as they expect him
to make his headquarters at Grez when he visits Europe again, and
also because so many celebrities visit them to play to Delius.

> Our Ibach piano is, of/course, shockingly bad.
> One can/hardly expect real artists/to play on it ...

[She includes composers and conductors and names Beecham, Klenau
and Schuricht as constant visitors.]

They are delighted that *The Song of the High Hills* has been given
at the Hollywood Bowl, although Goossens' 'tempi' do not always
please Delius. 'Kuosewitzky' [sic] she notes 'has/done the Song
of the H.H. in Boston/in March. ...'.

She regrets that, while many of Percy's works are given on BBC
Daventry, they never do *Father and Daughter*, which she remembers
vividly hearing at his mother's house in the King's Road, [Chelsea],
the place and time she always associates with his mother.

Only Beecham seems to be giving Delius works in London and she
praises his recent 'Seadrift' [sic]. Her characteristic summing
up is:-

> But for/him there seems great stag-/nation in
> London. ...

DELIUS, JELKA   99-6
To Percy Grainger
2.7.1927
Grez-sur-Loing (S & M)/[Station] Bourron [blue letterhead as above]
ALS   One single leaf
         27 x 21 cms.
         Envelope addressed: 7 Cromwell Place/White Plains/New York/
                              USA
         pmk Grez illegible
         pmk New York omitted

         Dearest Percy,/Our dear friend Ida/Gerhardi died
         on the 29th of June. ...

Ida was Jelka's oldest friend and she feels it 'as an/immense
sorrow ...'. Grainger's letters to Ida during her long illness
had cheered her greatly and she had been elated by his promise to
come to play for her but 'it is too/late - alas'.

Jelka thanks him also for his efforts 're Steinway and the/hope
about the Duo-Art. Fred would enjoy that immensely/it is such a
wonderful invention/and it is so glorious of you to/have recorded
his own things -/dear kind Percy'.

She is wondering whether the letter will reach him before he leaves
for Europe. 'Fred', who 'was happy reading/all you wrote about
N.C. Sk. [*North Country Sketches*] and/*Brigg Fair* and I played it
for him/on the Gramo, ...', 'is fairly well/greatly looking forward'
to seeing Percy again.

DELIUS, JELKA   99-7
To Percy Grainger
27.12.27
Grez-sur-Loing (S & M)/[Station] Bourron [blue letterhead as above]
ALS   Two single leaves
        27 x 21 cms.
        Envelope addressed: 7 Cromwell Place/White Plains/N. York/
                             U.S.A.
        pmk Grez 27-12 27
        pmk New York omitted

        Dearest Percy./This is to send you/all our love
        and millions of/the best wishes for all the
        import-/ant change in your life that/1928 is to
        bring you. May you/be really happy at last! ...

Balfour Gardiner and Frederick Austin visited over Christmas. The
Brooks family [from Grez] came in as well for the Christmas
Tree and carols were sung by the maid Hildegard and the Brother
[male nurse - see above]. She describes at some length their
struggles and triumphs with the Duo-Art piano and the rolls Grainger
and Balfour Gardiner had made for it from Delius's works. With
Balfour's roll, which contained Delius's *On Hearing the First
Cuckoo in Spring*, it would only play Balfour's own piece (Dance)
very loudly! But they were able to introduce Frederick Austin to
North Country Sketches by its means. The Duo-Art catalogue introduction to the Delius works written by 'Percy' pleases them very
much, as also the portrait they have printed of 'Fred'.

Balfour and Austin also played duet versions of the *Song Before
Sunrise* and *A Dance Rhapsody* (no. 2) for Delius. They hope
Barbirolli will include the latter in the Delius items he plans
to conduct for the BBC.

Klenau conducted *Paris* in Liverpool, but the new Daventry Experi-
mental Station was not clear. Klenau 'is going to do some Delius
in Russia' and is keen to make recordings.

        Toye/is to do the *Summer Garden* [*In a Summer Garden*]
        etc./ ... There is rather a rivalry ...

In Germany 'the *Mass of Life*/in Francfort does not seem to have/been
so very good. *The Village Romeo*/[*and Juliet*] in Wiesbaden
"middling". ...'.

JD to PG 11/5/1928 and Xmas Day 1928;
        28/5/1929 and 27/8/1929

        - copy DT/LC

DELIUS, JELKA   99-8/EG
To Ella Grainger
27.12.29
Address stamped: Frederick Delius/Grez-sur-Loing
ALS   Two single leaves of which the verso of the second is blank
        (dark blue paper)
        22 x 17 cms.

        My dear Ella,/I was so/astonished to see your/
        letter from London;   ...

Ella is in England on account of her niece's health. The Deliuses
wish Percy and Ella could have been at the Festival and are hoping
they heard all about it and its great success [the 1929 Delius
Festival in London].

        ... Fred trav-/elled so well and bore/up
        wonderfully in Lon-/don too. It was a great/
        experience. Beecham/was wonderful and/all
        his performances/were first rate ...

Grez, by contrast 'seemed so calm and uneventful'; and so Jelka
has neglected correspondence while attempting to keep Delius amused.

[This letter should be seen in the context of Eric Fenby's book,
Delius as I Knew Him.]

        JD to PG 23/4/1930
                - copy DT/LKC

        JD to PG 4/11/1930, n.d. [2?/6 or 7/1931], 20/12/1931
                and 17/3/1932
                - copy DT/LC

DELIUS, JELKA   99-9/PG & EG
To Percy and Ella Grainger
18.8.1934
Grez-sur-Loing (S & M)
ALS   Three single leaves
          27 x 21 cms.

        My beloved Percy and Ella,/At last your dear/
        letter arrived, for which I had longed,/knowing
        so well that you would under-/stand all the
        trouble that has come/over me. I am better
        now at last physi-/cally, tho' I shall never
        be other than/a semi-Invalid. ...

She tells the story of Delius's decline since February 1934 and
her own emergency operation after suffering increasingly for two
years from a tumour; Fenby's arrival on receiving her telegram with
Balfour Gardiner joining him later; Delius's new will made in the
belief that she was dying at the hospital; her return to be with
him as he died; his subsequent temporary burial at Grez pending
transference to a country churchyard in the south of England (his
wish); the current money problems due to probate delay; the
confusion between the original will and the second - as also other
clauses concerning Delius's music and its promotion, appointment of
executors and so on. There has been other sadness:- Norman O'Neill
died in March, also Ida Gerhardi's sister, Lilli, and Mr Stoop
whose 'hospitable little house in Hans/Place exists no longer'.

In a postscript she adds:

        It was lovely that you gave the Memorial Concert/
        at once. The article I have not yet received/
        and am greatly looking forward to it.

She notes that Balfour Gardiner 'will pay ... another visit in
September./Fenby will come in Octo-/ber and stay two/months.'

[This letter should be seen in the context of Eric Fenby's book,
Delius as I Knew Him.]

FREDERICK DELIUS, AGED 50
Portrait by Jelka Delius (née Rosen), 1912

Photograph reproduction by courtesy of the
Grainger Museum Board, University of Melbourne.

CHECKLIST AND INDEX of the letters of Jelka (Rosen) Delius to
Frederick (Fritz) Delius

DATE	CORRESPONDENTS	TYPE OF COMMUNI- CATION	GRAINGER MUSEUM NUMBER	PAGE
[20/6/1896]	JR/FD	ALS	178A-1	98
<26/5/1899>	JR/FD	ALS	178A-2	98
26/8/1900 Sunday	JR/FD	ALS	178A-3	98
1/9/<1900> continued on 'Sunday'	JR/FD	ALS	178A-4	98-99
25/7/1908	JD/FD	ALS	178A-5	99
29-31/7/1908 Wednesday [continued on Thursday, Friday]	JD/FD	ALS	178A-6	99
4/8/1908	JD/FD	ALS	178A-7	99
5/8/1908	JD/FD	ALS	178A-8	99-100
10/8/1908	JD/FD	ALS	178A-9	100
13/8/1908	JD/FD	ALS	178A-10	100
16/8/1908	JD/FD	ALS	178A-11	100
18/8/1908	JD/FD	ALS	178A-12	100
4/8/1908	Alvarez/FD	ALS	178A-12(b)	101
25/<8/1908>	JD/FD	PCS	178A-13	101
30/8/1908	JD/FD	ALS	178A-14	101
30/8/1908	JD/FD	PCS	178A-15	101-102
<1/9/1908>	JD/FD	PCS	178A-16	102
5/9/1908 <7/9/1908> Monday afternoon	JD/FD	ALS	178A-17	102

DATE	CORRESPONDENTS	TYPE OF COMMUNI-CATION	GRAINGER MUSEUM NUMBER	PAGE
<10/9/1908> 'Thursday afternoon'	JD/FD	ALS	178A-18	102
9/10/1908	JD/FD	ALS	178A-19	102-103
6/12/1908	JD/FD	ALS	178A-20	103
8/12/1908	JD/FD	ALS	178A-21	103
<9/12/1908>	JD/FD	ALS	178A-22	103
<30/5/1910>	JD/FD	ALS	178A-23	104
16/6/1910	JD/FD	ALS	178A-24	104
17/6/1910	JD/FD	ALS	178A-25	104
18/6/1910	JD/FD	ALS	178A-26	104
20/6/1910 Monday	JD/FD	ALS	178A-27	105
22/6/1910	JD/FD	ALS	178A-28	105
23/6/1910	JD/FD	ALS	178A-29	105
24/6/1910 Friday	JD/FD	ALS	178A-30	105
26/6/1910	JD/FD	ALS	178A-31	106
n.d.	FD/Tischer	ALS draft in German in Jelka's hand	178A-31(b)	106
27/6/1910	JD/FD	ALS	178A-32	106
[29?/6/1910]	JD/FD	PCS	178A-33	106
4/7/1910	JD/FD & IG/FD	ALS	178A-34	107
6/7/1910	JD/FD	ALS	178A-35	107
7/7/1910	JD/FD	ALS	178A-36	107
8/7/1910	JD/FD	ALS	178A-37	107-108

DATE	CORRESPONDENTS	TYPE OF COMMUNI- CATION	GRAINGER MUSEUM NUMBER	PAGE
8/7/1910 Friday afternoon	JD/FD	ALS	178A-38	108
4/1/1911	*JD/Leni*[?]	*AL in German unfinished*	*178A-JD/ Leni(i) 4 January*	108
<1/10/1912>)	JD/FD	ALS	178A-39	108
) <1 or 2/10/) 1912>))))	JD/FD	ALS written on blank pages of 40b	178A-40 and 40b	109
30/9/1912)	Collman/FD	ALS	178A-40b	109
4/10/1912	JD/FD	ALS	178A-41	109
7/10/1912	JD/FD	ALS	178A-42	109
1/6/1913	JD/FD	ALS	178A-43	109-110
6/7/1913	JD/FD	ALS	178A-44	110
8/7/1913 Wednesday [Tues- day]	JD/FD	ALS	178A-45	110
12/7/1913 Saturday	JD/FD	ALS	178A-46	110
14/7/1913 completed on 'Monday [Tues- day] morning'	JD/FD	ALS	178A-47	110-111
18/7/1913	JD/FD	ALS	178A-48	111
2<0>/7/1913	JD/FD	ALS	178A-49	111
[24/7/1913]	JD/FD	PCS	178A-50	111
[26/7/1913]	JD/FD	PCS	178A-51	111
<24/11/1913> Monday morning	JD/FD	ALS	178A-52	112
26/11/1913 Wednesday evening	JD/FD	ALS	178A-53	112

DATE	CORRESPONDENTS	TYPE OF COMMUNI-CATION	GRAINGER MUSEUM NUMBER	PAGE
[29/11/1913]	JD/FD	PCS	178A-54	112
24/6/1914	JD/FD	ALS	178A-55	113
26/6/1914	JD/FD	ALS	178A-56	113
[27/6/1914] 'Saturday 6 pm'	JD/FD	PCS	178A-57	113-114
29/6/1914	JD/FD	ALS	178A-58	114
30/6/1914	JD/FD	ALS	178A-59	114
4/7/1914 Saturday	JD/FD	ALS	178A-60	114
<5/7?/1914>	JD/FD	ALS	178A-61	115
7/7/1917	JD/FD	ALS	178A-62	115
10/7/1917 Tuesday	JD/FD	ALS	178A-63	115
11/7/1917	JD/FD	ALS	178A-64	115
15/7/1917	JD/FD	ALS	178A-65	116
17/7/1917	JD/FD	ALS	178A-66	116
<18 or 19/7/ 1917>	JD/FD	ALS	178A-67	116
20/7/1917	JD/FD	ALS	178A-68	116
21/7/1917	JD/FD	ALS	178A-69	116-117
22/7/1917 Sunday	JD/FD	ALS	178A-70	117
27/7/1917	JD/FD	ALS	178A-71	117
<1/2/1918> 'Friday morning'	JD/FD	ALS	178A-72	117-118
<February or early Spring 1918>	JD/FD	ALS	178A-73	118
<26/7/1919> 'Sat. morn'	JD/FD	ALS	178A-74	118

DATE	CORRESPONDENTS	TYPE OF COMMUNI-CATION	GRAINGER MUSEUM NUMBER	PAGE
28/7/1919	JD/FD	ALS	178A-75	118
5/10/1919	*Haym/JD*	*PCS*	*178A-Haym/ JD(i) 5 October 1919*	119
24/2/1920	JD/FD	ALS	178A-76	119
27/2/1920 Friday	JD/FD	ALS	178A-77	119
29/2/1920 Sunday	JD/FD	ALS	178A-78	119

CHECKLIST AND INDEX of the letters of Frederick (Fritz) Delius to Jelka (Rosen) Delius

DATE	CORRESPONDENTS	TYPE OF COMMUNI- CATION	GRAINGER MUSEUM NUMBER	PAGE
1/3/1896	FD/JR	ALS	178B-1	120
[March 1896] 'Samedi'	FD/JR	ALS	178B-2	120
2/4/1896	FD/JR	ALS	178B-3	120
11/4/1896	FD/JR	ALS	178B-4	120-121
[April 1896] 'Lundi'	FD/JR	ALS	178B-5	121
15/6/1896	FD/JR	ALS	178B-6	121
[end of June 1896]	FD/JR	ALS	178B-7	121
8/7/1896	FD/JR	ALS	178B-8	122
15/8/1896	FD/JR	ALS	178B-9	122
[15/9/1896]	FD/JR	PCS	178B-10	122
[end of Sep- tember 1896]	FD/JR	ALS	178B-11	122
[6/11/1896]	FD/JR	PCS	178B-12	123
[1896]	FD/JR	printed visiting card	178B-13	123
<1896>	FD/JR	printed visiting card	178B-14	123
1897	FD/JR	12 longhand copies	178B xv-xxvi	124-125
1898	FD/JR	15 longhand copies	178B xxvii-xliii	126-128
[5/1/1899]	FD/JR	ALS	178B-44	129
[January 1899]	FD/JR	ALS	178B-45	129

DATE	CORRESPONDENTS	TYPE OF COMMUNI- CATION	GRAINGER MUSEUM NUMBER	PAGE
<January 1899> 'Sunday'	FD/JR	ALS	178B-46	129
<January 1899> 'Monday'	FD/JR	ALS	178B-47	129-130
[8/3/1899]	FD/JR	PCS	178B-48	130
[18/3/1899]	FD/JR	carte- lettre	178B-49	130
<25 or 26/3/ 1899>	FD/JR	ALS	178B-50	131
[Spring 1899]	FD/JR	ALS	178B-51	131
[20/4/1899]	FD/JR	ALS	178B-52	131
[27/4/1899]	FD/JR	ALS	178B-53	131
[29/4/1899]	FD/JR	PCS	178B-54	132
[May 1899]	FD/JR	ALS	178B-55	132
7/5/1899	FD/JR	ALS	178B-56	132
[May 1899]	FD/JR	ALS	178B-57	132
<before 23/5/1899>	FD/Keary	ALS	178B-57(b)	132
[25/5/1899]	FD/JR	PCS	178B-58	133
[May 1899]	FD/JR	ALS	178B-59	133
[Summer 1899] 'Friday' <1902> ?	F(rederick)D/ JR	ALS	178B-60	133
14/8/1899	FD/JR	ALS	178B-61	133-134
[16/10/1899]	FD/JR	ALS	178B-62	134
[16/10/1899]	FD/JR	PCS	178B-63	134
<August 1900>	FD/JR	ALS	178B-64	134
23/8/1900 Thursday	FD/JR	ALS	178B-65	135
[Summer 1900] <27 or 28 August>	FD/JR	ALS	178B-66	135

85

DATE	CORRESPONDENTS	TYPE OF COMMUNI-CATION	GRAINGER MUSEUM NUMBER	PAGE
[20/9/1900]	FD/JR	ALS	178B-67	135
<25/10/1900> 'Thursday'	FD/JR	ALS	178B-68	135
21/10/1900	Buths/FD	ALS	178B-68(b)	136
1/11/1900	FD/JR & Gerhardi	ALS (in German)	178B-69	136
5/11/1900	FD/JR	ALS	178B-70	136
9/11/1900	FD/JR	ALS	178B-71	136
18/11/1900	FD/JR & Gerhardi	ALS (in English)	178B-72	137
[30/11/1900]	FD/JR & Gerhardi	ALS (in English)	178B-73	137
[December 1900]	FD/JR	ALS	178B-74	137
14/12/1900	FD/JR	ALS	178B-75	137
[24/12/1900]	FD/JR	PCS	178B-76	138
24/12/1900	FD/JR	ALS	178B-77	138
[26/12/1900]	FD/JR	PCS	178B-78	138
29/12/1900 cont. [30/12/ 1900] 'Sunday'	FD/JR	ALS	178B-79	138
n.d.	Mrs Julius Delius/FD	ALS	178B-79(b)	139
[2/1/1901]	FD/JR	PCS	178B-80	139
[4/1/1901]	FD/JR	ALS	178B-81	139
1/1/1901	Hess/FD	printed correspon-dence card (in French)	178B-81(b)	139
<14/1/1901>	FD/JR	ALS	178B-82	140
20/1/1901	FD/JR	ALS	178B-83	140

DATE	CORRESPONDENTS	TYPE OF COMMUNI-CATION	GRAINGER MUSEUM NUMBER	PAGE
24/1/1901	FD/JR	ALS	178B-84	140
1/2/[1901]	FD/JR	ALS	178B-85	141
8/2/1901	FD/JR	ALS	178B-86	141
<early February 1901>	FD/JR	ALS	178B-87	141
[February 1901]	FD/JR	ALS	178B-88	141
<March 1901>	FD/JR	ALS	178B-89	142
14/3/1901	FD/JR	ALS	178B-90	142
[20/3/1901]	FD/JR	PCS	178B-91	142
[Spring 1901]	FD/JR	ALS	178B-92	142-143
[Spring 1901]	FD/JR	ALS	178B-93	143

Cycling Tour with Maynard:

DATE	CORRESPONDENTS	TYPE OF COMMUNI-CATION	GRAINGER MUSEUM NUMBER	PAGE
[6/7/1901] (8.00 p.m.)	Maynard/JR	PPCS	178B-94 (i - Maynard)	143
[6/7/1901] (9.00 p.m.)	FD/JR	PPCS	178B-94	144
[6/7/1901] (10.00 p.m.)	FD/JR	PPCS	178B-95	144
[8/7/1901]	FD/JR	PPCS	178B-96	144
[8/7/1901] 'Lundi'	FD/JR	PPCS	178B-97	144
[8/7/1901]	FD/JR	PPCS	178B-98	144
[8/7/1901]	Maynard/JR	PPCS	178B-98 (ii - Maynard)	145
[8/7/1901]	FD/JR	PPCS	178B-99	145
[8/7/1901]	FD/JR	PPCS	178B-100	145

DATE	CORRESPONDENTS	TYPE OF COMMUNI-CATION	GRAINGER MUSEUM NUMBER	PAGE
<4 or 5/10/ 1901>	FD/JR	ALS	178B-101	145
9/10/1901	FD/JR	ALS	178B-102	146
n.d. [1902?] 'Tuesday'	FD/JR	ALS	178B-103	146-147
[27/3/1902]	FD/JR	carte-lettre	178B-104	147

From this point Delius signs himself 'Frederick'

[Spring 1902]	FD/JR	ALS	178B-105	147
[Spring 1902]	FD/JR	ALS	178B-106	148
[Spring 1902]	FD/JR	ALS	178B-107	148
[2/4/1902]	FD/JR	ALS	178B-108	148
[Spring 1902]	FD/JR	ALS	178B-109	148-149
[Spring 1902]	FD/JR	ALS	178B-110	149
[Spring 1902]	FD/JR	ALS	178B-111	149
[Spring 1902]	FD/JR	ALS	178B-112	149
[Spring 1902]	FD/JR	ALS	178B-113	150
[Spring 1902]	FD/JR	ALS	178B-114	150
[May 1902]	FD/JR	ALS	178B-115	150-151
[Spring 1902]	FD/JR	ALS	178B-116	151
14/5/[1902]	FD/JR	ALS	178B-117	151-152
3/6/[1902]	FD/JR	ALS	178B-118	152
31/5/1902	Kronig/FD	ALS	178B-118(b)	152
[June 1902]	FD/JR	ALS	178B-119	153
10/6/[1902]	FD/JR	ALS	178B-120	153
[middle June 1902]	FD/JR	ALS	178B-121	154

DATE	CORRESPONDENTS	TYPE OF COMMUNI-CATION	GRAINGER MUSEUM NUMBER	PAGE
<?Summer 1902>	F(rederick)D/ JR	ALS	Note 178B-60	154
n.d. [1902] <Summer>	FD/JR	ALS	178B-122	154
[July 1902]	FD/JR	ALS	178B-123	155
<mid-August 1902>	FD/JR	ALS	178B-124	155
10/8/[1902]	d'Humières/ FD	ALS	178B-124(b)	155
[September 1902]	FD/JR	ALS	178B-125	156
[Autumn 1902]	FD/JR	ALS with pressed flower	178B-126	156
n.d.	FD/JR	ALS [first leaf missing]	178B-127	156
9/2/1903	FD/JR	ALS	178B-128	157

Fritz Delius, from now onwards known formally as Frederick Delius, was married to Jelka Rosen on 25 September 1903.

[Autumn 1903]	FD/JD	ALS	178B-129	157
[14/6/1906]	FD/JD	PCS	178B-130	158
[28/6/1906]	FD/JD	PCS	178B-131	158
[9/7/1906]	FD/JD	PCS	178B-132	158
18/7/[1906]	FD/JD	ALS	178B-133	159
19/7/[1906]	FD/JD	ALS	178B-134	159
20/7/[1906]	FD/JD	ALS	178B-135	159-160
24/7/1906	FD/JD	telegram	178B-136	160
9/4/1907	FD/JD	ALS	178B-137	160
10/4/[1907]	FD/JD	PCS	178B-138	161

DATE	CORRESPONDENTS	TYPE OF COMMUNI-CATION	GRAINGER MUSEUM NUMBER	PAGE
11/4/[1907]	FD/JD	ALS	178B-139	161
[13/4/1907]	FD/JD	PCS	178B-140	161
14/4/1907	FD/JD	ALS	178B-141	162
[15/4/1907] <16/4/1907?>	FD/JD	PCS	178B-142	162
<17/4/1907>	FD/JD	PCS	178B-143	163
[18/4/1907]	FD/JD	PCS	178B-144	163
18/4/1907 'Friday'	FD/JD	ALS	178B-145	163-164
21/4/1907	FD/JD	ALS	178B-146	164-165
[22/4/1907]	FD/JD	PCS	178B-147	165
[24/4/1907]	FD/JD	PCS	178B-148	165
[29/4/1907]	FD/JD	PCS	178B-149	165-166
<October-November 1907>	FD/JD	ALS	178B-150	166
<October-November 1907>	FD/JD	ALS	178B-151	166
[8/1/1908]	FD/JD	PCS	178B-152	167
<9/1/1908> 'Thursday'	FD/JD	ALS	178B-153	167
<12/1/1908>	FD/JD	ALS	178B-154	167-168
<16 or 17/1/ 1908>	FD/JD	ALS	178B-155	168
<20/1/1908>	FD/JD	ALS	178B-156	168

Walking Tour with Beecham, Norway, 1908:

<29/7/1908>	FD/JD	PPCS	178B-157	169
<30/7/1908>	FD/JD	PPCS	178B-158	169
29?/7/1908 <30>	FD/JD	ALS	178B-159	169

DATE	CORRESPONDENTS	TYPE OF COMMUNI-CATION	GRAINGER MUSEUM NUMBER	PAGE
<1/8/1908>	FD/JD	PPCS	178B-160	169
2/8/1908	FD/JD	ALS	178B-161	170
[4/8/1908]	FD/JD	PPCS souvenir panorama	178B-162	170
4/8/1908	FD/JD	ALS	178B-163	170
<5 or 6/8/ 1908>	FD/JD	PPCS	178B-164	170
6/8/[1908]	FD/JD	ALS	178B-165	170-171
10/8/1908	FD/JD	ALS	178B-166	171
10/8/1908	FD/JD	PPCS	178B-167	171
12/8/1908	FD/JD	PPCS	178B-168	171
15/8/1908	FD/JD	PPCS	178B-169	171
[August 1908]	FD/JD	PPCS	178B-170	172
<16/8/1908?> 'Sunday'	FD/JD	PPCS	178B-171	172
18/8/1908	FD/JD	ALS	178B-172	172
18/8/1908	FD/JD	PPCS	178B-173	173
20/8/1908	FD/JD	PPCS	178B-174	173
22/8/1908	FD/JD	PPCS	178B-175	173
[27/8/1908]	FD/JD	PCS	178B-176	173
28/[8]/1908	FD/JD	ALS	178B-177	174
31/8/1908	FD/JD	ALS	178B-178	174
1908		PPCS (9)	178B-179/ i-ix	174

DATE	CORRESPONDENTS	TYPE OF COMMUNI- CATION	GRAINGER MUSEUM NUMBER	PAGE
<5/10/1908?>	FD/JD	PCS	178B-180	174
<7/10/1908?>	FD/JD	ALS	178B-181	175
[12/10/1908] 'Monday'	FD/JD	PCS	178B-182	175
13/10/1908	FD/JD	PCS	178B-183	175
<3/12/1908> 'Thursday night'	FD/JD	PCS	178B-184	175
<after 4/12/ 1908>	FD/JD	ALS	178B-185	176
[10/12/1908]	FD/JD	ALS	178B-186	176
[12/12/1908]	FD/JD	ALS	178B-187	176-177
[December 1908?]	FD/JD	ALS	178B-188	177

Walking Tour with O'Neill, Black Forest, 1909:

DATE	CORRESPONDENTS	TYPE OF COMMUNICATION	GRAINGER MUSEUM NUMBER	PAGE
<July 1909> 'Wednesday'	FD/JD	ALS	178B-189	177
[14/7/1909]	FD/JD	PCS	178B-190	178
<15/7/1909>	FD/JD	PPCS	178B-191	178
[16/7/1909]	FD/JD	PPC	178B-192	178
[16/7/1909]	FD/JD	PPC	178B-193	178-179
<16/7/1909>	FD/JD	PPCS	178B-194	179
[18/7/1909]	FD/JD	PCS	178B-195	179
[July 1909]	FD/JD	ALS	178B-196	179
[20/7/1909]	FD/JD	PCS	178B-197	180
[21/7/1909] 'Wednesday'	O'Neill/JD	PCS	178B-197 (i/O'Neill)	180
<23/7/1909>	FD/JD	PPCS	178B-198	180

DATE	CORRESPONDENTS	TYPE OF COMMUNI-CATION	GRAINGER MUSEUM NUMBER	PAGE
[24/7/1909]	FD/JD	PCS	178B-199	180-181
[26/7/1909]	FD/JD	PCS	178B-200	181
[27/7/1909]	FD/JD	PCS	178B-201	181
[27/7/1909]	FD/JD	PCS	178B-202	181
[28/7/1909]	FD/JD	PCS	178B-203	182
n.d. [1910?] <Friday, before 8.00 p.m.>	FD/JD	ALS	178B-204	182
n.d. 'Satur-day' <1910>	FD/JD	ALS	178B-205	182
[27/5/1910]	FD/JD	ALS	178B-206	183
[28/5/1910]	FD/JD	PCS	178B-207	183
<30/5/1910> 'Monday'	FD/JD	ALS	178B-208	183-184
17/6/1910	FD/JD	ALS	178B-209	184
[17/6/1910]	FD/JD	PCS	178B-210	184
18/6/1910	FD/JD	ALS	178B-211	184
20/6/1910	FD/JD	ALS	178B-212	185
[21/6/1910]	FD/JD	PCS	178B-213	185
23/6/1910	FD/JD	ALS	178B-214	185
23/6/1910	FD/Tischer	ALS incomplete draft	178B-214(b)	186
[24/6/1910]	FD/JD	PCS	178B-215	186
[27/6/1910]	FD/JD	PCS	178B-216	186
29/6/1910	FD/JD	ALS	178B-217	187
[30/6/1910]	FD/JD	PCS	178B-218	187

DATE	CORRESPONDENTS	TYPE OF COMMUNI- CATION	GRAINGER MUSEUM NUMBER	PAGE
[6/7/1910]	FD/JD	PCS	178B-219	187
[7/7/1910]	FD/JD	PCS	178B-220	187-188
[7/7/1910]	FD/JD	ALS	178B-221	188
[9/7/1910]	FD/JD	PCS	178B-222	188
[9/7/1910]	FD/Gerhardi	PCS	178B-223	188
[9/7/1910]	FD/JD	PCS	178B-224	189
<30/9/1912>	FD/JD	PCS	178B-225	189
2/10/1912	FD/JD	ALS	178B-226	189-190
[3/10/1912]	FD/JD	PCS	178B-227	190
[5/10/1912]	FD/JD	PCS	178B-228	190
<6/10/1912>	FD/JD	PPCS	178B-229	191
8/10/1912,	FD/JD	PCS	178B-230	191
<late May 1913>	FD/JD	ALS	178B-231	191-192
[31/5/1913] 'Saturday'	FD/JD	PCS	178B-232	192
4/6/1913	FD/JD	ALS	178B-233	192
[6/6/1913]	FD/JD	PCS	178B-234	193
[9/7/1913]	FD/JD	PCS	178B-235	193
[10/7/1913]	FD/JD	PCS	178B-236	193
10/[7]/1913	FD/JD	ALS	178B-237	194
[12/7/1913]	FD/JD	PPCS	178B-238	194
[12?/7/1913]	FD/JD	PPCS	178B-239	194
13/7/1913	FD/JD	ALS	178B-240	194
20/7/1913	FD/JD	ALS	178B-241	194-195
[21/7/1913]	FD/JD	PPCS	178B-242	195

DATE	CORRESPONDENTS	TYPE OF COMMUNI- CATION	GRAINGER MUSEUM NUMBER	PAGE
[July 1913]	FD/JD	PPCS	178B-243	195
24/7/1913	FD/JD	PPCS	178B-244	195
[22/10/1913]	FD/JD	PCS	178B-245	196
[24/10/1913]	FD/JD	PCS	178B-246	196
<25/11/1913>	FD/JD	ALS	178B-247	196-197
<25 and 26/11/ 1913> conclu- ded 'Wednesday morning'	FD/JD	PCS	178B-248	197
<27/11/1913>	FD/JD	ALS	178B-249	197-198
[23/6/1914]	FD/JD	ALS	178B-250	198
<26/6/1914>	FD/JD	ALS	178B-251	198
<27, 28 or 29/ 6/1914>	FD/JD	ALS	178B-252	198-199
<27 or 28/6/ 1914> [pmk 28/6/ 1914 1-AM]	FD/JD	PCS	178B-253	199
<2/7/1914>	FD/JD	ALS	178B-254	199
<3 or 4?/7/ 1914>	FD/JD	ALS	178B-255	199-200
<8/7/1914>	FD/JD	ALS	178B-256	200
<9/7/1914>	FD/JD	PCS	178B-257	200
<4/12/1914>	FD/JD	ALS	178B-258	200-201
<24/2/1915>	FD/JD	ALS	178B-259	201
<11/3/1915?>	FD/JD	ALS	178B-260	201-202

DATE	CORRESPONDENTS	TYPE OF COMMUNI-CATION	GRAINGER MUSEUM NUMBER	PAGE
From Tessé-la-Madeleine while 'taking a cure':				
<7/7/1917>	FD/JD	ALS	178B-261	202
<9/7/1917>	FD/JD	ALS	178B-262	202
13/7/1917	FD/JD	carte-lettre (blue)	178B-263	202-203
<15/7/1917?>	FD/JD	ALS	178B-264	203
[16/7/1917]	FD/JD	carte-lettre (blue)	178B-265	203
[18/7/1917]	FD/JD	carte-lettre (blue)	178B-266	203
<July 1917>	FD/JD	ALS	178B-267	203-204
<July 1917>	FD/JD	ALS	178B-268	204
[24/7/1917]	FD/JD	carte-lettre (blue)	178B-269	204
[24/7/1917]	FD/JD	carte-lettre (brown)	178B-270	204
<25/7/1917?>	FD/JD	ALS	178B-271	204-205
[28/7/1917]	FD/JD	carte-lettre (brown)	178B-272	205
<31/1/1918>	FD/JD	ALS	178B-273	205
22/7/<1919>	FD/JD	ALS	178B-274	206
23/7/1919	FD/JD	ALS	178B-275	206
[31/7/1919]	FD/JD	PCS	178B-276	206
<February 1920>	FD/JD	ALS	178B-277	207
<22?/2/1920>	FD/JD	ALS	178B-278	207
<27/2/1920>	FD/JD	ALS	178B-279	208
[28/2/1920]	FD/JD	ALS	178B-280	208

DATE	CORRESPONDENTS	TYPE OF COMMUNI- CATION	GRAINGER MUSEUM NUMBER	PAGE
<week of 2/3/ 1920>	FD/JD	ALS	178B-281	208
9/3/1920	FD/JD	ALS	178B-282	209
[March 1920]	FD/JD	ALS	178B-283	209
[17/3/1920]	FD/JD	PCS	178B-284	209
4/9/1920	FD/JD	ALS	178B-285	210
[4/9/1920]	FD/JD	PPCS	178B-286	210
5/9/1920	FD/JD	ALS	178B-287	210
7/9/1920	FD/JD	ALS	178B-288	210-211
<7/9?/1920> 'Tuesday'	FD/JD	ALS	178B-289	211
<8/9?/1920> 'Wednesday'	FD/JD	ALS	178B-290	211
[9/9/1920]	FD/JD	carte-lettre	178B-291	211
[18/11/1920]	FD/JD	ALS	178B-292	212
20/9/1921	FD/JD	ALS	178B-293	212
[25/10/1921] 'Tuesday'	FD/JD	ALS	178B-294	212

Frederick Delius (born Fritz Theodor Albert Delius of German parents in Bradford, Yorkshire) did not marry the painter Jelka Rosen until 1903. He anglicised his name to 'Frederick' in 1902-3.

ROSEN, JELKA   178A-1   (7)
To Fritz Delius
n.d. ['20th June 1896' - added by Jelka in pencil: see below]
Félicité/Grez par Nemours/S. et. M.
ALS   Two leaves folded of which one side of the second leaf is
        blank [a sketch, no longer extant, of Jelka's hands by Ida
        Gerhardi was included 'after/the last chord of/Plus vite,
        mon cheval; ...']
        17 x 11.4 cms.

        Dear Mr Delius,/Of course/you did not write;/I
        thought you were'nt going to so I was/not very
        disappoin-/ted; ...

        ... This/letter is supposed/to reach you just/on
        the longest day,/the 21st, I think? ...

She wonders if he is 'composing Nietzsche ...' and copies out a short poem 'Venedig (1888)' by 'Fr. Nietzsche' on the last page.

ROSEN, JELKA   178A-2   (60)
To Fritz Delius
n.d. <Friday, 26 May 1899>
The Grelix*, 80, Elm Park Road, S.W. [London] [letterhead]
ALS   One leaf folded of which two sides are blank
        18 x 11.4 cms.

        Dearest Fritz -/I am think-/ing all the time/of
        your music - ...

*The home of Jelka's Aunt and Uncle (Moscheles).

ROSEN, JELKA   178A-3   (68)
To Fritz Delius
Sunday 26 Août 1900
Grez
ALS   Two leaves folded
        17.4 x 11.2 cms.

        Dear Fritz, Your/letter only reached/me to-day (from/
        thursday to sunday!!!! ...

ROSEN, JELKA   178A-4   (70)
To Fritz Delius
1. Sept <1900> contd on 'Sunday' [1-2 September 1900]
Breskens.
ALS   Two single leaves
        23.5 x 14.8 cms.

Envelope addressed: Monsieur Fritz Delius/
                      Rotheneuf Hôtel/Rotheneuf/près
                      St. Malo/Bretagne
pmk Domburg 3 Sep 00
pmk Valenciennes à Paris 3 Sept <00>

Dear Fritz,/I have just/got to the sea, ...

DELIUS, JELKA   178A-5   (161)
To Frederick Delius
25th 7. 1908
Grez
ALS   One single leaf
         23 x 17.8 cms.

         Dearest Fred,/Here is Rosch's letter -/Of course
         it had to arrive/at once after your departure./
         How long it all takes, fancy/only beginning on
         the 18th Sept. ...

Signed:

         Lovingly/Jelkaaah!

DELIUS, JELKA   178A-6   (165)
To Frederick Delius
29.7.08 Wednesday [continued on 'Thursday' and 'Friday 31.7']
Grez
ALS   Two leaves folded
         21.3 x 13.5 cms.

         Dearest Fred,/To-day I/received your tele-/gram
         at 8 a.m. ...

DELIUS, JELKA   178A-7   (168)
To Frederick Delius
4.8.08
Grez
ALS   Two leaves folded
         21.3 x 13.5 cms.

         Dearest,/Yesterday I/received your 2 post-/cards - ...

DELIUS, JELKA   178A-8   (171)
To Frederick Delius
5.8.08
Grez
ALS   One leaf folded
         21 x 13.5 cms.
         Envelope addressed: Herrn Frederick Delius/Poste restante/
                              Molde/Norvège.
         Re-addressed to Kr.iania.
         pmk Grez 5-<8> 08
         pmk Molde 10 VIII 08
         pmk Kristiania 13.VIII.08

Dearest,/Just received/your delightful/letter
from Sve -/I remember it/all so well; we got/
such an enormous/and good supper/there and then/
took their carriage/back home. ...

DELIUS, JELKA   178A-9   (176)
To Frederick Delius
10. Aug. 08
Grez
ALS   Three leaves folded
         21.2 x 13.5 cms.

         Dearest Fred, Just got your/letter from Molde/and
         the panorama/card came yester-/day. ...

DELIUS, JELKA   178A-10   (178)
To Frederick Delius
13.8.08
Grez sur Loing
ALS   Two single leaves
         23 x 18 cms.
         Envelope addressed: Herrn Frederick Delius/Poste Restante/
                              Kristiania/Norvège
         pmk Grez illegible
         pmk Kristiania 16 VIII 08

         Dearest,/Just got your letter/from Saebe, which
         is aw-/fully nice. ...

DELIUS, JELKA   178A-11   (181)
To Frederick Delius
16.8.08.   'Fête de Grez, alas!'
Grez
ALS   Three single leaves
         23 x 18 cms.

         Dearest Fred,/Just got your letter from Hjelle
         (10.8). So/pleased to get it and the/lovely
         card from Trold fjord/also sent from Hjelle - ...

DELIUS, JELKA   178A-12   (183)
To Frederick Delius
18.8.08
Grez
ALS   One single leaf
         23 x 18 cms.

         Dearest Fred,/Enclosed a letter/from Florida -
         I hope that/you have meanwhile/heard from
         Gardiners/Father about the value/of the farm. ...

```
            ALVAREZ, P.H.              178A-12(b)
            To Frederick Delius
            August 4 1908
            Coolee/Florida
            ALS

                        Mr Frederic Delius/
                        Dear Sir/Your letter of the 30 July/
                        was receive [sic] ...

                        ... your estate/has all gone down
                        st. ...

                  He outlines cost and problems of repairs.


DELIUS, JELKA                     178A-13                (188)
To Frederick Delius
25.<8.08>
PCS       pmk Grez 25-8 08
          pmk Kristiania 30.VIII.08
          pmk Arendal 31 VIII 08
          pmk Fevig 15 IX 08
          addressed:  Herrn Fr. Delius/
                      Poste Restante/Kristiania/Norvège
          re-addressed to Arendal and Fevik, thence returned to Grez
                      misspelt Graz sur Loing

          Dear Fred,/your letter and cards/from Jendesheim
          all/came together.  ...


DELIUS, JELKA                     178A-14                (191)
To Frederick Delius
30.8.08
Grez
ALS       Two single sheets
          23 x 18 cms.
          Envelope addressed:  Herrn Fr. Delius/
                      Poste Restante/ as for PCS above and
                  similarly forwarded and returned
          pmk Grez 30-8 08
          pmk Kristiania 29.08.8
          pmk Fevig 15 IX 0<8>

          Dearest Fred/Your telegram received/Friday
          afternoon - I was/awfully disappointed to/have
          to miss you a whole/week longer - ...


DELIUS, JELKA                     178A-15                (192)
To Frederick Delius
30.8.08
Grez
PCS       pmk Grez illegible
          pmk Frederiksvaern 3 IX 08
          pmk Fevig 15 IX 08
          received again at Grez <20>9 08
```

addressed: Fredericksvaern [sic] and at side to Poste
              Restante/Arendal
re-addressed to Fevik and thence returned to Grez
              misspelt Graz

I wrote you a letter to-day to Xania/Poste
restante;   send you this/on the chance - ...

DELIUS, JELKA   178A-16   (195)
To Frederick Delius
<1 September 1908>
Grez
PCS   pmk Grez 1-9 08
          pmk Fevig <15> IX 08
          received again at Grez 20-<9> 08
          addressed: Arendal/Norvège and returned to Grez
                      misspelt Graz

          Just received your letter to Aren-/dal, wrote you
          ['2 days ago' deleted] yesterday to/Xania and
          Fredericksvaern, ...

DELIUS, JELKA   178A-17   (196)
To Frederick Delius
Monday afternoon 5.9.08 [a date error for 7.9.08 by JD?]
Grez
ALS   One single leaf
          23 x 18 cms.

          Dearest Fred, the enclosed/two letters came to-day
          and/also a nice one from Mrs/Cassirer. Their address
          is 29 Hol-/land Park Avenue; as she thinks/we are just
          going to London/she tells me to bring *Koanga*/along. ...

DELIUS, JELKA   178A-18   (197)
To Frederick Delius
Thursday afternoon <10 September 1908>
Grez
ALS   One single leaf
          23 x 18 cms.

          Dearest Fred, Just got/your telegram and/am
          disappointed not/to have you here/to-night. ...

DELIUS, JELKA   178A-19   (200)
To Frederick Delius
9.10.08
Grez
ALS   Two single leaves
          23 x 18 cms.

Dearest, The enclosed/nice letter from Ritters/
came to-day and also/the one from Harmonie. I
must say Szanto is/quite mad to order/all that
without ask-/ing you first. ...

Concludes:

A thousand loves/<u>Jelka</u>

DELIUS, JELKA   178A-20   (204)
To Frederick Delius
6.12.08
Grez
ALS   One single leaf
        23 x 18 cms.
        Envelope addressed: Fr. Delius Esq/c/o Th. Beecham Esq/
                            Highfield/Boreham Wood/Herts. [headed
                            'Angleterre']
        pmks illegible

        Dear Fred, Your card came/at last Saturday afternoon/
        and I am awfully glad/it was such a fine perform-/
        ance. ...

DELIUS, JELKA   178A-21   (205)
To Frederick Delius
8.12.08
Grez
ALS   One single leaf
        23 x 18 cms.
        Envelope addressed: Fr. Delius Esqre/c/o Th. Beecham Esq/
                            Highfield/Boreham Wood/Herts/Angleterre
        pmk Grez illegible
        pmk Boreham-Wood De 9 08

        Dearest Fred,/Here enclosed what/came from Harmonie
        this/morning. I hope you have/been able to get
        that man/from Hanley to copy out/the Tonic. Sol Fa!
        Tomorrow/you have your first re-/hearsal; I shall
        think/of you <u>very</u> much. ...

DELIUS, JELKA   178A-22   (206)
To Frederick Delius
n.d. <9.12.08> [in pencil: found in same envelope as 8.12.08]
[Grez]
ALS   One single leaf
        23 x 18 cms.

        Dearest Fred, I forgot/Harmonie's letter. Please/
        dont hate me for it - here/it is. Last night Ida
        came/with Mrs St.[?] and Kaesbach. ...

DELIUS, JELKA   178A-23   (231)
To Frederick Delius
n.d. <30 May 1910>
[Grez]
ALS   One leaf folded and one half leaf of which one side is blank
         23 x 18 cms.
         Envelope addressed: Herrn Frederick Delius/p.a. Frau H.
                              Haeberlin/Stocker Str 49/Zürich/Suisse
         pmk Grez 30-5 10
         pmk Zürich 31 V 10
         On verso: 'No news from Gardiner'

         Dearest Fred,/Your card/came just now. How/splendid
         all these per-/formances are! I am/so happy about
         Suters/*Messe* - and also/*Sea-Drift* Haym and/
         Schuricht - Andreae/too is splendid -/and above all
         that/you are well! ...

DELIUS, JELKA   178A-24   (232)
To Frederick Delius
16.6.1910
Grez
ALS   One leaf folded of which one side is blank
         20.2 x 12.5 cms.

         Dearest Fred,/How are you,/and how have you/arrived*
         and how/is everything? ...

*See 178B-209(233) et seq.

DELIUS, JELKA   178A-25   (234)
To Frederick Delius
17.6.1910
Grez
ALS   One leaf folded
         20.2 x 12.5 cms.

         Dearest Fred,/I hope you/are not flooded/I hear
         in the Matin/that the Bodensee/is all flooded. ...

DELIUS, JELKA   178A-26   (236)
To Frederick Delius
18.6.10
Grez
ALS   One leaf folded
         20.2 x 12.5 cms.

         Dearest,/I've just receiv-/ed your first letter,/
         you must try and/get them to change/your room ...

DELIUS, JELKA   178A-27   (238)
To Frederick Delius
Monday 20.6.10
[Grez]
ALS   One leaf folded and one half leaf
         17.8 x 11.3 cms.

         Dearest,/I just received/your letter and am/
         sending you the under-/drawers at once - ...

DELIUS, JELKA   178A-28   (241)
To Frederick Delius
22.6.1910
Grez
ALS   One leaf folded
         20.2 x 12.5 cms.

         Dearest/Your letter from/the 20th came yesterday/
         afternoon. I see that/you accustom your-/self a
         little - ...

DELIUS, JELKA   178A-29   (242)
To Frederick Delius
23.6.10
Grez
ALS   One leaf folded
         20.2 x 12.5 cms.

         Dear Fred,/Here is a trial-/letter for Tischer. ...

                    DELIUS, FREDERICK   178A-29(b)
                    To Sander
                    Draft letter by Jelka for her husband's
                         approval enclosed in Jelka Delius
                         to Frederick Delius 23.6.10
                    ALS   One leaf folded
                             20.2 x 12.5 cms.

                    In German

DELIUS, JELKA   178A-30   (244)
To Frederick Delius
Friday 24.6.1910
108 Bd Montparnasse/Sanct Haus.
ALS   Two ruled leaves folded
         21.4 x 13.5 cms.

         Dearest Fred,/Here I am/at Ida's and she is/
         spoiling me like/she always does. ...

DELIUS, JELKA   178A-31   (246)
To Frederick Delius
26.6.1910 [date added in pencil]
[Grez]
ALS   One leaf folded and one half leaf
        20.2 x 12.5 cms.

[The letter begins after seven lines of a draft letter to Herr Sander
deleted.]

>   Dear Fred -/I wrote you/another letter to/Tischer -
>   so you/can chose [sic] from/both, ...

                    DELIUS, FREDERICK   178A-31(b)
                    To Tischer
                    Draft letter by Jelka for her husband's
                        approval enclosed in Jelka Delius
                        to Frederick Delius 26.6.1910
                    ALS   One leaf folded
                            20.2 x 12.5 cms.

                    In German

DELIUS, JELKA   178A-32   (248)
To Frederick Delius
27.6.1910 'postet [sic] before 7 p.m.'
Grez
ALS   One leaf folded and one half leaf
        20.2 x 12.5 cms.

>   Dearest,/Inclosed [sic] came just/now. ...

Jelka announces that 'yesterday' she began to copy their Gauguin
picture, ['Nevermore']. She gives interesting details about the
problems involved; and also talks about their strawberry crop
and the 'servantless quiet' of the house at present.

DELIUS, JELKA   178A-33   (249)
To Frederick Delius
n.d. [29? June 1910]
PCS   pmk Grez 2[9]-6 10
        pmk Mammern (Thurgau) 30.VI.10.
        addressed: Mons. Fr. Delius/Wasserheilanstalt/Mammern/
                    untersee-Bodensee/Suisse [headed 'via Bâle']

>   Dearest Fred, I received your/card of the 27th
>   to-day./The weather is entirely abom-/inable
>   here too - storm/rain and high barometer/with
>   it all./I am going/to Paris to-night. ...

DELIUS, JELKA and GERHARDI, IDA   178A-34   (252)
To Frederick Delius
4.7.10
Grez s.L.
ALS   One leaf folded and one half leaf of which the verso is blank
         21.4 x 13.5 cms.
         Envelope addressed: Mammern. Stamps torn off. [Jelka's
                                                           holograph]
         pmk Grez destroyed
         pmk Mammern (Thurgau) on verso 6.VII.10

The first part of the letter is written by Ida Gerhardi in German
ending on page 4.

         Lieber Fritz!/Gestern Abend bin ich mit/Vater
         u. Tochter Groesch/ke ...

Jelka begins again in English on page 4.

         Dearest Fred, I am/very pleased so/far - If you
         could/only find us a/robust ordinary/servant ...

DELIUS, JELKA   178A-35   (253)
To Frederick Delius
6.7.1910
Grez
ALS   Two single leaves
         23 x 17.2 cms.

         Dearest Fred/I am awaiting news/from you rather anxiously ...

DELIUS, JELKA   178A-36   (255)
To Frederick Delius
7.7.1910
Grez
ALS   Two leaves folded and one half leaf
         20.2 x 12.5 cms.
         Envelope addressed: Mammern
         pmk Grez 7-7 10
         pmk Mammern (Thurgau) 9.VII.10

         My dear Fred,/I have just/received your/angry
         postcard/dated 6th, yester-/day and I hope/you
         have the/money now. ...

DELIUS, JELKA   178A-37   (258)
To Frederick Delius
8.7.1910
Grez sur Loing/S. et M.
ALS   Three leaves folded
         20.2 x 12.5 cms.
         Envelope addressed: Mammern
         pmk Grez 8-7 10
         pmk Mammern (Thurgau) 9.VII.10
         postscript on verso: 'Wire if I am to find a ménage!'

107

Dearest Fred-/Unfortu-/nately I have to/tell you
now/that Frl Bertha/is no good what-/ever and is
going. ...

DELIUS, JELKA   178A-38   (259)
To Frederick Delius
8.7.10 Friday afternoon
Grez
ALS   One leaf folded
          20.2 x 12.5 cms.

          Dear Fred,/The post brought/your nice letter,
          hap-/pily. Of course/our news crossed/and I am
          not/sure what you/propose now./Please wire if/I
          am to hunt up/servants on Mon-/day and Tuesday/
          in Paris or Frl/Bertha could stay/a little longer ...

DELIUS, JELKA   *178A-JD/Leni(i) 4 January 1911*
To Leni [?] in German
4.1.1911
Weisser Hirsch bei/Dresden
Villa Hohenzollern
AL   Two single leaves
          27 x 21 cms.

          Liebste Leni,/Du Siehst aus der Adres-/se, dass wir
          noch immer hier sind -/weil Fred immer noch Krank
          ist. ...

[unfinished]

DELIUS, JELKA   178A-39   (264)
To Frederick Delius
3.1.Oct. 1912 <3.0 p.m., 1 October 1912>
Grez
ALS   Two single leaves with verso of the second leaf blank
          25 x 20 cms.

          Dearest, Your card* just came/this afternoon and
          made me quite/happy on account of B. Splen-/did:
          it is a weight off my heart. ...

          ... I sup-/pose you will get this on the day/of
          Seadrift and I wish all/that is best, and more! ...

*The card received was 178B-225 [pmk Sep 30 12] written by Delius
from London en route for Birmingham where *Seadrift* was performed
at the Festival on 3 October. The composer arrived at the Festival
on 1 October: see 178B-226 [pmk Oct 2 12].

DELIUS, JELKA   178A-40 and 40b   (265)
To Frederick Delius
<1 or 2 October 1912>
ALS   One leaf folded
         21 x 14 cms.

Written on the remaining blank pages of a letter Jelka is forwarding
to Delius which, written in German, is from his cousin C. Collmann
of Voss and Delius, Manchester, England dated 30.9.1912 [40b].

Jelka continues below Collman's signature:

         Dearest, This just came/and also Harmonie's
         recti-/fied Abrechnung. ...

DELIUS, JELKA   178A-41   (268)
To Frederick Delius
4.10 12.
Grez
ALS   One leaf folded, of which one side is blank
         20 x 12.5 cms.

         Dearest,/I just got your/dear letter with all/the
         good news this/morning. I have/made rather a
         muddle; I have/sent you a letter/to the Cecil
         with/enclosure from Carl/Collmann, who wants/to
         know your London/address as he wants/to come on
         the 10th/to hear the Concerto.   ...

DELIUS, JELKA   178A-42   (271)
To Frederick Delius
7.10.12
Grez
ALS   Two single leaves
         27 x 21 cms.

         Dearest,/I was so delighted to get your/card and
         hear that *Seadrift* went/well and that you are all
         right. How/awfully stupid of them not to print/
         the words! How good too that B. does/the *Dance
         Rh.*, or did it last night,/so I suppose you do
         not find/it worth your while to stay for/Woods
         performance of it. ...

DELIUS, JELKA   178A-43   (275)
To Frederick Delius
1.6.1913
Grez
ALS   One leaf folded
         20 x 12.5 cms.

Dearest, Enclosed/2 letters came this/morning. Your
mother/is laconic. I do not/see at all why she/
should settle all your/affairs? ...

Concluded:

Your old/Jelka

DELIUS, JELKA   178A-44   (278)
To Frederick Delius
6.7.1913
Grez sur Loing/S. et M
ALS   One leaf folded and one half leaf
         20 x 12.5 cms.

         Dearest,/Here I am again/and have already/started
         painting my/spring scene - there/were such lovely
         straw-/berries and Rasberries [sic]/that I made 3
         little/conserve bottles to-/day, then painted/again
         and had a/terrible visit from/Heseltine*. I've
         left/orders that next time/he is not let in. ...

*'Joe' Heseltine, the painter, who lived at Marlotte: uncle to
Philip Heseltine (Peter Warlock).

DELIUS, JELKA   178A-45   (279)
To Frederick Delius
8.7.13 Wednesday [JD's error: In 1913 this was Tuesday]
Grez sur L-
ALS   One leaf folded and one half leaf
         20 x 12.5 cms.

         Dearest,/I imagine you/in Xania to-day -/and
         only hope the/sea journey was good. ...

DELIUS, JELKA   178A-46   (283)
To Frederick Delius
Saturday 12.7.1913
Grez
ALS   One single leaf and a second leaf added later, also signed
         25 x 20 cms.

         Dearest,/Your card came/quite quickly, this morning,
         and/I am happy that all went off well. ...

DELIUS, JELKA   178A-47   (287)
To Frederick Delius
14 Juilllet 13 [completed on 'Monday morning': but JD means
                    'Tuesday']
Grez
ALS   Three single leaves
         25 x 20 cms.

Dearest,/As everybody is/already drunk since the
after-/noon, maybe they will not make/too much
noise in the night!! ...

DELIUS, JELKA   178A-48   (288)
To Frederick Delius
18.7.1913
Grez
ALS   Two leaves folded
           20 x 12.5 cms.

           Dearest, I received/your splendid letter/from Gol*
           yesterday/afternoon and had/plenty of leisure/to
           think about it all/as I had to walk/to Marlotte
           and/get another tube of/white ...

*See 178B-240(286).

DELIUS, JELKA   178A-49   (289)
To Frederick Delius
2<0>.7.1913
Grez sur Loing
ALS   One single leaf
           25 x 20 cms.

           Dearest Fred,/I got your P.C./yesterday and am
           glad you/like it so much. It would be love-/ly
           if we had a little hut of our/own as it will
           be more and more/horrid about hotels if there
           are/always more visitors in Norway. ...

DELIUS, JELKA   178A-50   (294)
To Frederick Delius
n.d. [24 July 1913]
PCS   pmk Grez 24-7 13
           addressed: Poste Restante/Kristiania/Norvège
           re-addressed to Finse and re-postmarked 26.7.13

           Dearest, I received/no news to-day or yestr-/
           day. I hope all is well/and that it is because/
           you are further away. ...

Jelka plans to reach Bergen on Friday, 1 August.

DELIUS, JELKA   178A-51   (295)
To Frederick Delius
n.d. [26 July 1913]
PCS   pmk Grez 26-7 13
           addressed: Poste Restante/Kristiania/Norvège
           re-addressed to Finse and re-postmarked 28.7.13

           Dear, I received your letter/and card from Tyin
           just/now. And am sorry to/hear about the rain. ...

DELIUS, JELKA   178A-52   (298)
To Frederick Delius
Monday morning <24 November 1913>
          ['12?.10.1913' added in pencil is incorrect and caused by
          a confusion between the visit to Leipzig in October and the
          visit to Vienna in November.]
          ['Fred in Vienna' added by Jelka in pencil is correct for
          November: see 178A-53(301) below; also compare Delius to
          Grainger 18 November 1913 in this catalogue.]
Grez
ALS   One leaf folded
          25 x 20 cms.

          Dearest, When I came/back last night the/postwoman
          who also/arrived gave me a/telegram that had/come
          on friday aftr-/noon after we left:/Concert
          abgesagt,/Brief folgt. ...

For a full discussion of the evidence for dating these Vienna letters
of 1913 see Rachel Lowe-Dugmore: 'Documenting Delius' in *Studies in
Music* (Perth, W.A.) no. 12, 1978, pp. 115-116 and p. 128.

DELIUS, JELKA   178A-53   (301)
To Frederick Delius
26.11.1913 Wednesday evening
Grez
ALS   One leaf folded
          20.3 x 12.5 cms.

          Dearest,/Well, I saw your/handwriting on the/
          envelope of the letter/from Mrs Hertzka/and her
          pupils - but,/I dont understand/why there is no
          word/from you? ...

The letter concludes in the margin recto p. 1:

          so goodbye. Dont forget me! Jelka

At the head of the letter Jelka adds in pencil:

          Many kindest regards to th Hertzkas [sic]

DELIUS, JELKA   178A-54   (303)
To Frederick Delius
n.d. [29 November 1913]
PCS   pmk Grez 29-11 13
          pmk Vienna omitted
          addressed: Hotel Residenz/Teinfaltstr 6/Vienne I/Autriche

          ·Just got your splendid letter/and am delighted
          about/the Harmonie - arrange-/ment. I understand
          that/you then have no more to do/with them and
          Hertzka owns/the works. ...

DELIUS, JELKA   178A-55   (305)
To Frederick Delius
24.6.14
Grez-sur-Loing/Seine et Marne [letterhead]
ALS   One single leaf
         29 x 22.5 cms.

         Dearest, I have just come back from/Paris. I took
         the 6 a.m. train and/had an awful day of commissions/
         and am so delighted it is all done./When I came back
         here I found/Adine's[1] kind card and your/letter,
         which had come tantôt -/What a lot has been going on
         al-/ready in this short time - tremen-/dous! ...

         ... Is/Nijinsky to dance the $D. Rh.^{2}$ in/this concert
         or at Cambon's[3]/or when? ...

         ... I've been hard at work/and I think the Buchenwald/
         will be good now - I have to do/ferns and things still,
         but/the look through and tone/seems good now. ...

1.   Adine O'Neill, pianist wife of the composer, Norman O'Neill.

2.   *A Dance Rhapsody* (no. 1).

3.   The residence of Monsieur Jules Cambon, the French Ambassador
     in London.

DELIUS, JELKA   178A-56   (306)
To Frederick Delius
26.6.14
Grez
ALS   One single leaf (mauve colour, linen finish)
         23.3 x 17.7 cms.

         Dearest, This letter came from Bir-/mingham -
         otherwise nothing. It/is 9 p.m. and I've been
         in the/garden till now. It is so heaven-/ly.
         The lilies are phosphores/cent white and such
         masses/of them. The poppies and laven-/der so
         lavish. ...

The garden at Grez was a constant source of inspiration in Jelka's
paintings: see Lionel Carley and Robert Threlfall, *Delius: A Life
in Pictures* (O.U.P., London, 1977), illustrations, pp. 6 and 64.

DELIUS, JELKA   178A-57   (308)
To Frederick Delius
Saturday 6.p.m. [27 June 1914]
PCS   pmk Grez 27-6 14
         pmk London omitted
         addressed: 4 Pembroke Villas[*]/Kensington. W/Londres/
                     Angleterre.

*4 Pembroke Villas was the home of the composer Norman O'Neill.

113

Am just taking the/4 parcels containing/the
orchestral parts of/2 Act[*] to the post. In case/
you want Chorus voices too,/please wire how many/
of each.   ...

*Koanga, Act Two; this is revealed in the next letter 29.6.1914.

DELIUS, JELKA   178A-58   (311)
To Frederick Delius
29.6.1914
Grez-sur-Loing/Seine et Marne [letterhead]
ALS   One single leaf
         29 x 22.5 cms.

         Dearest, The enclosed came just/now; and it seems
         you must attend/to it at once. ...

         ... am painting the room-sketch/for the 8th scene[*];
         am also reading/the book ...

*The eighth scene of Fennimore and Gerda.

DELIUS, JELKA   178A-59   (312)
To Frederick Delius
30.6.1914
Grez-sur-Loing/Seine et Marne [letterhead]
ALS   One single leaf
         29 x 22.5 cms.

         Dearest, I just received your/card sent off on
         the 27th it went by/Portsmouth. Is that
         natural? ...

DELIUS, JELKA   178A-60   (315)
To Frederick Delius
4.7.14 Saturday
[Grez]
ALS ·   Two single leaves, the fourth side blank except for a
         pencilled: 'Many Grüsse from the girls'
         22.5 x 15 cms.

         Dearest, I just received/your lovely letter with so/
         much news. The only thing/I regret is this fearful/
         heat. ...

         ... Percy/wrote me such a kind/little letter and
         said you/looked perfectly splendid/and they were
         enjoying/you ever so much and/missing me! ...

DELIUS, JELKA   178A-61   (316)
To Frederick Delius
n.d. <5 July? 1914> ['June 1914' added in pencil is incorrect on
        internal evidence]
[Grez]
ALS   One single leaf
           22.5 x 15 cms.

           Dearest, The enclosed/just came - and perhaps/
           you prefer attending/to it at once -

           ... the Osbournes/... arrive/to-night, so I shall/
           walk over to Bourron/to say How d'you do/to them
           there - ...

           All my thoughts are/with you for the Con-/cert - ...

DELIUS, JELKA   178A-62   (323)
To Frederick Delius
7.7.1917
Grez
ALS   One single ruled leaf
           28.8 x 22.2 cms.

           Dearest, I had forgotten the pipeclay/so I send it
           to-day and also a letter/from M. Harrison. It is
           nice she/has the *Légende* and that Beatrice/loves
           her Cello-Sonata so much!/I am ever so anxious to
           hear/about Bagnoles and your journey ...

DELIUS, JELKA   178A-63   (325)
To Frederick Delius
Tuesday 10-7 1917
Grez
ALS   Two single ruled leaves (red ink)
           28.8 x 22.2 cms.

           Dearest, How are you? I do so/hope you are feeling
           much rested/and better. ...

DELIUS, JELKA   178A-64   (326)
To Frederick Delius
11.7.1917
Grez sur Loing
ALS   Two single ruled leaves (red ink)
           28.8 x 22 cms.

           Dearest, When the second post came/to-day without
           news from you I could/not wait any more ...

DELIUS, JELKA   178A-65   (329)
To Frederick Delius
15.7.1917
Grez
ALS   Two single ruled leaves (red ink)
         28.8 x 22.2 cms.

         Dearest, How are you? Is it all going/well? I am
         a little afraid that you/take the baths too long - ...

DELIUS, JELKA   178A-66   (331)
To Frederick Delius
17.7.1917
Grez
ALS   One single ruled leaf (red ink)
         28.8 x 22.2 cms.

         Dearest, I got your letter from sunday/just now ...

DELIUS, JELKA   178A-67   (333)
To Frederick Delius
n.d. <18 or 19 July 1917>
[Grez]
ALS   One ruled half leaf written on both sides (red ink)
         17.7 x 22.2 cms.

         Dear boy, Enclosed the account/from the Bank.   ...

DELIUS, JELKA   178A-68   (335)
To Frederick Delius
20.7.17
Grez
ALS   One single ruled leaf written on both sides (red ink)
         17.7 x 22.2 cms.

         Dearest, Just received your letter/from the 18th.
         I think it by far/the best for you to write to Dr/
         Bas 'Lá [deleted] Villa Vedetta' Rue de la Frégate/
         Biarritz and explain your state/and the effect of
         the baths ...

DELIUS, JELKA   178A-69   (336)
To Frederick Delius
21.7.1917
Grez
ALS   One single leaf of which one side is blank
         27 x 26.7 cms.

Dear boy/I opened the enclosed/from B.M.[*] What a
pity you/are not there. You had better/write at
once and say you/are at Bagnoles, maybe they/are
travelling about and/would go there to see you. ...

*Byres Moir mentioned again in full in the next letter - a Harley
Street specialist already consulted in 1915.

DELIUS, JELKA   178A-70   (337)
To Frederick Delius
22.7.1917 Sunday
Grez
ALS   One single ruled leaf
       29 x 22.2 cms; and
       Two single plain leaves numbered II and 3 respectively
       27 x 21 cms.
       (red ink)

       Dearest, There is so much always to say/I dont
       know where to begin ...

DELIUS, JELKA   178A-71   (342)
To Frederick Delius
27.7.17
Grez
ALS   Two single leaves of which one verso is blank (red ink)
       27 x 21 cms.

       Dearest boy, I received your 2/letters from tuesday
       and wednesday/and was very glad that you have/a room
       ordered at Val-André/so that we need not search
       straight/away. ...

DELIUS, JELKA   178A-72   (345)
To Frederick Delius
Friday morn. <1 February 1918>*
Lapparent [in the course of the letter Jelka gives her telephone
       number as Sasee 55-32]
ALS   One leaf folded (mauve ink)
       17.5 x 11 cms.

*This dating is corroborated by a letter from Jelka to Marie
Clews [Archive of the Delius Trust, transcript by Dr Lionel Carley]
headed 'Friday' pmk 1.2.1918. It is substantiated by Jelka's
description in 178A-73 below of the German raid on Paris, the
previous Wednesday night, which exactly agrees with that of Wednesday, 30 January 1918, as documented by Elizabeth Hausser in
Paris au Jour le Jour; Les événements vus par La Presse 1900-1919
(Les Editions de Minuit, Paris, 1968).

Dearest, There was no/raid which of course/you
heard out there -/I have been thinking/of you
all the time/of course and wonder-/ing how you
got on and/what he said this morn-/ing after -
examining/you and whether the food was good and/what
you did last/night. Do send a line/to tell me.

Mrs M.* was rather/shaken by the raid/and
proposed that/we should all go to/Grez ...

*See 178A-73(346) below; and, in the Delius-Clews correspondence
we find reference to a Mrs or Mme Mersey [?]. See also 178B-273
and footnote to 178B-274; and compare 178B-65(67) of 1900
'Cooper Meese', the hotelier.

DELIUS, JELKA   178A-73   (346)
To Frederick Delius
n.d. <February or early Spring 1918>
[Grez?]
ALS   One half leaf of brown paper (red ink)
        16.2 x 18.3 cms.

        Dearest, I send you the receipt/of the trunks -
        in the fear that/they have not arrived. ...

Jelka appears to be preparing to lock the house properly and join
Delius [in Paris?]. She is collecting up a gift of sugar for
'Mrs M.' and notes they will need sugar ration cards in Paris
as treacle will be rationed on Tuesday. She speaks of spring
warmth and blue sky and how well she slept with the air from her
open window 'so fresh and invigorating after Lapparent'.

DELIUS, JELKA   178A-74   (349)
To Frederick Delius
Sat. morn <26 July 1919> ['July 1919 - added by Jelka in pencil]
Grez*
ALS   Three single leaves of which the verso of the third is blank
        20 x 14.5 cms.

        Dearest Here I am sitting/on your bed (the only
        clean/place and writing with a love-/ly fountain
        pen my aunt gave/me. ...

DELIUS, JELKA   178A-75   (350)
To Frederick Delius
28.7.1919 [Monday]
Grez*
ALS   Three single leaves
        20 x 14.5 cms.

        Dearest, I am writing in/the night, so as not to
        loose [sic]/any time to-morrow. ...

*Jelka is at Grez-sur-Loing to make lists of everything missing in
their house after its occupation by the French Army as an officers'
mess. She remarks on the inflated post-war prices in France which
will affect replacement, e.g. 200 frs for a pair of sheets.

```
HAYM, HANS                          178A-Haym/JD(i)  5 October 1919
To Jelka Delius
5 Oct. 19
E. [Elberfeld]
PCS       pmk Elberfled 6.10.19
          addressed:  Frau Delius/p.a. Simon/Frankfurt A.M.
                      Untermainkai 3
```

Dr Haym cannot find the Apalachia *[sic] music. He sends greetings
for 18 October, the world première of Delius's sixth and last opera,*
Fennimore and Gerda, *in Frankfurt. Scheduled for 18 October, it
finally took place on 21 October. The Deliuses were in Frankfurt
for a whole month of rehearsals prior to that date and their address
is that of their old friend Dr Simon of the Frankfurter Zeitung.*

```
DELIUS, JELKA                       178A-76                    (354)
To Frederick Delius
24.2.20
Grez
ALS       One leaf folded
          19.5 x 15.5 cms.
```

Dearest, If anything could/give me pleasure in my/
present misery it/was your 2 letters from before/
and after the Double [Concerto]. They/arrived <u>together</u>
to-day./How splendid! All you tell sounds/so good
and The *Daily Mail*/interviewing you! ... Now all
wishes for the *S.H.H.*'s [*Song of the High Hills*] ...

```
DELIUS, JELKA                       178A-77                    (355)
To Frederick Delius
27.2.1920 Friday
Grez
ALS       One leaf folded and one half leaf
          19.5 x 15.5 cms.
```

Dearest - Now is n't it really/too hard on me,
this <u>beastly</u>/railway-strike - ...

```
DELIUS, JELKA                       178A-78                    (358)
To Frederick Delius
Sunday 29th 2 20
Grez
ALS       One leaf folded and one half leaf
          19.5 x 15.5 cms.
          Envelope addressed:  Frederick Delius Esq/c/o Norman O'Neill
                               Esq/4 Pembroke Villas/Kensington W/
                               Londres./Angleterre

          pmk Grez 29-[2] 20
          pmk London omitted
```

Dearest, since yesterday/I feel really much better,/ ...

FREDERICK DELIUS TO JELKA DELIUS

Until the Spring of 1902 Frederick Delius signs himself 'Fritz', his
baptismal name. It has generally been known that after his marriage
to Jelka Rosen in 1903 he anglicised his name to 'Frederick', but
the letters show that he had begun to use this name informally for
some time before that.

DELIUS, FRITZ   178B-1   (1)
To Jelka Rosen
le 1 Mars 96
33 Rue Ducouëdic [Paris]
ALS   One leaf folded of which two sides are blank
         17.8 x 11.5 cms.

         My dear Miss Rosen -/I thank you very much/for
         your kind note and/will, as you propose, come/
         on Monday night. ...

DELIUS, FRITZ   178B-2   (2)
To Jelka Rosen
Samedi ['March/Spring 1896' - added by Jelka in pencil]
33 Rue Ducouëdic
ALS   One leaf folded of which two sides are blank
         17.8 x 11.5 cms.

         Dear Miss Rosen -/I shall be unable to/leave
         before Tuesday, so/am sorry that I cannot/
         accompany you - but will/come on Tuesday
         morning/11.50. ...

Delius is to meet Jelka for a country walk. The first sentence
suggests it is at some distance from Paris, while the rest of the
letter shows it is Grez-sur-Loing.

DELIUS, FRITZ   178B-3   (3)
To Jelka Rosen
le 2 Avril 96
33 Rue Ducouëdic
ALS   One leaf folded of which two sides are blank
         17.8 x 11.5 cms.

         Dear Miss Rosen -/Will you come up to/my place
         at 6-30 on/Saturday evening - the/Sterners' are
         coming - ...

DELIUS, FRITZ   178B-4   (4)
To Jelka Rosen
le 11/96 ['11.4.96' - added by Jelka in pencil]
Bourron -/Hotel de la Gaité [the oblique sign is written by Delius]
ALS   One leaf folded of which outside pages are blank
         17.8 x 11.5 cms.

> Dear Miss Rosen -/Your letter was forwarded here
> to me - I left Paris/last Tuesday and intend/
> staying until Monday.   ...

On his return to Paris they will 'arrange a walk'.

DELIUS, FRITZ   178B-5   (5)
To Jelka Rosen
Lundi ['Spring 1896/April' - added by Jelka in pencil]
33 Rue Ducouëdic
ALS   One leaf folded of which three sides are blank
        17.8 x 11.5 cms.

> Dear Miss Rosen -/Some friends came/unexpectedly
> to see me, which/prevented me from coming/round
> to see you - ...

He wishes her well for her visit to 'the fatherland'.

DELIUS, FRITZ   178B-6   (6)
To Jelka Rosen
le 15 Juin [1896]
Haugen/S. Aurdal/Valders [Norway]
ALS   Two leaves folded of which one side is blank
        20 x 12.5 cms.
        A pressed flower enclosed.

> Dear Miss Rosen -/You will be surprised, no/
> doubt, that I kept you so long/without news. ...

DELIUS, FRITZ   178B-7   (8)
To Jelka Rosen
n.d. ['End of June/1896' - added by Jelka in pencil]
Haugen -/S. Aurdal/Valders/Norvège
ALS   Two leaves folded of which two sides are blank
        20 x 12.5 cms.
        A pressed flower enclosed.

> Dear Miss Rosen -/You must have got my letter/
> about the same time that I got/yours ie the 23rd
> June. Sankt Haus ...

The letter of the 23rd June mentioned has not survived in this
archive. 'Sankt Haus' is the address of JD to FD 24 June 1910,
the home of Jelka's great friend, Ida Gerhardi at 108 Bd.
Montparnasse, Paris.

```
DELIUS, FRITZ                        178B-8                    (9)
To Jelka Rosen
8 July 96
Haugen/S. Aurdal/Valders [Norway]
ALS      One leaf folded and one half leaf
         20 x 12.5 cms.
         A pressed flower enclosed.

         Dear friend -/I am glad to learn from/your letter
         that you are having a/good time in Grez doing some/
         work & enjoying your beautiful/little garden with
         Marcelle in it ...


DELIUS, FRITZ                        178B-9                   (10)
To Jelka Rosen
le 15 Aout 96
Haugen/S. Aurdal/Valders [Norway]
ALS      Two leaves folded
         20 x 12.5 cms.
         A pressed flower enclosed.

         Dear friend -/You must excuse my silence/as I have
         been out in the wilds/& only came back a couple of/
         days ago - I went with a/knapsack into
         Jotunheimen ...


DELIUS, FRITZ                        178B-10                  (11)
To Jelka Rosen
n.d. [15 September 1896]
<33 Rue Ducouёdic> [Paris]
PCS      pmk Paris 6$^e$  15 Sept 96  Av. d'Orléans
         pmk Nemours 16 Sept 96
         addressed:  Mademoiselle/Jelka Rosen/Grez/près Nemours

         Dear friend - I am back again in Paris.  ...


DELIUS, FRITZ                        178B-11                  (12)
To Jelka Rosen
n.d. ['End of August September/1896' - added by Jelka in pencil]
33 Rue Ducouёdic
ALS      One leaf [the torn half of a folded leaf]
         21.5 x 14 cms.

         Dear friend -/I have been working hard/at
         my opera - & therefore could not/yet make up
         my mind to quit/Paris - The filthy weather too/
         kept me here - ...

When the fine Autumn weather comes Delius plans to visit Grez.
```

```
DELIUS, FRITZ                    178B-12                    (13)
To Jelka Rosen
n.d. [6 November 1896]
33  Rue Ducouᵭdic
PCS      pmk Paris 6ᵉ  6 Nov 96  Av. d'Orléans
         addressed:  Mademoiselle/Jelka Rosen/4 Rue Honoré
                     Chevalier [Paris]

         Dear friend - I cannot come to night as I am/
         working very successfully at something.  ...


DELIUS, FRITZ                    178B-13                    (14)
To Jelka Rosen
A printed visiting card in the name of 'Fritz Delius' of '33 rue
Ducouᵭdic' with pencilled message:

         Gare de Sceaux -/1 25 Monday.

Jelka's hand has added '1896' at the top.  On the back of the card
is a list of train times.


DELIUS, FRITZ                    178B-14                    (15)
To Jelka Rosen
A printed visiting card as above with pencilled message:

         I will come to-morrow with/pleasure - Au revoir/
         thanks for your letter.

On the back of the card Delius has written in pencil 'Mlle Rosen',
and on the front Jelka has added '1896'.
```

THE LETTERS OF 1897 AND 1898 HAVE SURVIVED IN COPY FORM ONLY IN
THIS ARCHIVE. INFORMATION AS TO THE FATE OF THE ORIGINALS WOULD
BE WELCOMED BY THE BOARD OF THE GRAINGER MUSEUM AND THE OFFICERS
OF THE DELIUS TRUST.

THE OPENING LINE OF EACH COPY WILL BE QUOTED AS IF IT WERE AN
ORIGINAL; BUT, AS THE COPIES HAVE BEEN FOUND TO AMOUNT TO PARA-
PHRASES IN MANY INSTANCES IN THE OTHER YEARS WHERE ORIGINALS EXIST
FOR COMPARISON, THESE OPENING LINES MUST BE TREATED AS APPROXIMATE
ONLY. FOR THE SAME REASON THE DATES OF LETTERS EXISTING IN COPY
FORM ONLY MUST BE TREATED WITH CIRCUMSPECTION. THE ADDRESSES,
WHILE SELDOM COPIED EXACTLY AS WE KNOW DELIUS WROTE THEM, MAY BE
TAKEN TO BE CORRECT.

DELIUS, FRITZ   1897   12 items in longhand
To Jelka Rosen   copy, autograph unknown

GRAINGER MUSEUM CATALOGUE NUMBERS
178B xv-xxvi

    xv [1897 April] copyist's conjectural date.
        Solana Grove/Piccolata/St Johns Co./Fla.

        My dear friend, Your letter was forwarded to me here.
        I left in January for Florida and have been basking
        in the sunshine and enjoying this lovely place for the
        last three months. ...

   xvi [End of May, 1897] copyist's conjectural date.
        33 Rue Ducouᵉdic, Paris.

        Dear friend, I arrived yesterday in Paris and found
        your letter awaiting me. So you have really settled
        in Grez ...

  xvii Thursday
        33 Rue Ducouᵉdic

        Dear friend, I leave tomorrow Friday by the 11.55
        train for Bourron station en route for Grez, ...

 xviii [Beginning of July] copyist's conjectural date.
        33 Rue Ducouᵉdic

        Dear friend, I nearly missed the train last Monday and
        had a real race on your bicycle. I expect to come on
        the 15th. Gunnar Heiberg, the poet, will come to Grez
        for a short time. ...

  xviv Oct. 1st 1897
        Grand Hotel, Christiania

        Dear friend, Here I am after three nights on the
        train! ...

        Delius is in Norway for the performance of *Folkeraadet*,
        the play by Gunnar Heiberg for which he wrote the
        incidental music.

    xx Oct. 16th
        Christiania

        Dear friend, Thanks for your postcard - since I
        wrote you last I have been very busy with rehearsals
        and day after tomorrow, the 18th, the première
        comes off. ...

xxi [Oct.]
   Oslo [Delius would have written Kristiania or Christiania]

   Dear friend, Well! the first two performances have
   been and the result is tremendous, they hissed and
   had a real demonstration against the piece and
   especially against the <u>music</u>. ...

xxii [End of Oct. 1897]
   Holmenkollens Turisthotel

   Dear friend, No one speaks any more of Heiberg's
   piece, now it is only my music. ...

xxiii Nov. 10th 1897
   Elberfeld

   Dear friend, I arrived here from Copenhagen this
   morning and have just come from Dr. Haym ...

   Delius is in Elberfeld for the first performance of his
   overture *Over the Hills and Far Away*.

xxiv [1897]
   33 Rue Ducouëdic, Paris

   Dear friend, Thanks for the paper, that is right and
   the only one I want. I am working at the finishing
   of my concerto ...

   The letter concludes:-

   ... The recital of Falke will only come off on the
   3rd or 4th of January, so that will suit Miss Gerhardi.
   My love to you all, Yours as ever, Fritz Delius.
   I hope your work is going well.

xxv [1897]
   33 Rue Ducouëdic, Paris

   Dear friend, Thanks for your letter. I shall await
   you on Sunday at four and we will spend the evening
   together. I have an invitation card for you from
   the Princess, ...

xxvi Dec. 25th 1897
   33 Rue Ducouëdic, Paris

   My dear friend, Many thanks for your letter - it found
   me in about the same mood as you were. No answer from
   home or from my brother - bad news from Anderson ...

   Anderson was the caretaker of Delius's estate in Florida,
   Solana Grove, see item xv above.

DELIUS, FRITZ   1898   15 items in longhand
To Jelka Rosen   copy, autograph unknown

GRAINGER MUSEUM CATALOGUE NUMBERS
178B xxvii-xliii

xxvii   Jan. 2nd. 1898
        33 Rue Ducouëdic

        Dear friend, The recital is postponed until Friday
        on account of sickness. Next Friday at five [?].
        I will come to Rue Bara tomorrow after lunch, F.D.

xxviii Jan. 1898
        33 Rue Ducouëdic

        Dear friend, I am so sorry to hear Marie is ill ...

        ... I am spending a lot of time with Busoni who is
        playing my concerto with me tomorrow a deux pianos. ...

        ... Busoni was quite begeistert with my Nietzsche
        songs ...

xxix   Jan. 25th 1898
        33 Rue Ducouëdic

        Dear friend, Many thanks for your letter and the
        little flower which gave me a great longing for
        Grez. ...

        Delius is working on the cadenza of his 'concerto Fantasie'
        and 'annihilating the alterations ... made for Falke'. He
        is taking the work to Harold Bauer instead of continuing
        with Falke. His 'Fantasie Ouverture' is being copied and
        he has re-orchestrated 'a little Serenade' which he has
        sent to Jebe in Norway as entr'acte music for Heiberg's
        play *Balkongen*. He plans to arrive in Grez on 4 February.

xxx   Jan. 28th 1898
        33 Rue Ducouëdic

        Dear friend, I sent you the libretto of 'Romeo and Julie',
        read it and give me your opinion on it. ...

xxxi   [End of Jan. 1898] copyist's conjectural date.
        33 Rue Ducouëdic

        Dear friend, I cannot come back until Wednesday 11.45.
        Dr. Robin wants me to dine with him on Tuesday. ...

xxxii   [Early Feb.] copyist's conjectural date.
        33 Rue Ducouëdic

        Dear friend, Enclosed a wire which I do not understand.
        Do you? It is about Starke. ...

xxxiii   [Spring 1898] copyist's conjectural date.
          33 Rue Ducouëdic

          Dear friend, I shall only come back on Wednesday
          morning as I dine with Dr. Robin on Tuesday night. ...

xxxiv   Oct. 11th 1898
          Paris

          Dear friend, I shall come to Grez on Sunday ...

          ... I do not leave for England until the middle of
          November. ...

xxxv   Oct. 12th 1898
          Paris

          I have ordered another cask of wine ...

xxxvi   Oct. 13th 1898
          Paris

          Dear Jelka, How kind of you to send me the roses and
          the grapes - ...

          Delius is collecting introductions to people in London
          through Dr. Robin. Lady de Grey is mentioned. He also
          alludes to his legacy of 25,000 francs which he anticipates
          spending on bringing out an opera in London. The name
          of the opera is not mentioned, but this project was
          shelved, as we now know, in favour of the 1899 all-
          Delius concert in London.

xxxvii   [Nov. 15th-18th 1898] copyist's conjectural date.
          Paris

          Dear Jelka, I shall not be able to come out to Grez
          before leaving as I have to meet Lady de Grey here.
          I go often to Dr. Robins who is getting me some
          valuable introductions. ...

          Delius is leaving for London on 'Monday night' ...

xxxviii   Nov. 20th 1898
          London. 25, Montpelier Street S.W.

          Dear Jelka, I had a quiet passage and arrived on
          Tuesday morning. Keary received me very kindly
          and got me lodgings close to his own. I feel awfully
          out of my water here, and pretty hopeless. ...

          Keary was the librettist of Delius's opera *Koanga*.

xxxiv Nov. 28th 1898
       London

       Dear Jelka, Thanks for your letter, book and
       beautiful leaf. What a bother about Koanga!
       The best thing would be not to let the dog loose
       until you take him out with you ...

       'Koanga' in this case refers to their pet jackdaw, and not
       to the opera so called.

   xl Dec. 18th 1898
       London

       My dear Jelka, Many thanks for your kind letter.
       I am sorry you are low-spirited - my spirits are
       not very elevated I can tell you in this beastly
       town ...

  xli Dec. 19th 1898
       London

       Dear Jelka, No good news to tell you - I went
       twice to Lady de Grey in vain - they told me at the
       door that her ladyship was very busy this week ...

 xlii Dec. 20th 1898
       London

       Dear Jelka, I wonder whether you could translate
       my opera into German from the piano-score? There
       is no chance here and no interest. ...

xliii [Christmas 1898]
       Stone-Gappe, Cononley

       Dear Jelka, I shall be back shortly. We will
       translate it together if you care to try. ...

       He also suggests that they should work on the libretto of
       A Village Romeo and Juliet together as he finds Keary is
       not moving ahead with it sufficiently fast. He is
       spending Christmas with his sister Clare Delius Black
       near the site of the Brontë book *Wuthering Heights*.

FROM THIS POINT A DATE IN SQUARE BRACKETS MEANS THAT A POSTMARK
(pmk) HAS BEEN FOUND, USUALLY IN THE CASE OF A POSTCARD, OR THAT A
DATE ADDED IN PENCIL EITHER BY JELKA DELIUS OR A PREVIOUS HANDLER
OF THE LETTERS IS BEING ACCEPTED AS CORRECT OR APPROXIMATELY
CORRECT. OBLIQUE BRACKETS < > WILL BE USED FOR DATINGS DEDUCED,
CONJECTURED OR PREFERRED BY THE CATALOGUER ON INTERNAL EVIDENCE
OR AFTER CROSS-REFERENCE WITH OTHER LETTERS.

DELIUS, FRITZ   178B-44   (45)
To Jelka Rosen
n.d. [5 January 1899]
25 Montpelier Str/S.W. [London]
ALS   Two leaves folded of which two sides of the second leaf are
         blank
         17.9 x 11.3 cms.

         Dear Jelka -/I received your letter/this evening on
         my return/from Stone Gappe. ...

DELIUS, FRITZ   178B-45   (46)
To Jelka Rosen
[January 1899]
London & Paris Hotel, Newhaven, Sussex [letterhead]
ALS   One leaf folded
         20 x 12 cms.

         Dear Jelka -/We left Newhaven/for Dieppe yesterday/
         morning at 11-30 -/Very stormy weather ...

The ship had to put back to Newhaven.

DELIUS, FRITZ   178B-46   (47)
To Jelka Rosen
n.d. Sunday [dated by Jelka as 'end of August', on the copy, but on
         internal evidence it precedes the 'Monday' letter which
         follows here.]
33 Rue Ducouedic [sic]
ALS   One leaf folded
         21.5 x 13.5 cms.

         Dear Jelka -/I arrived last night/after a fairly
         decent/crossing this time - ...

DELIUS, FRITZ   178B-47   (48)
To Jelka Rosen
n.d. Monday <January 1899> [Jelka has pencilled 'end of August' over
         an erasure which can be seen to have read 'early Autumn'.
         Internal evidence suggests January. See notes below.]
33 Rue Ducouedic
ALS   One leaf folded of which one side is blank
         21 x 13 cms.

Dear Jelka - Unless Peters[1] turns/up to morrow Tuesday
I/shall come out by the 5/train with Jebe[2] - Please/
get him a room at/Charlots ...

In this letter Delius mentions his Gauguin picture ('Nevermore')
'now framed'. This, the first fruits of his legacy from his
Uncle Theodor, was purchased 8-11 November 1898 from Daniel de
Monfreid and framed within a few days of the purchase. [See
Lionel Carley, *Delius: The Paris Years* (London, Triad Press,
1975).]

1. Peters, a prospective tenant or buyer for Solana Grove (found
    by Miss Gerhardi), has also been mentioned in the previous
    letters and appears to be the cause of Delius's delayed
    return, as he had hoped to meet him in London.

2. Jebe's coming to Paris has been forecast in the letters from
    London, for Delius wanted Jelka to entertain him in his
    absence. Furthermore, Jebe, as we learn from dated letters
    of August 1899 to follow, was settled once more in Christiania
    in August 'waiting for something to turn up'.

DELIUS, FRITZ   178B-48   (49)
To Jelka Rosen
n.d. [8 March 1899]
[Paris]
PCS   pmk Paris 25 8 Mars 99 R. Danton
        pmk Grez sur Loing Seine et Marne 9 Mars 99
        addressed: Mademoiselle/Jelka Rosen/Grez sur Loing/Seine
                    et Marne

        I shall come back by the 5 train[*] ...

*This is the 5 train on 'Saturday', i.e. the 11th, after lunching
with 'Mrs Maddison' (Adela Maddison).

DELIUS, FRITZ   178B-49   (50)
To Jelka Rosen
n.d. [18 March 1899] ['1899 18.3.' has been added in pencil on the
        evidence of the postmark]
[Paris]
Carte-lettre addressed: Mlle Jelka Rosen/Grez sur Loing/Seine
                    et Marne
        pmk Paris 6 18 Mars 99 R. de Vaugirard
        pmk Grez 19 Mars 99

        Dear Jelka - I cannot come/until Monday morning
        9-/30 - As I dine with the/Detelbacks on Sunday/[*]
        night -

*18.3.99 was a Saturday. Delius goes on to say that he must return
to Paris again on the following Wednesday to see the Princess[e]
de Polignac.

DELIUS, FRITZ   178B-50   (51)
To Jelka Rosen
n.d. <25 or 26 March 1899> ['March 1899' - added by Jelka in pencil]
33 Rue Ducouёdic
ALS   One leaf folded
          17.5 x 11.2 cms.

          Dear Jelka -/Thanks for your/letter which I
          thoroughly/understood -

Delius describes an afternoon at Mrs Maddison's where 'Gabriel Fauré
& a few of the best young french musicians' played his 'opera' before
a small musical audience which included the Prince and Princesse de
Polignac.

DELIUS, FRITZ   178B-51   (52)
To Jelka Rosen
n.d. [Spring 1899]
33 Rue Ducouedic [sic]
ALS   One leaf folded, of which one side is blank, and one half
          leaf (torn)
          21 x 13.1 cms.

          Dear Jelka -/Thanks for the telegram & letter/ -
          I met Hauge in Paris - ...

DELIUS, FRITZ   178B-52   (53)
To Jelka Rosen
n.d. [20 April 1899]
6 Colosseum Terrace/Regents Park/London -
ALS   One leaf folded of which one side is blank
          18 x 11.5 cms.

          Dear Jelka -/I arrived this morning after a good/
          passage - London/very dreary & raining/heavily -
          Hertz lives/in the same house/as I do ...

[Delius is in London for the concert of his works at the St James's
Hall on 31 May 1899 with Alfred Hertz as the conductor and Halfdan
Jebe leading the orchestra. The composer himself financed this
concert from his recent legacy.]

DELIUS, FRITZ   178B-53   (54)
To Jelka Rosen
n.d. [27 April 1899]
6 Colosseum Terrace/Regents Park
ALS   One leaf folded of which one side is crossed
          17.8 x 11.3 cms.

          Dear Jelka -/Miss Gerhardi/wrote me about
          Peters - ...

DELIUS, FRITZ   178B-54   (55)
To Jelka Rosen
n.d. [29 April 1899]
[London]
PCS   pmk London.W Ap 29 99
        pmk Grez 1 Mai 99
        addressed: Mademoiselle/Jelka Rosen/Grez sur Loing
                    Seine et Marne/France and re-addressed to
                    4 Rue Honoré Chevalier/Paris

        Please send "Dansen Gaar" at once - ...

DELIUS, FRITZ   178B-55   (56)
To Jelka Rosen
n.d. [May 1899]
6 Colosseum Terrace/Regents Park
ALS   One ruled leaf folded
        20.3 x 12.7 cms.

        Dear Jelka -/Your letter & enclosed letter just/
        to hand - I cannot/stand Mrs Mowinckel ...

DELIUS, FRITZ   178B-56   (57)
To Jelka Rosen
7 May 1899
Pagani's/restaurant/44 & 48 Great Portland St. W./London [letterhead]
ALS   One leaf folded
        17.5 x 11.5 cms.

        Dear Jelka -/Thanks for your/two letters - I do
        hope Koanga/is better - ...

DELIUS, FRITZ   178B-57   (58)
To Jelka Rosen
n.d. [May 1899]
6 Colosseum Terrace/Regents Park
ALS   One ruled leaf folded
        20 x 12 cms approx.

        Dear Jelka -/Your letter & little/flower were very
        welcome/in this Pandemonium ...

                    DELIUS, FRITZ   178B-57(b)   (58(b))
                    To Keary
                    n.d. <before 23 May 1899>
                    6 Colosseum Terrace/Regents Park
                    ALS   One leaf folded
                            17.9 x 11.2 cms.

                            Dear Keary -/I have been so/overwhelmed
                            with/work & worry ...

                            132

```
DELIUS, FRITZ                    178B-58                    (59)
To Jelka Rosen
n.d. [25 May 1899]
[London]
PCS      pmk London.W  My 25 99
         addressed:  Miss Jelka Rosen/80 Elm Park Road/Chelsea/London

         Hertz & I will lunch/with you on Sunday/at
         1-30 - Write/if it does not suit -/Fr.D.

[Sunday would be 28 May.]


DELIUS, FRITZ                    178B-59                    (61)
To Jelka Rosen
n.d. [May 1899] <29 or 30 May, assuming that the 'Wednesday' is the
         day of the concert, 31 May 1899>
6 Colosseum Terrace/Regents Park
ALS      One ruled leaf folded of which two sides are blank
         20 x 12 cms.

         Dear Jelka -/I & Hertz will/come & lunch with/you
         on Wednesday/at - 1-30 - If/you cant do with/Hertz -
         wire - ...


DELIUS, FREDERICK                178B-60                    (62)
To Jelka Rosen
Friday ['1899.  Summer.  Antwerp on his way to Norway'[1] - added in
         pencil in Jelka's hand]
[illustrated letterhead of the Hotel de l'Europe, Place Verie,
         Anvers, proudly boasting 'Electric Light' as one of its
         attractions]
ALS      One ruled leaf of which one side is blank
         21.4 x 14 cms approx.

         Dearest Jelka -/The 3.40/train/is shockingly bad -/
         12-40 - or 6- p m/

         ... au revoir in Fredriksvarn[2] ...

1.  <1902 Summer> is suggested by the cataloguer as more likely
    because of the style of the opening and the signature
    'Frederick'.  See 1902 letters to follow.  However, the
    suggestion of 1899, by Jelka, indicates that they holidayed
    together in Norway that year.

2.  Fredriksvaern - see pmk of 178B-131, etc.


DELIUS, FRITZ                    178B-61                    (63)
To Jelka Rosen
14 August 99
Hotel Phønix/Copenhagen
ALS      One leaf folded
         21 x 13.5 cms.

         Dear Jelka/I arrived here last/night & leave to night/
         for Bünde - ...
                              133
```

As no envelope survives, it must remain a mystery as to where Jelka was staying when this was written, but Delius volunteers to stay in Paris until Jelka's return, although he is longing to get back to work in Grez. He notes that he has bought 'the danish books' and adds:

I saw Jebe/Just before leaving Christiania ...

DELIUS, FRITZ   178B-62   (64)
To Jelka Rosen
n.d. ['1899 16.10' - added by Jelka in pencil]
33 Rue Ducouedic [sic]
ALS   One leaf folded of which one side is blank
        17 x 11 cms.

        My dear Jelka/Please write/a card to Miss/Gerhardi
        & ask/her to fetch my/piano concerto./It will be
        ready/on Friday afternoon/I come out to morrow/
        evening - ...

If the pencilled date is correct, 'to morrow evening' is Tuesday. Delius is busying himself on behalf of the painter, Hauge, and has called on the critic 'Berend' and 'Me Robin' to no avail.

DELIUS, FRITZ   178B-63   (65)
To Jelka Rosen
[16 October 1899]
[Paris] <33 Rue Ducouedic>
PCS   pmk Paris depart 16 Oct 99
        pmk Grez 17 Oct 99
        addressed: Grez
        message headed 'Later than letter.'

        I may not be able to come/to morrow so dont expect/
        me for certain - ...

DELIUS, FRITZ   178B-64   (66)
To Jelka Rosen
n.d. <August 1900> [A pencilled '1899' on the original seems less
        likely on internal evidence than Jelka's note 'August 1900'
        added to the longhand copy.]
33 Rue Ducouedic [sic]
ALS   A leaf of squared paper (torn from a notebook) folded and
        with one side blank
        20.7 x 13 cms.

        Dear Jelka/Got two telegrams/for you from Lobach/
        just before getting into/the train - ...

DELIUS, FRITZ   178B-65   (67)
To Jelka Rosen
                        *
Thursday <23 August 1900 > [Jelka writes 'August 1900' after
        Delius's 'Thursday']
Cooper Meese/Bristol Palace/Paramé/France [letterhead]
ALS   Two leaves folded
         18.5 x 11.5 cms.

         My dear Jelka/I left Paris by/an excellent rapide/
         10 pm. yesterday ...

Delius thinks he will stay a week there and then bicycle on to Mont
Michel.

*See 178A-3 Sunday 26 Août 1900 which acknowledges this letter.

DELIUS, FRITZ   178B-66   (69)
To Jelka Rosen
n.d. [1900 Summer] <27 or 28 August: see 178A-3 and 178A-4>
Grand Hôtel de Rotheneuf ['avec Plage à 5 minutes de Paramé':
         letterhead]
ALS   One leaf
         21.5 x 13.5 cms.

         Dear Jelka -/I am now here/since this morning.
         I received/your letter - à l'instant - ...

DELIUS, FRITZ   178B-67   (71)
To Jelka Rosen
n.d. [20 September 1900]
Grez sur Loing
ALS   One leaf folded
         17.5 x 11.0 cms.
         Envelope addressed: Mademoiselle/Jelka Rosen/Pension
                               Bellevue/Domburg/près Middelburg/
                               Hollande
         re-addressed: 4 Rue Honoré Chevalier/Paris
         pmk Grez 20 Sept 00
         pmk Domburg 22 Sep 00

         Dear Jelka/I just received/your wire so that I/
         shall come in on/Sunday morning/& will come & see/
         you after lunch at/2 if it suits you ...

DELIUS, FRITZ   178B-68   (72)
To Jelka Rosen
Thursday <25 October 1900> ['26.10.1900' added by Jelka must be
         the receiving pmk as 26 October 1900 was a Friday]
Elberfeld
ALS   One leaf folded
         18 x 11.5 cms.

         My dear Jelka -/I arrived here at/2.30 am after
         a rather un/pleasant journey: the train/was
         overcrowded - The/Emperor of course had/arrived
         the same day ...
                              135

BUTHS, JULIUS   178B-68(b)
To Fritz Delius
21.10.1900.
Ddf. [Düsseldorf]
ALS   One single leaf torn from a folded leaf
        17.5 x 11 cms.

In German, it concerns the *Mitternachtslied*
and a possible performance after the 1900/1901
season.
Enclosed in 'Thursday <25.10.1900>' above, in
which we learn that it was received just before
Delius left Paris.

DELIUS, FRITZ   178B-69   (73)
To Jelka Rosen and her artist friend Ida Gerhardi
1 Nov 1900
9 Landgrafen Str/Berlin W -
ALS   One leaf folded and one half leaf
        18 x 11.5 cms.

In German.

DELIUS, FRITZ   178B-70   (74)
To Jelka Rosen   *
5 Nov 1900/Monday [Delius writes the oblique sign]
Hôtel Monopol/Breslau [letterhead with coat of arms]
ALS   One leaf folded
        22 x 14 cms.

        Dear Jelka -/I arrived here on/Saturday night
        Hertz met/me at the station & was/very glad to
        see me again ...

*Jelka's pencil note '3.11.1900' is incorrect as 5 November 1900
was a Monday.

DELIUS, FRITZ   178B-71   (75)
To Jelka Rosen
9.11.1900
Hôtel de Prusse/Leipzig [illustrated letterhead]
ALS   Two leaves folded of which one side is blank
        22 x 14 cms.

        Dear Jelka -/I arrived here last night:/before
        leaving Breslau I spoke/with Director Loewe who
        was/very amiable - but seemed to/know nothing
        about my Opera/(Pose of course) ...

DELIUS, FRITZ   178B-72   (76)
To Jelka Rosen and Ida Gerhardi
18th Nov 1900
26 Winterfeldt Str^I [Berlin]
ALS   Two leaves folded
        17.8 x 11.4 cms.

        My dear Girls/I am now in my new lodgings:/
        a nice large room: ...

DELIUS, FRITZ   178B-73   (77)
To Jelka Rosen and Ida Gerhardi
n.d. [30 November 1900]
26 Winterfeldt St^I ['Datum unbestimmt' is written, apparently by
        Delius himself, below address]
ALS   Two leaves folded
        17.8 x 11.4 cms.

        My dear Girls - I will/answer both your letters/
        at once - I should not/have asked Albertine/before
        the arrival of Ida/if Marie had not already/done
        so ...

Albertine was Delius's aunt from whom he was trying to obtain the
promise of an allowance instead of a possible legacy. Ida's tact
was to be engaged in the matter, and as the later letters show, was
successfully employed with Tante Albertine on his behalf; but, in
the meantime, his cousin's widow, Marie Krönig (later Marie
Heinitz) generously, but we gather, rather tactlessly, entreated
her mother-in-law on Delius's account.

DELIUS, FRITZ   178B-74   (78)
To Jelka Rosen
n.d. [Dec 1900]
26 Winterfeldt Str^I
ALS   One leaf folded
        18 x 11.5 cms.

        My dear Jelka -/I sent you a portrait/of
        Nietzsche & also a little/hamper of eatables ...

DELIUS, FRITZ   178B-75   (79)
To Jelka Rosen
14/12/1900
26 Winterfeldt Str^I
ALS   Two leaves folded
        22 x 14.3 cms.

        My dear Jelka/I am glad you liked/the things I
        sent - ...

```
DELIUS, FRITZ                    178B-76                      (80)
To Jelka Rosen
n.d. [24 December 1900]
[Berlin]
PCS       pmk Berlin.W. 24.12.00.
          pmk Grez illegible
          addressed to Grez as above

          Dear J.  I have not yet/received your letter or the/
          packet - A thousand/thanks!  ...


DELIUS, FRITZ                    178B-77                      (81)
To Jelka Rosen
24/12/1900            I
49 Eisenacher Str
ALS       One leaf folded
          18 x 11.4 cms.

          Dearest Friend -/I received your letter/to day -
          not yet the packet -/I am so glad everything is/
          going on well in Grez - I/am working in my new/
          lodging at Dansen Gaar - ...


DELIUS, FRITZ                    178B-78                      (82)
To Jelka Rosen
n.d. [26 December 1900]
[Berlin]
PCS       pmk Berlin.W. 26.12.00
          pmk Grez 28./12/.00
          addressed:  Mademoiselle/Jelka Rosen/Grez sur Loing/
                      Seine & Marne

          Dr. J.  I forgot to tell you that/Marie is in the
          Heil Anstalt of/Nassau a. Rhein since 8 or 10 days/
          undergoing a cure - ...


DELIUS, FRITZ                    178B-79                      (83)
To Jelka Rosen
29/12/1900 continued on 'Sunday' [30/12/1900]
49 Eisenacher Str
ALS       Two leaves folded;  the second headed 'Sunday' has one side
          blank
          17.9 x 11.5 cms.

          My dear girl -/At last the packet/of fruit & cakes
          has/arrived ...

Delius signs:  'yrs ever/FD' at the foot of the fourth page and begins
again on the fifth page, (the second leaf), with the heading 'Sunday' -

          M^r Nicolas has just left - ...

Jelka has noted in pencil 'containing mother's letter'.  See below.
```

DELIUS, MRS JULIUS   178B-79(b)
To Fritz Delius
n.d.
Claremont. [Bradford, Yorkshire]

> My dear Fritz!/Thank you for your
> good/wishes for a happy Cristmas/
> which I return. ...

It concerns Delius's request for a renewal
of his monthly allowance and hotly denies
that there has been family gossip concerning
his relationship with Jelka.

DELIUS, FRITZ   178B-80   (84)
To Jelka Rosen
n.d. [2 January 1901]
Berlin
PCS   pmk Berlin.W. 2 1.01
          pmk Grez 4 Jany 01
          addressed: Grez

> Dear J. I wrote you Marie's address - ...

He concludes: 'A happy new year to all - yrs ever Fr D'.

DELIUS, FRITZ   178B-81   (85)
To Jelka Rosen
[4 January 1901]
49 Eisenacher Str
Schöneberg/Berlin
ALS   One leaf folded
          18 x 11.4 cms.

> Dear girl -/Your letter just to hand/I knew my mother
> to be/one of the largest liars but I, now,/also think
> she is one of the/falsest women; her letter does not
> ring true to me either - ...

HESS, OTTO   178B-81(b)
To Fritz Delius
A correspondence card dated '1.I.1901' with
the printed name and address of the sender:-

'Otto Hess, Tauentzienstr. 49a^{I} Breslau'

Hess writes in French that, failing to
find Delius at his old address in Berlin,
he has mailed the piano arrangement of
his opera [*Koanga*] to him at the new
address. He sends a message from Alfred
Hertz that it is vital to make a new libretto,
the present German text rendering a performance in Breslau impossible.

DELIUS, FRITZ   178B-82   (86)
To Jelka Rosen
n.d. <14 January 1901>
ALS   First leaf missing, but a longhand copy dated 'January 14th
         1901', while being much edited, tallies with this letter at
         the salient points, suggesting that this was the date of
         the original.
         One extant leaf
         17.9 x 11.4 cms.
         begins in mid-sentence:-

         ... in this way - Shortness/is my best quality as/
         you know - so expect nothing/from me in this line - ...

The letter concludes:-

         My love to Ida/& to you./When does Ida leave?
         yours as ever/Fritz Delius

At the foot is a drawing of the pet jackdaw Koanga, which is followed
by the message: 'love to Koanga/(shew him this)'.

DELIUS, FRITZ   178B-83   (87)
To Jelka Rosen
20/1/1 -
Eisenacher Str 49.
ALS   One leaf folded
         22 x 14.2 cms.

         Dear Jelka -/I send you the contract/which I have
         just received/Nicolas & Fröhlke sail on the 29th ...

Nicolas and Fröhlke were to be the new tenants of Delius's estate in
Florida. They were found through the good offices of Ida Gerhardi,
even though her efforts over 'Peters' (see 1899-1900 letters) had
not been satisfactory.

DELIUS, FRITZ   178B-84   (88)
To Jelka Rosen
24/1/1
49 Eisenacher Str
ALS   One leaf folded
         17.9 x 11.5 cms.

         My dear Jelka/Many thanks for/your letter &
         the sweet/little flower - it still/had some
         perfume -/I still am in the dark/as to what I
         have done -/what things have I done/not equal
         to my nature? ...

DELIUS, FRITZ   178B-85   (89)
To Jelka Rosen
1 Feb. [1901] [1.2.1901 - added in pencil]
49 Eisenacher Str/Berlin/Schöneberg
ALS   One leaf folded and one single leaf
        17.9 x 11.5 cms.

        Dear Jelka -/Many thanks for/the nice letter.
        If Ida/is still in Grez thank/her also & tell
        her/that what she writes/about Nikisch is all/
        very true - ...

DELIUS, FRITZ   178B-86   (90)
To Jelka Rosen
8/2/1
49 Eisenacher Str/Berlin/Schöneberg
ALS   One leaf folded
        18 x 11.4 cms.

        Dearest friend - Many/thanks for your letter &
        pretty/flower - The thing now is/to get *Paris*
        back from Nikisch. ...

DELIUS, FRITZ   178B-87   (91)
To Jelka Rosen
n.d. <early February 1901, possibly 15 or 22, certainly after the 8th>
        [Jelka's addition of 'January' to the longhand copy of this
        letter cannot be right on internal evidence when one studies
        the sequence of information concerning Ernest Newman, Busoni
        and the forthcoming concert at the Salle Erard in Paris.]
Eisenacher Str 49 -
ALS   One leaf folded
        18 x 11.4 cms.

        Dear Jelka - Many/thanks for your letter - Ida/
        wrote me to day saying she would/arrive on
        Tuesday - ...

DELIUS, FRITZ   178B-88   (92)
To Jelka Rosen
n.d. ['Febr. 1901' - added in pencil by Jelka]
49 Eisenacher Str
ALS   One leaf folded
        17.9 x 11.5 cms.

        Dearest girl - Many/thanks for your nice/letter
        & flower - Ida is/here & looks very well - ...

The letter ends:-

        With love to all -/always yours/Fritz Delius/
        It is too late for a concert in London.

                              141

DELIUS, FRITZ   178B-89   (93)
To Jelka Rosen
n.d. <March 1901> ['Winter 1901' - added in pencil by Jelka]
49 Eisenacher Str
ALS   One leaf folded
          23 x 14.4 cms.

          Dearest Jelka -/Excuse me for not/answering your
          letters. I/have been a good deal/bothered with
          this Concert/which does not come off/(and as you
          know I never/believed it would/Busoni/is sick
          in London ...

A postscript reads:-

          Ida's Picture of you/is very good indeed. But/
          Koanga disturbs the/whole - In any case he ought/
          not to be on the floor He draws/the eyes from
          the face.

DELIUS, FRITZ   178B-90   (94)
To Jelka Rosen
14/3/1
49 Eisenacher Str/Schöneberg/Berlin
ALS   One leaf folded
          23 x 14.4 cms.

          Dear Jelka -/The 13th seems to/be a good number
          for/me. Yesterday the 13th./2125 Marks suddenly/
          arrived for the Courbet from Elberfeld - ...

DELIUS, FRITZ   178B-91   (95)
To Jelka Rosen
n.d. [20.3.01]
[Berlin]
PCS   pmk Berlin.W 20.3.01
          pmk Grez 22 Mars 01
          addressed: Grez

          I wired for the parts of my *Folkeraadet* Suite
          per Express - It will be played instead of *Paris*
          which required too many rehearsals ...

DELIUS, FRITZ   178B-92   (96)
To Jelka Rosen
n.d. ['Spring 1901' - added in pencil by Jelka]
Berlin -
ALS   One leaf folded of which one side is blank
          20.2 x 12.6 cms.

          Dearest friend -/Many thanks/for your kind letter -/
          I am also longing to/be back in Grez &/at my work.
          I am/sick of this place - ...

                              142

The letter ends:-

>Love to/all - your friend/Fritz/Ida sends her
>love

DELIUS, FRITZ   178B-93   (97)
To Jelka Rosen
n.d. ['Spring 1901' - added in pencil by Jelka]
1 Rue Leopold Robert [Paris]
ALS   One leaf folded of which one side is blank
        21 x 13 cms.

>Dearest Jelka/I arrived this morning/at 9
>after a rather/unpleasant journey -/Ida saw
>me off at/the station: we were/both a little
>anxious/about your health ...
>
>... I shall come out/on Monday by the/5 train -
>I shall/go & fetch my/songs first - ...
>
>... It is a relief to be/back in France ...

A series of nine picture postcards (seven from Delius, two from
the painter Guy Maynard) sent to Jelka Rosen (at Grez-sur-Loing)
from the Loire Valley during a cycling tour. The exact order in
which the composer and his companion visited the chateaux is hard
to determine as the postmarks are often barely legible. Dates added
in pencil, which do not tally with such postmarks as are visible,
further complicate matters. The following order seems to be most
likely and differs slightly from that in which the cards were filmed.

>MAYNARD, GUY   178B-94(i/Maynard)
>To Jelka Rosen
>PPCS   pmk Pithiviers Loiret 6 Juil 01
>   picture: Pithiviers. - Kiosque
>   de la Musique.
>   Message below in Maynard's hand
>
>   8 heures/du Soir/On joue du/
>   Delius à Neuf. [unsigned]
>
>[Jelka's pencilled date '2.7.01' appears
>to be a misreading of the posting time
>for the date.]

DELIUS, FRITZ   178B-94   (98)
To Jelka Rosen
PPCS   pmk Pithiviers Loiret 6 Juil 01
         picture: Pithiviers. - Statue du Mathématicien Poisson.
         message below in Delius's hand

         9 heures - Tout va bien. - Maynard/se vaporise. F.D.

DELIUS, FRITZ   178B-95   (99)
To Jelka Rosen
PPCS   pmk Pithiviers Loiret 6 Juil 01
         picture: Pithiviers en 1540
         message below in Delius's hand

         10 heures - Maynard change/son gilet - depart
         prochain pour/Orleans F.D.

DELIUS, FRITZ   178B-96   (100)
To Jelka Rosen
PPCS   pmk Blois Loir et Cher 8 Juil 01
         picture: Château de Blois, Aile de Louis XII.
         message below in Delius's hand

         I cannot possibly be back for dinner/to morrow.
         Tuesday - late in the/evening - if not I will
         wire - FD

DELIUS, FRITZ   178B-97   (101)
To Jelka Rosen
Lundi 8 Juillet
PPCS   pmk Amboise 8 Juil 01
         pmk Grez 9 Juil 01
         picture: Château d'Amboise - Vue Générale
         message below in Delius's hand

         Having a delightful time -
         Ot as ell
         But alls well   Yrs. FD. -

DELIUS, FRITZ   178B-98   (102)
To Jelka Rosen
PPCS   pmk Amboise Indre-et-Loire 8 Juil 01
         picture: Chateau d'Amboise - La Chapelle et la Tour de César
         message below in Delius's hand

         Dont forget the roses - the salades!/will be
         back on Tuesday night -/Hoping all's well with
         you - F.D.

                    MAYNARD, GUY   178B-98(ii/Maynard)
                    To Jelka Rosen
                    PPCS   pmk Amboise 8 Juil 01
                            picture: Château d'Amboise/Intérieure
                                      de la Chapelle.
                            message alongside in Maynard's hand

                            Amboise/Lundi 8<u>me</u>/Priez pour lui./
                            Guy Maynard

DELIUS, FRITZ   178B-99   (103)
To Jelka Rosen
PPCS   pmk Chaumont-s-Loire Loir et Cher 8 Juil 01
        pmk Grez 10 Juil 01
        picture: Château de Chaumont-s-Loire.
        no message

DELIUS, FRITZ   178B-100   (104)
To Jelka Rosen
PPCS   pmk Chaumont-s-Loire Loir et Cher 8 Juil 01
        pmk Grez 10 Juil 01
        picture: Château de Chaumont-s-Loire.
        no message

DELIUS, FRITZ   178B-101   (105)
To Jelka Rosen
n.d. <Friday, 4 October or Saturday, 5 October 1901 prior to Julius
        Delius's burial on Monday 7 October> [a pencilled '1899?' is
        incorrect]
Claremont/Bradford
ALS   One leaf folded
        17.6 x 11.2 cms.

        Dearest Jelka -/I missed the/train of course & left/
        next morning - had/a fair crossing &/stayed the
        night in/London - arrived/here to day & found/my
        family quite cool/& gefasst - which was/quite
        pleasant - ...

        ... The funeral is on/Monday ...
        ... The clans will begin/to gather to morrow ...

Concluded:

        ... Believe me/as ever/Fritz Delius
        [but 'Fritz' looks as if it is written over 'Fred']

Delius is anticipating that the funeral will be a civic occasion.

In a postscript Delius asks what Runciman has said about 'the libretto'.

DELIUS, FRITZ   178B-102   (106)
To Jelka Rosen
Oct 9. 1901 [From the contents it appears that he is writing on a
          Thursday which would make it 10 October 1901]
Harrogate [staying with his sister, Clare Black]
ALS   One leaf folded
         17.8 x 11.4 cms.

         Dearest Jelka/I really have not/had time to write
         before ...

         ... We/buried the old man/on Monday and/indeed he
         died just/in time to save the/whole family from/
         ruin - ...

         ... Is Runciman/still in Grez? ...

Delius leaves for London 'tomorrow/Friday'.

The letter ends:-

         With best love/I remain/as ever yours/Fr Delius.

DELIUS, FRITZ   178B-103   (107)
To Jelka Rosen
n.d. [Headed 'Tuesday' by Delius. 're. Sonata prob. 1902' - added
          in pencil by Jelka on the envelope. In the longhand copies
          this letter is placed at the end of the 1902 group, as is
          usual with undated letters which contain no internal
          evidence for dating. See below for discussion of dating.]
[Paris?]
ALS   One leaf folded of which two sides are blank
         21 x 13.5 cms.
         Envelope: buff colour, unfranked
         Addressed: 4 Rue Honoré Chevalier, Paris [Jelka's mother's
                     house]

         Dear Jelka - Le Voici. le Notaire/Monsieur Camille
         Tollu/9 Rue de Grenelle -

Delius goes on to say that he has received the orchestral parts of
the *Légende* and the score of the 'Sonata'[*]. Of the latter he says:

         On looking/it through I dont like it any more &/
         shall not present it -/I dont believe in having/
         things played/which I find not up to/my present
         standard - ...

He 'shall fetch the Songs/to morrow after lunch ...' for a 'Mrs
Runkel' to sing.

The letter is signed 'Ever your friend/Fr. Delius ...'.

*The Sonata is, presumably, the 1892 Violin Sonata rejected by
Delius but published by Boosey and Hawkes 1976.

                                 146

The style is that of 1896-1898 rather than that of 1902 and the contents (discussion of items to be submitted for a concert) could as well come from then. On the other hand, the more formal style may simply have been dictated by family circumstances which made it desirable for Delius to conceal his close relationship with Jelka.

Again, the mention of a notary might lead one to think that Delius is offering his assistance after Jelka's mother's death later in 1902; but, equally, he might have been suggesting this notary in late 1896 or early 1897 to assist with the conveyancing of the Grez property or some matter arising from the property.

Since there is no proof of the earlier date, the 1902 date has been accepted for this catalogue but it is placed here at the beginning of the group because of the mention of 'Mrs Runkel' and because there is no mention of Rosen family affairs such as dominates the letters after Jelka's mother's death.

DELIUS, FRITZ   178B-104   (108)
To Jelka Rosen
n.d. pmk Grez 27 Mars 02
[Grez]
Carte-lettre addressed: Mademoiselle/Jelka Rosen/4 Rue Honoré
        Chevalier/Paris [Jelka's mother's house]

        Just received your letter - Will/bring everything
        tomorrow after/lunch -

is written on the same side as the address.

The message begins on the verso:-

        Dear Jelka - I come in to/morrow & will call
        on you/after Dejeuner - in the 2^d Act/of *Koanga*
        Pracher makes/a mistake of 185 pages/40.-50 frcs -
        Will you kindly/count the pages of the/Concerto
        which is at your/mother's -

He notes that the dahlias have been planted; and he asks Jelka to wish her mother a speedy recovery.

[On the film the two sides of this card have been separated - the verso appearing after letter number 101 (film order), at which point the recto has been photographed again.]

DELIUS, FREDERICK   178B-105   (109)
To Jelka Rosen
n.d. ['Spring 1902' - added in pencil by Jelka]
ALS   One leaf folded
        18 x 11.3 cms.

        Dearest Jelka/How unfortunate that/you cannot
        get a/nurse! This seems/extraordinary in a
        place like Paris - ...

Signed:
        As ever yours/Frederick.

147

DELIUS, FREDERICK   178B-106   (110)
To Jelka Rosen
n.d. ['Spr. 1902' - added in pencil by Jelka]
[Grez]
ALS   One leaf folded
         18 x 11.3 cms.

         Dearest Jelka -/Enclosed a letter/from Busoni,
         which/please return - I/suppose this concert/will
         clash with Buths. ...

Signed:

         With best/love - yrs ever/Frederick

DELIUS, FREDERICK   178B-107   (111)
To Jelka Rosen
n.d. ['Spring 1902' - added in pencil by Jelka]
[Grez]
ALS   One leaf folded
         18 x 11.3 cms.

         Dearest Jelka/Your letter just/received with the
         postal/order for which many/thanks - ...

Signed:

         yrs ever/Frederick

DELIUS, FREDERICK   178B-108   (112)
To Jelka Rosen
n.d. [2 April 1902]
[Grez]
ALS   One leaf folded
         18 x 11.3 cms.

         Dear Jelka - You/will be grieved to hear/that
         poor little Koanga/is dead - he fell off/his
         perch at 7.30 yester/-day morning April 1st. ...

Concluded:

         Farewell - as ever yours/Frederick

DELIUS, FREDERICK   178B-109   (113)
To Jelka Rosen
n.d. [Spring 1902 - added in pencil by Jelka]
Grez sur Loing -/S & M
ALS   One leaf folded of which one side is blank
         22.4 x 14 cms.

         Dearest Jelka/I arrived last night,/everything
         is alright but/it is very cold & nothing/has
         come out in the/garden - no roses - ...

I am at/my opera again - you ought to try and
see the Götterdämmerung/once - This is more im-/
portant than Pelleas/but try and see them/both -
Dont over/strain yourself - Yrs always/Frederick

DELIUS, FREDERICK   178B-110   (114)
To Jelka Rosen
n.d. [Spring 1902 - added in pencil by Jelka]
[Grez]
ALS   One leaf folded
         18 x 11.3 cms.

         Dear Jelka -/I enclose a letter from/Bamberger - I
         suppose/Ida has been up to/her little games again ...

Signed:

         Ever yours/Frederick

DELIUS, FREDERICK   178B-111   (115)
To Jelka Rosen
n.d. [Spring 1902 - added in pencil by Jelka]
Grez sur Loing/Seine & Marne
ALS   One leaf folded
         20.4 x 12.6 cms.

         Dearest Jelka/I have just received/a card from
         Schmitt/asking for the 3rd Act -/Please send it
         off/if you have time to/Florent Schmitt Villa/
         Medicis [sic], Rome -/D'Humières has just/left ...

Signed:

         Always your:/Frederick Delius

Florent Schmitt made the vocal score of *Koanga* and *Le Jardin du
Paradis*, later called *A Village Romeo and Juliet* [see RL Cat.
pp. 76-78 and RT Cat. pp. 34-41]. Robert d'Humières, we learn from
these letters, is making the French translation of the latter to be
inserted into Schmitt's score. See: Delius to Jelka 10 June 1902
and d'Humières to Delius, 10 August 1902 below. See also L(K)C/
The Paris Years, p. 75.

DELIUS, FREDERICK   178B-112   (116)
To Jelka Rosen
n.d. ['Spring 1902' - added in pencil by Jelka]
[Grez]
ALS   One leaf folded
         18 x 11.3 cms.

         Dearest Jelka - What/a nuisance that you/are kept
         there so/long - How long does/the doctor think
         the/illness will take? ...

He concludes:

         Take care of yourself/yours ever/Frederick

DELIUS, FREDERICK   178B-113   (117)
To Jelka Rosen
n.d. [Spring 1902 - added in pencil by Jelka]
[Grez]
ALS   One leaf folded
           18 x 11.3 cms.

           Dearest Jelka - I do/hope you have now/found a
           nurse and/that you will not make/yourself ill
           by sitting/up nights - ...

The letter concludes in the side and lower margins of page 1.

           Side margin: 'Jebe's address is 10 R. Charles d'Ivry
                             XIVe arrond$^{\underline{t}}$'

           Lower margin: 'Ida interests/me no more - If I were
                             you I/would gradually cease any correspo/
                             ndence with her - it only bothers you
                             Yrs ever Frederick.

DELIUS, FREDERICK   178B-114   (118)
To Jelka Rosen
n.d. ['Spring 1902' - added in pencil by Jelka]
[Grez]
ALS   One leaf folded
           22.4 x 14 cms.

           Dearest Jelka/The packet goes off/by this post
           so you/may get it to night. ...

He ends:

           Ever your friend/Frederick

DELIUS, FREDERICK   178B-115   (119)
To Jelka Rosen
n.d. [May 1902]
Grez sur Loing/S & M
ALS   One leaf folded of which one side is blank
           22.4 x 14 cms.

           Dearest Jelka -/I left in the afternoon/of Friday
           as I had to lunch/with Me Runkel. Certainly/
           propose the Grez dinner/to the Princess - ...

There has been a late frost in Grez which has killed off much of
the fruit on their vines but spared their potato crop.

Delius has seen *Pelléas et Mélisande* which he terms 'exquisite' -
the 'best thing' he has seen 'for years' - 'full of poetry and
dlicacy', and he urges Jelka to see it.

150

He concludes:

> ... How is your mother -/Yours as ever/Frederick

Note: The 'Princess' mentioned appears to be organising a performance of Delius's music, but he wants to meet the people concerned
first informally and for this purpose feels a dinner is better
than her 'stiff' 'afternoons'.

DELIUS, FREDERICK   178B-116   (120)
To Jelka Rosen
n.d. [Spring 1902 - precedes that of 14 Mai]
Grez sur Loing/Seine & Marne
ALS   One leaf folded
        22.4 x 14 cms.

> My dearest Jelka -/I am so sorry you are/so
> miserable ...

Achille Ouvré and a Miss Warwick appear to have offended both Jelka
and Delius equally.

The cold spring continues and frost has attacked the flowers, even
the roses.

In addition to nursing her dying mother, Jelka seems to be generally
overburdened by her family and the claims of friends. Delius urges
her to speak her mind, for, he maintains, she is too often the victim
of her own good nature. He goes on to say that of all her friends
he only really approves of Maud Ede. By this he appears to
mean that he finds all the others take from her and give nothing in
return. While stressing that he cares for her 'immensely' and is
her 'real friend', he also says:

> You really ought/to have somebody to love/you
> in the way you desire -

He concludes:

> ... It is as cold as/heaven here! - I am well/
> ever your friend/Frederick

[This letter is very interesting for what it implies rather than
what it says, for it is clear that the writers have reached a
turning point in their relationship. Unfortunately we do not
have Jelka's letter which prompted this reply.]

DELIUS, FREDERICK   178B-117   (121)
To Jelka Rosen
14 Mai [1902]
Grez sur Loing/Seine & Marne
ALS   One leaf folded of which one side is blank (very thin quality)
        22.4 x 14 cms.

151

> Dearest Jelka -/I have just received/news from
> Milly Bergh* - She/has the "Hytte" in the/Dovre
> Fjeld - ...

Delius is going to accept the hut for the summer holiday and is also
about to come to Paris (15 Rue Jacob) in order to see *Pelléas et
Mélisande* again. He notes that 36 Rue St Sulpice is now too
expensive. He hopes that Jelka is more cheerful, and offers to
take her out somewhere if she likes.

He concludes:

> Ever your friend/Frederick

*See Delius to Jelka pmk 17/vii/06.

DELIUS, FREDERICK   178B-118   (122)
To Jelka Rosen
3 Juin - [1902]
Grez sur Loing/Seine & Marne
ALS   One leaf folded
        21 x 13.3 cms.

> Dearest Jelka -/Of course a 'dénouement'/must be
> close at hand now/after your description it/cannot
> last long - your garde malade is a treasure!

The opening above is referring to Jelka's mother's terminal illness.
Delius goes on to talk of the 'Princess' of the previous letters.
She appears to have let them down, or to have taken offence
(concerning the dinner?). He attempts to explain the temperament
of his 'faithful friend', the Princess, to Jelka. In this context
the Princesse de Cystria would seem to be indicated rather than
the Princesse de Polignac of the 1899 letters above.

Delius plans to sail to Norway on 19 June. He hopes Jelka can
follow and entrusts his correspondence to her in the meantime.
He signs himself 'always yours/Frederick'.

                    KROENIG, ALBERTINE [TANTE]   178B-118(b)
                    To Fritz Delius
                    31/5.02
                    Berlin
                    ALS   One leaf folded of which one side
                            is blank

                    In German.

DELIUS, FREDERICK   178B-119   (123)
To Jelka Rosen
n.d. [June 1902]
Grez sur Loing/Seine & Marne
ALS   One leaf folded
        21 x 13.4 cms.

        Dearest Jelka -/You must be having a/terrible time
        of it - what a/frightful struggle she is having ...

He encloses 'a letter to Albertine' for Jelka's approval (presumably
the draft discussed in 178B-118) and asks if she received the roses
he sent 'on Friday night'.

He announces:

        My Opera was quite finished on the 6th of June.*

The rest of the letter is gardening and holiday planning talk. He
notes that with nothing left in the garden after the frost, he has
'lived off the things the Princess sent'.... for the 'last week',
and the weather is still 'beastly - rainy and cold'.

*At this point in the longhand copy '(Margot)' has been written,
implying that he refers to *Margot la Rouge* rather than *A Village
Romeo and Juliet*, but John Coates' copy of *Margot la Rouge*
inscribed in Delius's autograph reads 'finished April 1902'.
[see RT Cat. p. 43]. Since Delius did not write that dedication
until '15th Dec 1907' it is possible he was confusing the two
works, to both of which finishing touches were being made in the
Spring of 1902.

DELIUS, FREDERICK   178B-120   (124)
To Jelka Rosen
10th June [1902]
Grez sur Loing/Seine & Marne
ALS   Two leaves folded
        21 x 13.3 cms.

        Dearest Jelka -/Your letter just to hand/I sent
        off Albertines letter   I/suppose the Prologue*
        & 1st Act/must remain with Badoux [?] until I
        come and I will leave it with you so that you
        may take/it with you to Norway & put the/words
        in at your leisure - D'Humieres/then wants it
        to translate - He/may come up and spend a/fortnight
        with us in Norway & do/the Requiem with me - ...

He concludes:

        yrs ever/Frederick Delius

*The work referred to is *A Village Romeo and Juliet* for which Robert
d'Humières wrote the French translation appearing on the manuscript
vocal score made by Florent Schmitt at this time and entitled
Le Jardin du Paradis. See RL Cat. pp. 76-78 and RT Cat. pp. 34-41
and compare letters 178b-111(115) and 178B-119(123) above.

DELIUS, FREDERICK   178B-121   (125)
To Jelka Rosen
n.d. [Jelka has added in pencil 'middle of June after my mothers death']
Grez sur Loing/S & M
ALS   One leaf folded
          21 x 13.4 cms.

          Dearest Jelka - your card/just received   I am glad/
          you arrived all right at the/frontier & hope
          everything will/go off smoothly - ...

Delius gives Jelka more information about holiday plans and letting
the house while they are away. Jelka, one presumes, has gone to
Germany to settle her mother's affairs.

He concludes:

          Believe me/as always/y^{rs}/Frederick

DELIUS, FREDERICK   178B-60   (62)
To Jelka Rosen
Friday ['1899. Summer. Antwerp on his way to Norway' - added in
          pencil in Jelka's hand]
          <1902 Summer> is suggested by the cataloguer as more likely
          because of the style of the opening and the signature
          'Frederick'. However, the suggestion of 1899, by Jelka,
          indicates that they holidayed together, presumably for the
          first time, in Norway that year.
ALS   One ruled leaf of which one side is blank
          21.4 x 14 cms approx.

          Dearest Jelka -/The 3.40/train/is shockingly bad -/
          12-40 - or 6- p m/are the trains - or/8.20 a.m. - ...

          ... au revoir in Fredriksvarn [Fredriksvaern]

DELIUS, FREDERICK   178B-122   (126)
To Jelka Rosen
n.d. [1902]
Nevlingshavn
ALS   One leaf folded (a pocketbook leaf)
          18 x 10.8 cms.

          Dearest Jelka -/I came straight/on here to day
          and have/found lodgings of a/very primitive
          description./The food is awful and/the cooking
          worse, no/beer even. But the sea/bathing is
          immense - ...

He concludes:

          Au revoir bientôt/yrs ever/Frederick

DELIUS, FREDERICK   178B-123   (127)
To Jelka Rosen
n.d. ['Norway July 1902' - added by Jelka in pencil]
no address
ALS   One ruled leaf folded of which two sides are blank
         18 x 10.8 cms.

         Dearest Jelka -/I have removed to/another house ...

He concludes:

         - No/work as yet - too lazy/Frederick

DELIUS, FREDERICK   178B-124   (128)
To Jelka Rosen
n.d. <mid-August 1902> [see d'Humières below]
         ['Autumn, 1902' - added by Jelka in pencil]
[Grez]
ALS   One leaf folded
         20.4 x 12.6 cms.

         Dearest Jelka - I expected/a letter this morning
         but/none arrived, so I suppose/you are busy with
         the/division - ...

         ... Yesterday morning/I received a letter from/
         Humières. he has finished/the Prologue - and
         wants/me to change the names/of Sali & Vrenchen -
         I cant/see why? ...

He concludes:-

         ... - Let me know how/things are going on &/when
         the coast will be/clear - Always yours/Frederick

                         D'HUMIÈRES, ROBERT   178B-124(b)
                         To F. Delius
                         10 août [1902]
                         Brétel - St. Valery sur Somme
                         ALS   One grey leaf folded of which two
                                sides are blank
                                20.4 x 12.6 cms.
                                Enclosed in 178B-124(128) above

                                Cher ami - J'ai fini la traduction/
                                du Prologue de votre Opéra. ...

                         He notes that it will be necessary to change
                         the names of the hero and heroine to some-
                         thing at once Tyrolean and harmonious and
                         requests that Mlle Rosen shall handle this
                         and fill in the names where he has left
                         blank spaces.

The opera under discussion in 178B-124 and 124b is *Le Jardin du Paradis*
(A Village Romeo and Juliet).

DELIUS, FREDERICK   178B-125   (129)
To Jelka Rosen
n.d. [September 1902]
[Grez]
ALS   Two grey leaves folded, the side of one being blank
         20.4 x 12.6 cms.

         Dearest Jelka -/Your letter just to hand -/Your
         Berlin brother is a/misérable & F. not much/better.   ...

Signed:

         ... always yours/Frederick

The letter is full of advice to stand her ground over the 'division'
[of the property].

DELIUS, FREDERICK   178B-126   (130)
To Jelka Rosen
n.d. ['Autumn 1902' added by Jelka]
Grez sur Loing/Seine & Marne
ALS   Two grey leaves folded, the side of one being blank
         20.4 x 12.6 cms.
         A pressed flower enclosed

         Dearest Jelka -/Yours just to hand -/You forgot
         to send me the/address of my mother.   ...

Jelka is expected home at Grez 'on Wednesday'. The letter is a
tale of small events:- the roses and petunias; a cellar running
with cider when Marie forgot to drive home a 'spicket'; Maynard
'all the time at Marlotte' and 'getting a bit slow'; plans for
the re-decoration of the house; sighs for ready cash. It is
signed: 'Your loving/Frederick'.

DELIUS, FRITZ   178B-127   (131)
To Jelka Rosen
n.d. [The intimate and almost ardent manner suggests late 1902,
        yet the conclusion might be read as indicating an earlier
        date.]
no address
ALS   of which the first leaf is missing and the extant leaf
         folded has one side blank
         21 x 13.4 cms.

The conclusion is 'I am just longing to/be with you again -/your
loving friend' with no signature and a postscript reads: 'Burn
this letter at once dearest'.

The core of·the letter seems to lie on page (2):

         What a brave girl you/are - I admire you more/
         & more every day: perhaps/we are only now
         beginning/to really know & appreciate/one
         another - ...

DELIUS, FREDERICK   178B-128   (132)
To Jelka Rosen
9 Fev 1903 [Jelka has clarified in pencil as 9 Febr]
Düsseldorf [letterhead of the Café Cornelius]
ALS   One single leaf
        27 x 21.2 cms.

        Dearest Jelka - Arrived here this/afternoon & was
        very heartily received by Buths/I received your
        letter & enclosures - d'Humières/is idiotic ...

Delius is introducing one of his operas [*Koanga*?] to Hans Gregor.
He is writing the letter at the café while his friends, the
conductor Julius Buths and his wife are at a choral rehearsal.
Other names mentioned are Isidore de Lara, with whom he shared
the train journey as far as Liège, and Hans Haym, with whom Delius
has spent Sunday evening.

He concludes:

        Am longing to be/back with you again your
        affectionate/Fred.

FRITZ DELIUS, from now onwards known formally as FREDERICK DELIUS,
WAS MARRIED TO JELKA ROSEN ON 25 SEPTEMBER 1903.

DELIUS, FREDERICK   178B-129   (133)
To Jelka Delius
n.d. [Autumn 1903 has been added in pencil by Jelka]
110 Avenue d'Orléans
ALS   One leaf folded of which two sides are blank
        20 x 12.5 cms.
        Envelope addressed: Madame/Jelka Delius/Clinique
                             du Dr Millée/8 Rue de Strasbourg/
                             Paris
        pmk Paris illegible

        Dearest Jelka/I quite forgot to tell/you that
        I have to be/at the dentist at 2/to morrow &
        dont suppose/I can be with you before/4. ...

Signed:

        With best love/yrs ever/Frederick

DELIUS, FREDERICK   178B-130   (134)
To Jelka Delius
[14 June 1906]
[Norway]
PCS   pmk Larvik   14 VI 06
          addressed: Fru Jelka Delius/Hotel Victoria/Aasgaardstrand/
                       Norway

          It might be better to tell/Marie[*] to address
          the/knapsack directly/here ...

Jelka is painting at this well-known resort, which was also the
home of their great friend Edvard Munch. Delius is staying a little
further south.

*'Marie' was the housekeeper at Grez.

DELIUS, FREDERICK   178B-131   (135)
To Jelka Delius
[28 June 1906]
[Frederiksvaern, Norway]
PCS   pmk Frederiksvaern   28 VI 06
          addressed: Fru Jelka Delius/Victoria Hotel/Aasgaardstrand

          Harmonie writes that each/piece is counted
          separately/The music has arrived/also. Please
          tell me/what I shall write on/Schilling's copy
          as a/dedication*.   ...

*Sea Drift, completed 1903 (or 1904 according to the vocal score
and Max Chop's monograph on Delius of 1907), was first performed
on 24 May 1906 at Essen and published by Harmonie shortly afterwards.
Delius dedicated the work to Max Schillings.

DELIUS, FREDERICK   178B-132   (136)
To Jelka Delius
[9 July 1906]
[Kristiania (Oslo)]
PCS   pmk Kristiania   9 VII 06
          addressed: Fru Jelka Delius/Hotel Victoria/Aasgaardstrand

          If you get this in time/please put my
          knicker-/bockers & the pair of stockings/I
          wore last in the knapsack & send it/to
          Storfjeldsaeter: Atna St [Station]

Delius is off to the mountains and arrives at Atna at 11 o'clock
that night. The weather is hot and he needs cooler clothes.

DELIUS, FREDERICK   178B-133   (137)
To Jelka Delius
18/7. [18 July 1906]
Storfjeldsaeter [Norway]
ALS   One leaf folded
           17 x 13 cms.
           Pressed flowers enclosed: yellow violets and white heather
           Envelope addressed: Hotel Victoria, Aasgaardstrand, as above
           pmk Atna   18 VII 06

           Dearest Jelka - I received/your letter last night with/
           Munchs & the criticism./I am sorry you are in/low
           spirits - it must/be the bad weather. Buy/a good
           pair of boots/& walk more. ...

The weather, despite the last letter, is quite cold in the mountains.
'Mrs. B', a mutual friend who has already appeared in the correspondence, has just arrived and her husband is to follow in a few
days. Delius writes that he is being well supplied with books and
is reading Obstfjelder's works. In the previous letter 'Mrs. B'
was going to send books to Jelka. See 'Milly Bergh' in 178B-117(121)
1902.

DELIUS, FREDERICK   178B-134   (138)
To Jelka Delius
19 July [1906]
Storfjeldsaeter
ALS   One leaf folded (grey paper)
           20 x 12.7 cms.

           Dearest Jelka. Your letter with Arons'/Abrechnung
           just received. ...

DELIUS, FREDERICK   178B-135   (139)
To Jelka Delius
20/7.[1906]
Storfjeldsaeter
ALS   One leaf folded (grey paper)
           20.5 x 12.7 cms.

           Dearest/Your letters received safely the/one
           from "Harmonie" I enclose. ...

It appears that negotiations are in progress for the publication
of a score at present in the hands of Hermann Suter (conductor).
Leuckart is being considered as an alternative to Harmonie Verlag
as Delius's publisher. *A Mass of Life* was published in the following year, 1907, by Harmonie Verlag, but *Paris* was published in
1909 by Leuckart.

Jelka is depressed about her painting and Delius encourages
her:-

... Stick at your work/I am sure you will do
something/good. Dont be so easily discouraged./
Remember that every Artistic Effort/is a new
great endeavour. Like/bearing a child. At least
it ought/to be to bear fruit. Only those/that
continually repeat themselves/work easily & without
worry &/great endeavour. ...

He concludes:-

Now, write soon/again & keep your pecker up/
yrs ever/Fred

DELIUS, FREDERICK   178B-136   (140)
To Jelka Delius
Telegram from Atna 24 7.1906 3.55 pm
To Fru Delius, Aasgaardstrand

Kommer med Farlsberg/imorgen eftermiddag./
Delius

DELIUS, FREDERICK   178B-137   (141)
To Jelka Delius
9 April 07
90 Oakley Str/Chelsea S W
ALS   Paper borrowed from his landlady, one leaf folded
         17.5 x 11.5 cms.

Dearest!/Here I am. The place/is quite
comfortable. The/landlady & servant/quite
typical. I had/a very rough passage/& nearly
everybody was/sick.

He has seen his librettist, Keary, that morning and dines with him
that night. Henry Wood has written a welcoming letter and needs
biographical notes and a photograph for publicity purposes. He
asks Jelka to obtain a copy of the biography by Max Chop written for
Kahnt, or, alternatively, that to be published by Harmonie Presse
'if it is ready'.

He concludes this letter by promising to visit Jelka's aunt
(Moscheles) [see '1899 visit' letters] and ends in very English
fashion:

Lots of love from/yrs ever/Fred

Delius is using this visit not only to further his music but also
to re-equip himself with clothes and to purchase household items
for Jelka. The letters of this group are therefore very informa-
tive about goods available and current prices at such stores as
the Army and Navy and Harrods. Items purchased included curtain
material and 'Silurian' writing paper!

160

DELIUS, FREDERICK   178B-138   (142)
To Jelka Delius
10th/4 [1907]
90 Oakley Str. Chelsea
PCS   addressed: Grez
           pmk Chelsea S.W 10 4 07
           pmk Grez illegible

           Please send me a few of my/visiting cards in your
           letter. ...

DELIUS, FREDERICK   178B-139   (143)
To Jelka Delius
11 April [1907] ['11.4.1907' added in pencil]
90 Oakley Str/Chelsea SW.
ALS   One leaf folded (grey paper)
           21 x 13.5 cms.

           Dearest Jelka./Your letters just received/and
           also the Music. I/have written to RУsch &/
           Harmonie. ...

           ... I lunch with Wood tomorrow/& will write you
           the result. ...

           ... The climate agrees wonder/fully well with me.
           Mothers/milk I suppose! ...

He concludes:

           your loving/Fred

and in postscript says 'This is the Silurian/paper'.

DELIUS, FREDERICK   178B-140   (144)
To Jelka Delius
Apri [13 April 1907]
[London]
PCS   pmk London.W. Apr 13 07
           pmk Grez illegible
           addressed: Grez

           Please send a photo of mine/(sitting down) to
           Wood. ...

He notes that he lunched with Wood the previous day and is 'pretty
sure' that Wood will conduct his Piano Concerto.

DELIUS, FREDERICK   178B-141   (145)
To Jelka Delius
14th/4/07 [Sunday]
90 Oakley Str/Chelsea S W
ALS   One leaf folded (grey paper)
         21 x 13.5 cms.

         Dearest Jelka!/Enclosed a letter from Wood/as you
         see he likes the Concerto./They only pay solists
         [sic] 5 guineas/for the promenade Concerts/I hope
         Szanto will play/it in spite of the small fee./It
         is an opening & Wood/says it is the best public/in
         London ...

         ... I went today, Sunday, to Hampton Court with
         Keary ...

A vivid word picture of the flowers follows, showing an artist's
eye for his surroundings.

The following day Delius is to lunch with Percy Pitt and dine with
Balfour Gardiner with whom he will meet 'some musicians'.

DELIUS, FREDERICK   178B-142   (146)
To Jelka Delius
n.d. <16 April 1907?> ['15 April 1907' added by Jelka in pencil]
[London]
PCS   pmk illegible
         addressed: Grez

         I have no news of Cassirers[1]. I wrote to/the
         Adelphi Theatre but received no answer. ...

Two statements on this postcard are significant:-

         It would be worth while to come over here/only
         to see the Turners in the Tate Gallery -/Some
         are quite remarkable & one sees where/Monet got
         his Thames bridge from. ...

         I dined/with Balfour Gardiner last night[2] & they
         played/*Appalachia* thro (a few musicians were there)
         all/were tremendously taken with it - This really
         is/my field. ...

1. Fritz Cassirer and his wife. Cassirer conducted the first
    performance of the opera *A Village Romeo and Juliet* in Berlin
    on 21 February 1907, and was now expected in London in the course
    of a British tour. Delius and Cassirer are, at this point in
    the letters, planning to give *Appalachia* in London in the Autumn
    in an effort to establish Delius in his own country, for not a
    note of his music had been played in public in England since the
    1899 concert. This had been too much ahead of public taste to
    do more than introduce Delius's name to a few discerning musicians.

2. This statement, together with that of 178B-141 about dining
    'tomorrow' with Balfour Gardiner, suggests 16 April 1907 as
    the date for this PCS rather than 15 April.

DELIUS, FREDERICK   178B-143   (147)
To Jelka Delius
n.d. <17 April 1907>   [Jelka's pencilled '18 April 1907' is the
          receiving postmark]
[London]
PCS   pmk London illegible
           pmk Grez 18-4 07
           addressed: Grez

           Received your letter last night. Am/glad all
           is well. ...

           ... I lunch with your/aunt today. No Cassirers.
           I shall/take no more notice of them. Very/
           strange!! ...

Delius wants Jelka to write to Harmonie Verlag to remind them to send
the signed contracts and gives her advice about bottling their wine.

DELIUS, FREDERICK   178B-144   (148)
To Jelka Delius
n.d. [18 April 1907, possibly written late on 17 April]
[London]
PCS   pmk Chelsea. S.W 18 Ap 07
           pmk Grez omitted
           addressed: Grez

           It is alright with the Cassirers/They only just
           arrived in a special/train with the whole troupe
           (LPO)/I lunched with the Grelix*. They were/very
           nice. ...

He concludes:

           ... This is my real field & I/ought to be here
           every year. Je suis/plus connu que je croyais. ...

*'The Grelix' was the name of the house in Chelsea where Jelka's
Moscheles relations lived. See 1899 - Jelka Rosen to Fritz Delius
178A-2.

DELIUS, FREDERICK   178B-145   (149)
To Jelka Delius
Friday 18th/4/07
90 Oakley Str/Chelsea
ALS   One leaf folded
           21 x 13.5 cms.

           Dearest Jelka -/Your letter just received./I am
           very sorry you have had/a grippe again. It is
           very/cold here also. Would you/like to come or do
           you prefer/to stay in Grez? I think/of leaving
           here end of next/week. Sunday week. ...

Delius wants Jelka to write to Harmonie Verlag to say that *A Mass of Life* must be translated into English in readiness for possible performance at English festivals. He feels that he does not write German well enough to do this.

He lunches with the critic of *The Daily Telegraph* the following day. He notes:-

> Everybody/seems very keen on me/here. Especially
> all the/young lot. Cyril Scott/I have also seen &
> he/is really very nice. ...

He concludes by urging Jelka to send her paintings to some exhibitions and advises on choice, ending:

> your loving/Fred

DELIUS, FREDERICK   178B-146   (150)
To Jelka Delius
21/4 07
90 Oakley Str/Chelsea
ALS   One leaf folded (grey paper)
         21 x 13.5 cms.

> Dearest /I received your two/letters this morning.
> Perhaps/it is just as well to postpone/your visit
> until the autumn,/as I want to get back as/quick
> as I can to do a little/work before Dresden & it/
> would be a pity for you/to stay only 3 days. ...

He asks Jelka to meet him in Paris on 'Monday evening' and sums up his visit to London as 'most successful' even concluding:

> ... I should have no difficulty here to take the
> first place./Everyone wants me to come/and live
> in London. ...

A full and enthusiastic account of his first meeting with Percy Grainger occupies page two of the letter:

> ... I also/met Percy Grainger, a most/charming
> young man &/more gifted than Scott &/less affected.
> An Austra/-lien [sic] - you would like him/
> immensely. We all meet/at his house on Thursday/
> for music. My Concerto &/*Appalachia*. I have
> become acquainted with the musical/critic of the
> daily Telegraph -/Robin Legge. He has a very/
> charming wife & daughter & they/have invited me
> already/several times. He is all/fire & flame. I
> left him/the score of *Appalachia* &/he & Percy
> Grainger are quite/enthusiastic about it./Enclosed
> a little note*/Grainger left at my house/after he
> had seen &/played the score. He is/impulsive & nice. ...

*See Percy Grainger to Frederick Delius (i) in the Archive of the Delius Trust listed in this catalogue.

Other points mentioned: Delius has hopes of engaging Frederick
Austin to sing *Sea Drift* at Sheffield and later in the 'Messe';
Kalisch requires a copy of his songs for a female singer, and also
the score of the 'Messe'; he is so busy that he cannot complete
correcting 'the voices' of *Sea Drift* and he insists that they 'must
be in no hurry for an/Editor' for the Concerto.

DELIUS, FREDERICK   178B-147   (151)
To Jelka Delius
n.d. [22 April 1907]
[London]
PCS   pmk Chelsea. S.W. 22 Apr 07
           pmk Grez illegible
           addressed: Grez

           Please send at once to Robin Legge/Esqre. What
           we have concerning the Ver-/fassung etc of the
           Tonkünstler Verein - Their rules. & finances etc. ...

Delius gives Legge's address at 33 Oakley Street, and notes that
Kalisch will translate the 'Messe' of which he will write to Harmonie
Verlag.

DELIUS, FREDERICK   178B-148   (152)
To Jelka Delius
n.d. [24 April 1907]
[London]
PCS   pmk Chelsea. S.W. 24 Apr 07
           pmk Grez illegible
           addressed: Grez

           It strikes me that the/man in St Augustine[*]/
           has not sent me my/quittance for Taxes. ...

Delius notes that he has no time to visit his mother as he lunches
with Wood 'to morrow' to show him the 'Messe' and he leaves on
'Monday morning'. A final line reads:

           ... Cassirer may give my Opera/as an Oratorio.

[*]Solana Grove, Delius's orange farm in Florida, was within the
jurisdiction of St Augustine for tax purposes.

DELIUS, FREDERICK   178B-149   (153)
To Jelka Delius
n.d. [29 April 1907]
[London]
PCS   pmk Chelsea. S.W. 29 Apr 07
           pmk Grez illegible
           addressed: Grez

           I leave here on Monday morning/& arrive in Paris
           between 7 & 8. ...

Jelka is to meet him in Paris and to bring both summer and winter underclothing for him so that he is ready for any weather change. Delius's extreme sensitivity to changes in temperature necessitated frequent changes of the weight of his clothing.

DELIUS, FREDERICK   178B-150   (154)
To Jelka Delius
n.d. <October-November 1907. After 29 Oct. and before 6 Nov.>*
        [Jelka has added 'Dec. 1907' in pencil; but see editorial
        note to the next letter.]
Broad Meadow/Kings Norton [Birmingham] [Granville Bantock's letter-
        head]
ALS   One leaf folded to make four, of which the fourth is blank
        and page 2 is written right across sides two and three of
        the paper.
        14.5 x 11 cms.

        Dearest Jelka -/It is delightful here/& the Bantocks
        are/most charming people./They at once made/me
        telegraph for you. ...

Bantock is anxious to view the score of *Paris*, and he is described by Delius as being both 'very keen' on his music and 'one of the nicest men I ever met'.

An amusing postscript reads:

        Dont forget *Paris* & have the letters addressed
        here: bring my tooth & nail brush.

DELIUS, FREDERICK   178B-151   (155)
To Jelka Delius
n.d. <October-November 1907, as above>*
        [Edited in pencil by Jelka as above, 'Dec. 1907'.]
Broad Meadow/Kings Norton [letterhead as above]
ALS   One leaf folded, of which one side is blank
        14.4 x 11.3 cms.

        Dearest Jelka -/Dont bring *Paris*/now. ...

        ... Bring *Brigg fair*

*Envelope addressed to 7 Pembroke Villas, Kensington, Balfour Gardiner's house at that time. Norman O'Neill, with whom Delius also became acquainted this year, lived at number 4. On the evidence of the Bantock correspondence in the archive of the Delius Trust, I date these letters as after the London debut of the Piano Concerto on 22 October rather than after the first London performance of *Appalachia* on 22 November 1907.

DELIUS, FREDERICK   178B-152   (156)
To Jelka Delius
n.d. [8 January 1908]
[London] <7 Pembroke Villas?>
PCS   pmk Kensington. W. Ja 8 08
         pmk Grez illegible
         addressed: Grez

    I arrived safely here. The passage was/rough, ...

Delius would appear to be staying with Balfour Gardiner in order to
attend a rehearsal on 'Thursday morning'. After the rehearsal he
plans to travel to Liverpool, staying at the North Western Hotel and
thence to Adbolton near Nottingham, the home of a sister and brother-
in-law. He notes: 'London is just as dull & dirty & rainy' and
'Gardiner in excellent spirits ...'.

He signs himself '... yr loving Fred.'

DELIUS, FREDERICK   178B-153   (157)
To Jelka Delius
Thursday <9 January> ['1908 Jan 5th' added in pencil by Jelka is
         an error, as it obviously follows the postcard above]
7, Pembroke Villas, Kensington, W. [letterhead]
ALS   One leaf folded, of which one side is blank
         17.4 x 12.2 cms.

         Dearest Jelka/Just a word to say/that all is going
         well -/I was at a rehearsal/this morning which
         went/very well -/Beecham takes/good tempi & the
         orchestra/likes the piece - ...

He leaves the next day for Liverpool, rather than immediately as
planned, as the rehearsal to be attended there is in the evening.
He praises Beecham and notes that he plans to give *Paris, Brigg
Fair, Appalachia,* the *Légende* for Violin and Orchestra and possibly
the Danish Songs, in the near future. Bradford [Yorks], Delius's
home town, is interested in *A Mass of Life* for a May performance
and Beecham has helped to produce and distribute leaflets about
the work. He concludes:

         Lebenstanz is given/at the Albert Hall on/Sunday
         19th inst/With best love to you/& Helene/yr
         loving Fred/Write a word -

DELIUS, FREDERICK   178B-154   (158)
To Jelka Delius
n.d. Sunday <12 January 1908> ['Jan/1908?' added by Jelka in pencil]
Broad Meadow/Kings Norton [letterhead]
ALS   Two single leaves 22.5 x 17.4 cms.

         Dearest Jelka -/I received your letter & enclosures/
         yesterday in Liverpool - I decided/to go with
         Bantock to Birmingham/first & then to Nottingham/on
         Thursday & from there to Liver/pool again -

Delius has been in Liverpool for Beecham's presentation of *Paris* and
a first rehearsal of *Brigg Fair* under Bantock to be given there the
ensuing Saturday, after which he will return to 7 Pembroke Villas
to hear *Lebenstanz* in rehearsal at the Albert Hall on the Sunday
morning at 10.30 and in performance in the afternoon. He plans to
leave for Grez on Tuesday 21st [spelt 'Thuesday'].

Of *Paris* he says '... The success was mediocre. ...' but he
anticipates that Beecham will manage a more finished performance
of *Paris* in London. Here, as always, Delius is emphasising the need
for adequate rehearsal time and Bantock is allowing an extra
rehearsal for *Brigg Fair*, but he may also be indicating that the
audience was not quite ready for *Paris* when he says: 'I/dont
think anybody but a few musicians understood it. ...'.

DELIUS, FREDERICK   178B-155   (159)
To Jelka Delius
n.d. <16 or 17 January 1908> ['Autumn 1908' added in pencil is
        incorrect, for this letter flows on from the one above with
        its talk of contracts to be sent to 'Rüsch' and Beecham's
        plans to give *Appalachia* at Hanley (spelt Henley) on 2 April]
Adbolton, Nottingham. [letterhead]
ALS   One leaf folded
        20.4 x 12.8 cms.

        Dearest Jelka -/I received all your/letters &
        bought here/to day the wool &/cloth & pencil etc ...

He notes that Beecham's forthcoming London engagements with the New
Symphony Orchestra include *Paris* on 26 February, *Brigg Fair* in March
and *Appalachia* on 13 May.

DELIUS, FREDERICK   178B-156   (160)
To Jelka Delius
n.d. <20 January 1908, after first performance of *Brigg Fair* at
        Liverpool, 18 January 1908> ['1908 January' added by Jelka
        in pencil]
7, Pembroke Villas, Kensington, W. [letterhead]
ALS   One leaf folded
        17.5 x 12.2 cms.

        Dearest Jelka -/I arrived here yesterday morning,
        having left Liver/-pool at 12 at night/*A Dance of Life*
        was splen-/didly played by the Symphony/Orchestra &
        admirably/conducted by Arbos -/first class - better
        than/Haym or Buths. ...

Bantock's conducting of *Brigg Fair* was excellent, but, as with
Beecham's *Paris* performance, the general audience was not very understanding:- 'It was no public success, but found enthusiastic/
admirers among the young lot.' Delius, however, was very pleased
with the sound of his new work at this, its first performance
(Liverpool Orchestral Society), and it is clear that he feels in
complete command of his medium and happy about the future.

DELIUS, FREDERICK   178B-157   (162)
To Jelka Delius
n.d. <29 July 1908> ['1908 20.8' pencilled is possibly a confusion
      with F.D.'s 20/8/09 *about* Gjende]
PPCS   pmk illegible
        addressed: Grez
        picture: Gjendesheim

        Just arrived in/Lillehammer/we leave for Otta
        tomorrow. ...

Delius notes that he has had a 'lovely passage', arriving on 'Wednesday
morning'. He has received 'Letter & buttons' and concludes 'Heaps
of love/Fred'.

DELIUS, FREDERICK   178B-158   (163)
To Jelka Delius
n.d. <30 July 1908> ['1908 July' pencilled]
PPCS   pmk illegible
        addressed: Grez
        picture: Snehaetten

        Just left Lillehammer ...

DELIUS, FREDERICK   178B-159   (164)
To Jelka Delius
29th [?]/7/08 [Internal evidence suggests the date should have been
      written as '30th']
Sve/Vaage
ALS   One ruled leaf folded
        22 x 14 cms.

        Dearest Jelka - We/arrived here a/couple of hours
        ago. It is the place/where we two stopped at
        after/our walk over the Vidder from Dom/baas. ...

Delius concludes:

        Miss you very much/old girl -/your loving Fred.

DELIUS, FREDERICK   178B-160   (166)
To Jelka Delius
n.d. <1 August 1908?> ['1908.7.8' added in pencil is the receiving pmk]
PPCS   pmk Grotlien I VIII 08
        pmk Grez 7-8 08
        addressed: Grez
        picture: Gjeldedalstinderne, Falketind og Uranøset -
                 Jotunheimen

        Very cold, & some rain since we left Otta. ...

DELIUS, FREDERICK   178B-161   (167)
To Jelka Delius
2 August 1908
Hotellerne "Union" og "Geiranger"/Geiranger [letterhead]
ALS   Two single leaves, of which one side is blank
        28.5 x 22 cms.

        Dearest Jelka - We have just arrived here from/
        Grotlien where we stayed last night - ...

DELIUS, FREDERICK   178B-162   (169)
To Jelka Delius
A 'Souvenir-Panorama' of Molde addressed to Fru Jelka Delius at Grez
sur Loing and postmarked Molde/4 VIII 08

DELIUS, FREDERICK   178B-163   (170)
To Jelka Delius
4 August 08
Molde/Søstrene Hansen's Hotel
ALS   One ruled leaf folded
        21.7 x 13.4 cms.

        Dearest Jelka -/We arrived here this morning/
        Weather fine & warm again - ...
        ... We stayed/last night in Vestnaes on/the
        other side of the Fjord ...
        ... My next address/will be Gendesheim (Jotunheim)
        & then post restante Kristiania ...
        ... Beecham/is a splendid travelling com/-panion &
        one never tires of him - ...
        ... We sleep & eat like ogres - ...

DELIUS, FREDERICK   178B-164   (172)
To Jelka Delius
n.d. <5 or 6 August 1908*> [The pencilled '1908.10.08' is the
        receiving pmk]
PPCS   pmk Aalesund 6[?] VIII 08
        pmk Grez 10-8 08
        addressed: Grez
        picture: Helland pr Vestnaes.

        We left Molde today. Got your letter/with Bergers
        answer. ...

*In the letter above, 4 August, they plan to leave Molde 'tomorrow'
or the day after.

DELIUS, FREDERICK   178B-165   (173)
To Jelka Delius
6th August [1908] ['1908.4.08' pencilled at the head is incorrect
        and hard to explain!]
Saebe Hjørundsfjord

ALS   One leaf folded
    .   21 x 17 cms.

         Dearest Jelka - We arrived here this/evening - We
         left Aalesund at 4/a.m. (awfully hard to get up) ...

DELIUS, FREDERICK   178B-166   (174)
To Jelka Delius
10/8/1908
Hjelle Hotel / Hjelledalen./Nordfjord [letterhead]
ALS   One ruled leaf
         26.8 x 21 cms.

         Dearest Jelka - We have just arrived here/and
         we are waiting for a guide ...

DELIUS, FREDERICK   178B-167   (175)
To Jelka Delius
10/8/08
Hjelle
PPCS   pmk illegible
         addressed: Grez
         picture: Indseiling Troldfjord.

         It is pouring with rain/& we must stay here/until
         it stops - ...

DELIUS, FREDERICK   178B-168   (177)
To Jelka Delius
12/8./[08].
Skaare
                      *
PPCS   pmk Grotlien 12 VIII 08 [The pencilled '17.8.1908 must
         indicate the receiving date]
         pmk Grez illegible
         picture: Videsaeter Hotel, Opstryn (Nordfjord)

         Rain, rain, We went up to Vide Saeter/yesterday.
         This is the view/from the Saeter itself - very comfortable - ...

*The Grotlien pmk is quite in accord with their being at Skaare in
Stryn. The postcard was perhaps carried down by someone else.

DELIUS, FREDERICK   178B-169   (179)
To Jelka Delius
15/8/08.
<Aanstad, Gudbrandsdal>
PPCS   pmk illegible [Since Delius writes the date quite clearly
         it is hard to understand the pencilled '1908.13.8']
         addressed: Grez
         picture: girl milking a goat

         Arrived here in/Aanstad, Gud/brandsdalen after a
         glorious 2 days/march, across/Jostedalbrae/to Sota Sr -
         13th-/14th - Sunshine/On our way to Rodsheim, Galdhøpig -
         will/write when I can/with love/Fred

DELIUS, FREDERICK   178B-170   (180)
To Jelka Delius
[August 1908] <before Sunday, 16 August, 1908: post delayed>*
[Røysheim]
PPCS   pmk partially obscured 1[7] VIII 08[?]
          pmk Grez illegible ['1908.1.8' in pencil is a misreading of
          the legible figures of the Grez pmk without allowing for a
          missing figure]
          addressed: Grez
          picture: Lomseggen

          Just arrived at Røsheim, came past Andvord & the
          road/where we had that night walk. - We are
          presently going/off to Gjuvas/Hytten. ...

*despite pmk, probably written before the 'Sunday' item below, on the
evidence of 172-174. See also 173 on postal arrangements.

DELIUS, FREDERICK   178B-171   (182)
To Jelka Delius
n.d. Sunday. <16 August 1908?> [a pencilled 1908.2.8 is a misreading
          of an illegible pmk: possibly Øie 2[O VIII] 08]
PPCS   addressed: Grez
          picture: Knud Yole

          Sunday./Glorious weather. Just down/from Galdhøpig*. ...

*The highest peak in the Jotunheim range.

DELIUS, FREDERICK   178B-172   (184)
To Jelka Delius
18/8./08
Gendeboden [Delius's spelling]
ALS   Two leaves folded
          21 x 13 cms.
          Envelope addressed: Grez
          pmk Øie 20 VIII 08
          pmk Grez illegible
          On verso Jelka has pencilled: 'letter typed for E. Smyth/
          5.1.1935'

          Dearest Jelka - We arrived here/yesterday evening at
          6. after a/glorious walk thro' Uladalen/from Spiterstulen -
          The weather since Sunday is blazing hot ...

Delius recounts in detail the whole walk across the Jostedalsbrae
(beginning from Skaare in Stryn), and their ascent of Galdhøpig.

This is the letter published by Ethel Smyth in her book *Beecham
and Pharaoh* (London: Chapman and Hall, 1935), pp. 19-21. Also
see: Christopher Palmer, *Delius: Portrait of a Cosmopolitan*
(London: Duckworth, 1976), pp. 43-44.

DELIUS, FREDERICK   178B-173   (185)
To Jelka Delius
18/8/08 [written on the picture side of the card by Delius in ink]
<Gjendeboden>
PPCS   pmk Øie 20 VIII 0[8]
          pmk Grez illegible
          picture: Gjendeboden

          Just received your/letter. Have written you/to day -
          but the letter/only goes off day after/to morrow ...

DELIUS, FREDERICK   178B-174   (186)
To Jelka Delius
20/8/08
no address
PPCS   pmk Te ..nden 23 VIII 08
          pmk Grez illegible [a pencilled date '23' agrees with the
                             pmk and ignores Delius's own date.]
          addressed: Grez
          picture: Glittertind, Jotunheimen

          Lovely, sunny, cloudless/weather. Perfect! We/
          stayed 2 nights at Gjende/boden, & then went to/
          Gjendesheim over Besseggen ...

He concludes:

          Sail/on the 28th. With love./Fred

DELIUS, FREDERICK   178B-175   (187)
To Jelka Délius
22/8/08
Fagernaes.
PPCS   pmk Valdresbanen Peks.. 22 VIII 08
          pmk Grez illegible
          addressed: Grez
          picture: Besseggen

          Arrived here last/night. ...

Delius notes that it is raining, but that they have only had three
days of rain out of twenty-two. They will probably wait for the
boat at Fredriksvaern.

DELIUS, FREDERICK   178B-176   (189)
To Jelka Delius
n.d. [27 August 1908]
Fredriksvaern
PCS   pmk Chr.a-Bergen 27 VIII 08
          pmk Grez illegible
          addressed: Grez

          I have been here since Sunday. and leave/tomorrow
          morning for Arendal, taking/the boat on Friday for Antwerp - ...

DELIUS, FREDERICK   178B-177   (190)
To Jelka Delius
28th [August] 1908
Grand Hotel/Arendal [letterhead]
ALS   One ruled leaf folded
           22 x 14 cms.

           Envelope addressed: Grez [also hotel's letterhead]
           pmk Chr.a-Bergen 28 VIII 08
           pmk Grez illegible

           Dearest Jelka/I arrived here just now - there/
           is a big storm blowing so I think it/wiser to
           postpone my trip across the/North Sea until next
           Friday 4th Sept ...

DELIUS, FREDERICK   178B-178   (193)
To Jelka Delius
31/8/08
Fevik
ALS   Two leaves folded, of which one side is blank
           18 x 11.3 cms.

           Dearest Jelka -/Since I wrote you from Arendal/
           I have come out here: ...

DELIUS, FREDERICK   178B-179/i-ix   (194/
To Jelka Delius   i-ix)
Nine picture postcards of scenes on the walk of 1908. No message.

DELIUS, FREDERICK   178B-180   (198)
To Jelka Delius
n.d. <5 October 1908?>
[Kensington, London W.]   <7 Pembroke Villas?>
PCS   pmk Kensington Oc 5 08 [?]
           pmk Grez 6-10 08
           addressed: Grez

           Arrived safely after long passage./Just as we
           left Amiens a young/Englishman shot himself in
           the/train & we had to return & de/posite the
           body at the station. ...

           ... Gardiner & Ella/are well - We leave for Sh^{fd}*/
           to morrow 1-30. Tonight/we go to the Adelphi to
           hear/O'Neills music. ...

*Delius appears to be staying with Balfour Gardiner with whom he
is travelling to Sheffield for the first English performance of
Sea Drift conducted by Wood at the Festival.

DELIUS, FREDERICK   178B-181   (199)
To Jelka Delius
n.d. <7 October 1908?: the date of *Sea Drift* in Sheffield>
Kings Head Hotel/Sheffield (written in Delius's hand) on the
        letterhead of 29, Tavistock Square, W.C. deleted
ALS   One single leaf
        20.5 x 13.5 cms.

        Dearest, Just a word/to say the performance went/
        of [sic] very well - It was a huge/success - altho'
        I dont be/lieve any one really understood/it - ...

Delius goes on to say that the [Queen's Hall] Orchestra and the
baritone, 'Frederic Austin', performed well, but Henry Wood 'did
not always take/the right tempi -'.

DELIUS, FREDERICK   178B-182   (201)
To Jelka Delius
n.d. Monday [12 October 1908]
[Kensington]
PCS   pmk Kensington.W Oc 12 08
        pmk Grez 14-10 08
        addressed: Grez

        Just received your card - Alright. come to Paris/
        and get a room at the Beaux Arts. I must/have
        this tooth out all the same. ...

DELIUS, FREDERICK   178B-183   (202)
To Jelka Delius
13/10/08
[London]
PCS   pmk London.W. illegible
        pmk Grez 15-10 08

        Please bring my gray hat with/you to Paris - ...

DELIUS, FREDERICK   178B-184   (203)
To Jelka Delius
Thursday night <3 December 1908>
[Stoke on Trent]
PCS   pmk Stoke on Trent   9.15 am   4 De 08
        pmk Grez 5-12 08

        Just had a lovely performance of/*Sea-drift* -
        Beecham & Orchestra/wonderful also Chorus - Go
        to/Manchester tomorrow - Had a lovely crossing.
        Stayed with O'Neill/go on Saturday to London &/
        stay with Beecham - Send papers - Love from/Fred

DELIUS, FREDERICK   178B-185   (207)
To Jelka Delius
n.d. <after 4 December> ['1908' 'December' in pencil]
Highfield, Boreham Wood, Herts. [Thomas Beecham's letterhead]
ALS   One leaf folded
         18 x 11.2 cms.

         Dearest -/I have been rushing/about so that I
         had/no time to write./The Hanley performance/
         was splendid - At/Manchester the Hallé/people
         had evidently/boycotted the Concert ...

DELIUS, FREDERICK   178B-186   (208)
To Jelka Delius
n.d. ['10.12.1908' - added in pencil]
7, Pembroke Villas, Kensington, W. [Balfour Gardiner's letterhead]
ALS   One leaf folded
         17.5 x 11 cms.

         Dearest -/Have just come from/the rehearsal - it
         went/quite well - I seem/to have more control/
         over myself than at/Hanley. Perhaps it/is
         ascetism!! ...

         ... I have not the slightest idea - How it will/
         go tomorrow* - ...

He notes that there is a 'League Committee' meeting the next day in
the afternoon. This was the newly formed 'Musical League' for the
promotion of the work of British composers, with Elgar as President
and Delius as Vice President. It had been suggested in the first
place by Delius.

*In a Summer Garden (first version) was the work under rehearsal for
its première at a Philharmonic Concert the next day, 11 December 1908,
in the evening. Hence the dating of this letter. The Hanley performance to which Delius refers is that of Appalachia on 2 April 1908
where he had first tried his hand at conducting. The performers on
that occasion were the Hallé Orchestra and the North Staffordshire
Choral Society.

DELIUS, FREDERICK   178B-187   (209)
To Jelka Delius
n.d. [12 December 1908] ['1908.12.12' and 'Fred conducts Summer
         Garden/Ist perf.' written in pencil by Jelka at the head
         of this letter]
7, Pembroke Villas, Kensington, W. [letterhead]
ALS   One leaf folded
         17.5 x 11 cms.

         Dearest Jelka -/Just a word in haste/to tell you
         about the/Concert - I was quite/cool when I found/
         myself on the conducting/stand & made no/mistake - ...

Delius notes that he travels back 'tomorrow 13th [Sunday] with
Busonis & shall stay the night in Paris - ...'. He will go out
to Grez by the '5 train on Monday'.

DELIUS, FREDERICK   178B-188   (210)
To Jelka Delius
n.d. ['1908 December' - added in pencil]
Savile Club, 107, Piccadilly, W. [letterhead]
ALS   One leaf folded, of which one side is blank
        18 x 11.2 cms.

        Dearest -/Just a note to tell/you that everything
        went/well - I have been awfully/busy & rushing
        about/I shall leave here on Thursday morning at/
        9.5 & come straight to Grez. ...

This letter has been left where it was found but it is by no means
certain that it belongs here. It could belong earlier in the year,
as Delius says: 'Nearly all the notices on *Sea-drift* are
excellent -', but the Delius Trust archivist, Dr Lionel Carley,
feels that the reference to correspondence with Harmonie Verlag
(over the alterations to the Concerto which Szanto has made without
the composer's consent), fit at this point. It would seem,
therefore, that Delius's plans of 12 December 1908 for his return
to Paris were not carried out.

THE JULY 1909 WALKING TOUR WITH O'NEILL IN THE BLACK FOREST

DELIUS, FREDERICK   178B-189   (211)
To Jelka Delius
Wednesday ['1909' added in pencil]
Grand Hôtel/et Hôtel Euler/Basel [letterhead]
ALS   One leaf folded, of which one side is blank
        21.5 x 13.5 cms.

        Dearest - I arrived here/safely yesterday. ...

        ... Suter/came to fetch me & we/spent the
        evening together -/I feel much better to-day/
        & cough less - ...

Delius asks Jelka to send his only score of the *Dance Rhapsody*
(no. 1) to Ernest Austin, as 'he must do it as soon/as possible &
send the parts & Score insured/to Schou's Denmark -'.
[Presumably, in this case, 'do' means 'copy'.]

DELIUS, FREDERICK   178B-190   (212)
To Jelka Delius
[14 July 1909]
[Freiburg (Breisgau)]
PCS   pmk Freiburg 14.7.09
          pmk Grez 15-7 09
          addressed: Grez

          My address til Sunday/is Feldberger hof/Feldberg/
          Baden ...

Mention of 'Little O'Neill had the whooping cough' shows this is
the start of the Black Forest walking tour of that year with Norman
O'Neill.

DELIUS, FREDERICK   178B-191   (213)
To Jelka Delius
<15 July 1909> ['16.9.09' added in pencil is the wrongly transcribed
          receiving pmk]
<Freiburg>
PPCS   pmk illegible
          pmk Grez 16-7 [0]9
          addressed: Grez
          picture: Feldsee i.Schw.

          Dont send my/dance Rhapsody/off before I write/
          again - as I/am first writing/to Dr Sinclair/for
          a Heckelphone - ...

DELIUS, FREDERICK   178B-192   (214)
To Jelka Delius
[16 July 1909]
[Freiburg]
PPC   pmk Freiburg 16/7 09
          pmk Grez 17-7 09
          addressed: Grez
          picture: 'Badische Volkstrachten- Schonach' [girl spinning]

          Dont forget boot/trees - Mrs Griegs/address - My/
          Dowson Partitur* ...

*Songs of Sunset

DELIUS, FREDERICK   178B-193   (215)
To Jelka Delius
[16 July 1909]
Hinterzarten
PPC   pmk Freiburg 16/7 09
          pmk Grez 17-7 09
          addressed: Grez
          picture: 'Badische Volkstrachten-Gutachtal' [four girls]

Find the parts of my/Danish Songs &/send them to/
4 Pembroke Villas*/They must be in Grez - Also the/
piano score to/Miss Evans/5 Sandringham/Court 50,
Maida Vale. NW ...

*The home of the composer Norman O'Neill and his wife, the pianist,
Adine O'Neill.

DELIUS, FREDERICK   178B-194   (216)
To Jelka Delius
<16 July 1909>
<Hint[erzarte]n>
PPCS   pmk Hint[erzarte]n   [16 [7] 09]
        pmk Grez 18-7 [09]
        addressed: Grez
        picture: Gasthaus zum Himmelreich

        The weather is still rainy ...

His cough is still 'pretty bad' and the weather cold 'up here'.

Delius asks Jelka for a prescription and reminds her to bring his
syringe with her on the Scandinavian holiday they are taking jointly
after this walking tour is over.

DELIUS, FREDERICK   178B-195   (217)
To Jelka Delius
[18 July 1909]
[Feldberg]
PCS   pmk Feldberg (Schwarzwald) 18 7 09
        pmk Grez 20-7 09
        addressed: Grez

        Your letters received - I am glad you are no worse/
        I am better to day, but the last 2 days were/very
        bad - We are on the Feldberg, very high/but too many
        tourists - ...

        ... The Philharmonic can play *Paris* as Beecham/
        wrote - I am not going to give them a new work ...

DELIUS, FREDERICK   178B-196   (218)
To Jelka Delius
n.d. [July 1909]
Feldberger Hof/(Feldberg Schwarzwald) [letterhead]
ALS   Two leaves folded of which one side is blank except
        for Jelka's pencil note: 'Trip to Black Forest with O'Neill'
        21.9 x 13.8 cms.

        Dearest Jelka -/All your letters arrived here/
        safely - ...

Delius wants to know when to meet Jelka in Hamburg, 31 July or 1
August. He is evidently longing for the Scandinavian scene, and
says: 'All this is nothing/to Denmark & Norway ...'

DELIUS, FREDERICK   178B-197   (219)
To Jelka Delius
[20 July 1909]
[Feldberg]
PCS   pmk Feldberg (Schwarzwald) 20 7 09
          pmk Grez 21-7 09
          addressed: Grez

          Just received your card. I/think Beecham has the
          parts/of Danish songs. ...

Delius gives orders for fencing their field against cattle which will
harm their trees while they are away.

                    O'NEILL, NORMAN   178B-197(i/O'Neill)
                    To Jelka Delius
                    Wednesday [21 July 1909]
                    Feldberger Hof
                    PCS   pmk Feldberg (Schwarzwald) 21 7 09
                            pmk Grez 23-7 09
                            addressed: Grez

                            Dear Mrs Delius, Just a p.c./to tell
                            you that we are/being lazy & have
                            been lazy!/Fred is much better &
                            cough nearly gone. We move on/
                            tomorrow on our way to Triberg./...
                            It is glorious weather ...

DELIUS, FREDERICK   178B-198   (220)
To Jelka Delius
<23 July 1909>
<Amt Neustadt?>
PPCS   pmk not very clear: E..enbach 23[?] 7.09
          pmk Grez 25-7 09
          addressed: Grez
          picture: Gasthaus zum Engel auf dem Hochberg, Amt Neustadt,
                    (Schwarzwald)

          We are on our way to Triberg/& staying here for
          the night/a lovely place 4000 ft up/& lovely pine
          woods &/such air. ...

DELIUS, FREDERICK   178B-199   (221)
To Jelka Delius
[24 July 1909]
[Triberg]
PCS   pmk Triberg 24.7.09
          pmk Grez 26-7 09
          addressed: Grez

Dearest. Many thanks for your/letters & papers -
We have just/arrived here in Triberg, but it/is
very hot & too many tourists/so we leave to morrow
mor/-ning - I will meet you on/Saturday in Hamburg/
Hotel Continental as you/propose - Dont send the
score of/Danish songs anywhere - Beecham/has the
right score. ...

... Dont forget <u>Dowson</u>/Cucumber & glycerine ...

... walked 20 miles to day -

DELIUS, FREDERICK   178B-200   (222)
To Jelka Delius
[26 July 1909]
Hotel u. Pension z. Waldhorn/Schönmünzach (Murgthal) [letterhead]
PCS   pmk Schönmünzach (Württ) 26 Jul 09
        pmk Grez 28-7 09
        addressed: Grez

Gernsbach-Baden/I leave here for Gernsbach/to morrow.
& shall be there/until Friday morning -/I shall leave
Frankfurt/on Saturday morning/early & get to/Hamburg/
in the afternoon ...

DELIUS, FREDERICK   178B-201   (223)
To Jelka Delius
[27 July 1909]
[Gernsbach]
PCS   pmk Gernsbach (Murgthal) 27.7.09
        pmk Grez 28-7 09
        addressed: Grez

Dearest -/Your letter enclosing 'Harmonies' just/
arrived - ...
... I shall be in Ham/-burg perhaps on Friday night
12 pm. Mrs. O.Neill is not here ...
... The Schwarz/wald is rather expensive. 7 Mks a
day as a rule - I/am looking forward to the North - ...

DELIUS, FREDERICK   178B-202   (224)
To Jelka Delius
[27 July 1909]
[Gernsbach]
PCS   pmk Gernsbach (Murgthal) 27.7.09
        pmk Grez 28-7 09
        addressed: Grez

Letters & medicine & paper/arrived tonight - I
dont suppose/we shall be infectious! I had/that
pain in my chest for a/long time -

He will leave Gernsbach with O'Neill on Friday for Frankfurt and
then continue alone.

181

DELIUS, FREDERICK   178B-203   (225)
To Jelka Delius
[28 July 1909]
[Gernsbach]
PCS   pmk Gernsbach (Murgthal) 28.7.09.
         pmk Grez 29-7 [09]
         addressed: Grez

         Dearest, I am so sorry you have such/a pain in the
         chest - If we dont like it/at Schous we will go on
         to Thisted & stay/in a small bathing place - write
         to Mrs/Schou & tell her we arrive on Aug 1st - 4/p m -
         at Horsens - I hope we are not in-/fectious -
         Austin's children are also/there - ...

Delius wishes he had not accepted the Hereford engagement [the
performance of *Dance Rhapsody* (no. 1) at the Festival]. He does
not want to have to spend all September in England.

DELIUS, FREDERICK   178B-204   (226)
To Jelka Delius
n.d. <Friday, before 8.0 p.m.; see following letter>
        [a pencilled '1910?' at the head]
no address <Paris: Hotel Terminus Nord?>
ALS   One leaf folded of which two sides are blank
         17.5 x 11.4 cms.

         Delius writes in pencil and in haste:

         Dearest -/No fur - given orders/to send it to
         108.*/Monday morning or/latest at 6 p m -

The hotel is filthy and he has had to change rooms, but it appears
that he is only there one night. He notes that his 'douleur' is
cured.

*108 B^d Montparnasse/Paris: see 178B-218(251) and 178B-223(261)
below.

DELIUS, FREDERICK   178B-205   (227)
To Jelka Delius
n.d. Saturday <1910?>
Hotel Terminus Nord/Paris [letterhead]
ALS   One leaf, of which the verso is blank
         18.4 x 13.5 cms.

         Dearest -/my fur arrived at/8 o clock - just
         fancy/after having told me at/the Louvre that
         it was/impossible to get it/before Monday - ...

DELIUS, FREDERICK   178B-206   (228)
To Jelka Delius
n.d. [The pencilled editing first suggests '28' then deletes and
      superimposes '27.5.1910', which would make this a Friday.]
49, Stockerstrasse, Zürich. [letterhead of Carl Haeberlin]
ALS   One cross-ruled leaf folded, of which two sides are blank
       27 x 21.5 cms.

      Dearest Jelka - I arrived safely last/night at
      7.40 - Mrs Haeberlin is very kind/& nice & I am
      very comfortable & feeling quite/well - This
      morning had a rehearsal of/*Brigg Fair* - Andreae
      is awfully good/& the tempi perfect - ...

He has had a medical examination and possible gall stone trouble
has been diagnosed as a cause of his 'attacks' of debility
following upon influenza. Bodensee Sanatorium has been advised for
a thorough examination.

DELIUS, FREDERICK   178B-207   (229)
To Jelka Delius
[28 May 1910]
[Zürich]
PCS   pmk Zürich 28.V.10
       pmk Grez illegible

      Dearest Jelka - Everything is going well. The/
      Haupt Probe was very good, but Andreae/says the
      performance will be better - ...

      ... The con-/cert is to night - ...

Delius gives an impressive list of forthcoming performances of his
works in Germany and Switzerland.

DELIUS, FREDERICK   178B-208   (230)
To Jelka Delius
Monday <30 May 1910>
Zurich [sic]
ALS   One black edged leaf folded
       17 x 13 cms.

      Dearest Jelka -/Your letter just arrived:/I am
      glad everything is alright/& that you are
      better again -/The performance of *Brigg Fair*/
      was wonderful - the best I/have heard - ...
      a tremendous effect -/quite a triumph - ...

An excellent account of the way Zürich is entertaining its musician guests at the Festival. Delius is enjoying himself.

Wolf has acquired the first rights for the performance of *Brigg Fair* in Berlin and Hamburg, and so Delius notes that Nikisch will have to do it. Compare the 1900-1901 letters from Berlin which report that Nikisch was averse to performing Delius's music.

FROM THE SANATORIUM AT MAMMERN BODENSEE

DELIUS, FREDERICK   178B-209   (233)
To Jelka Delius
17/6/10
Mammern
ALS   One leaf folded
         21.5 x 13.5 cms.

         Dearest Jelka/I arrived here last night/at 10.19.
         The train left/Basle at 6-15 & not 7-5/Suter was
         at the station &/I had a nice chat with him/& a
         cup of tea - He is doing/*Brigg Fair* & *Appalachia*
         again - ...

Delius describes the other patients and finds them very dull: 'how ugly humanity is' he writes in disgust. The doctor has diagnosed that his central nervous system has been affected, but the cause is not certain.

DELIUS, FREDERICK   178B-210   (235)
To Jelka Delius
[17 June 1910]
Mammern
PCS

         pmk Mammern (Thurgau) 17.VI.10
         pmk Maurice s. Seine 18-6 10
         pmk Grez 19-6 10
         addressed: Grez

         Your letter just arrived/Send me written off/the
         2 Verlaine Songs/& a few others you/think likely - ...

DELIUS, FREDERICK   178B-211   (237)
To Jelka Delius
18/6/10
Mammern
ALS   One ruled leaf folded.   (The hand is very shaky.)
         21.6 x 13.4 cms.

         Dearest Jelka/I had my first Electric bath/today ...

DELIUS, FREDERICK   178B-212   (239)
To Jelka Delius
20 Juin 1910
Mammern
ALS   One ruled leaf folded
           21.6 x 13.4 cms.

           Dearest Jelka - I received your 2 letters/to day -
           one this morning & the other this after-/noon - I
           will do the corrections of *Seadrift** when/I feel
           up to it - ...

*See 178B-214(243) and 178B-215(245) below.

DELIUS, FREDERICK   178B-213   (240)
To Jelka Delius
[21 June 1910]
Mammern
PCS   pmk Mammern 21.VI.10
           pmk Grez 22-6 10
           addressed: Grez

           I have just received the Songs - but "Jeg hører/i
           Natten" I cannot send like that - The words/(German)
           must be written where the Norwegian/are - I will have
           it copied on my return - "Schneller/mein Ross" is
           too old to go with the Verlaine ones - ...

Delius reiterates that Jelka must send the seven 'German Songs'
'published by B & H separately' and he can send the Verlaine songs.

[The reference here is to the 'Seven Songs from the Norwegian'
published with German texts which, when re-issued by Breitkopf and
Härtel (London), some time after 1903, were entitled 'Seven German
Songs'. For all song references see RT Cat. pp. 88-123.]

DELIUS, FREDERICK   178B-214   (243)
To Jelka Delius
23/6 1910
Mammern
ALS   One ruled leaf folded
           21.6 x 13.4 cms.

           Dearest Jelka -/Enclosed I send you the Kor/rector
           Bogen [sic]* of *Sea Drift*, kindly correct/& send to
           Harmonie - I received/The *Dance Rhapsody* & the songs
           today/Send me the letter to Tischer here &/I will
           copy it off & send it - enclosed/is what I want to
           write - I will/offer him the 7 German songs &/the
           4 new ones for 1500 MK/or the 7 German for 1000 - ...

*Korrekturbogen? - proofsheet.

185

DELIUS, FREDERICK   178B-214(b)
To Dr Tischer
n.d.
Incomplete draft letter

The draft letter to Dr Tischer of the same
date enclosed reveals that the Verlaine songs:
'Il pleure dans mon coeur' and 'Le Ciel est,
pardessus le toit' are the subject of the
negotiations, in addition to the Seven German
Songs ('From the Norwegian'). Tischer took
over the 'Seven Songs' in 1910; and the two
Verlaine songs, previously published in
France in 1896, were also taken over that
year and given German translations. See RT
Cat. pp. 95-99 and 109.

DELIUS, FREDERICK   178B-215   (245)
To Jelka Delius
[24 June 1910]
[Mammern]
PCS   pmk Mammern   24.VI.10
         pmk Grez illegible [a pencilled 26.6.1910 suggested reception
                             date]
         addressed: Grez

When you send the Korrecten Bogen [sic]*/to Harmonie
tell them to send/copies to Schuricht & to/Dr. Haym ...

*Korrekturenbogen? - proofsheets.

DELIUS, FREDERICK   178B-216   (247)
To Jelka Delius
[27 June 1910]
[Mammern]
PCS   pmk Mammern   27.VI.10
         pmk Grez   29-6 10
         addressed: Grez

I suppose you stayed a day or 2 longer in
Paris:/ ...

... I am so glad your dress is going/to be
so beautiful ...

The severe rains have caused the Rhine to overflow. The park at
Mammern is flooded.

DELIUS, FREDERICK   178B-217   (250)
To Jelka Delius
29/6/10
Mammern
ALS   One leaf folded
           18.9 x 14.7 cms.

           Dearest -/Just got your letter dated 27 - The
           one/you posted at 12 in Grez got here the/next
           day at 12 - That is the quickest - ...

Delius is glad that Jelka is working hard at her painting and
encourages her task of copying their Gauguin picture:- 'It may be
better than the Gauguin - ...'.

A new society for promoting modern music has formed in Manchester
and Delius has been asked to be President. He requests more
information.

DELIUS, FREDERICK   178B-218   (251)
To Jelka Delius
[30 June 1910]
[Mammern]
PCS   pmk Mammern 30.VI.10
           pmk Paris omitted
           addressed to Jelka at 108 Bd Montparnasse/Paris (the home
           of their great friend, Ida Gerhardi)

           I sent a letter to Grez - If you/get this in time
           get money/and send me 4 hundred/francs. ...

Jelka is to thank Ida Gerhardi for sending papers. He is refusing
the Manchester proposal mentioned above: 'I have/nothing to do
with local/musical affairs - ...'.

DELIUS, FREDERICK   178B-219   (254)
To Jelka Delius
[6 July 1910]
Mammern
PCS   pmk Mammern 6.VII.10
           pmk Grez   7-7 10
           addressed: Grez

           I just received a letter from Ida, with/a few
           words from you - Why dont you/send me money? -
           Since 8 days/I have no news & no news-/paper -
           Can't you send off/a paper once a day? ...

DELIUS, FREDERICK   178B-220   (256)
To Jelka Delius
[7 July 1910]
[Mammern]
PCS   pmk Mammern 7.VII.10
           pmk Grez   8-7 10
           addressed: Grez

I shall leave here on Sunday/next at 2 pm - ...
... I have had enough/of this place - Since 8
days it/is raining & storming. I am/writing to
Ida -/No money/Fred

DELIUS, FREDERICK   178B-221   (257)
To Jelka Delius
n.d. ['7.7.1910] added in pencil]
ALS   One leaf folded
        18.9 x 14.7 cms.

        Dearest Jelka/I wrote you a card this morning/
        saying that I should leave here on/Sunday noon
        & arrive in Grez on/Tuesday evening for dinner -/
        Have some nice vegetable soup - ...

DELIUS, FREDERICK   178B-222   (260)
To Jelka Delius
[9 July 1910]
[Mammern]
PCS   pmk Ambulant 9.VII 10 ['Mammern' added in pencil by Jelka]
        pmk Grez 11-7 10

        Dearest - Have just got your letter/& I see
        that Bertha* is going - Dont/worry - Let us go
        to Norway/& shut up the house - ...

Delius has heard from their friend Mrs Bergh who says that the
weather is good in Norway.

*Bertha is the maid.

                        DELIUS, FREDERICK   178B-223   (261)
                        To Ida Gerhardi
                        [9 July 1910]
                        [Mammern]
                        PCS   pmk Ambulant 9.VII 10 ['Mammern'
                               added in pencil by Jelka]
                               addressed: Frl Ida Gerhardi
                                           108 Bd. Montparnasse/
                                           Paris/France
                        In German

                        Delius says that he has written to Jelka
                        to suggest shutting the Grez house and
                        going to Norway. Delius will arrive in
                        Paris on Monday [11 July 1910].

DELIUS, FREDERICK   178B-224   (262)
To Jelka Delius
[9 July 1910]
[Mammern]
PCS   pmk Mammern 9.VII.10
           pmk Grez   11-7 10   •

           We can picnic until we go away -/dont overstrain
           yourself - ...

Delius says that if Jelka prefers to go somewhere else other than
Norway he will fall in with her plans. He also discusses the idea
of employing a Swiss maid and ends: 'à Mardi/with love/Fred'.

[A small album of eight picture postcards:- 'Kuranstalt Mammern'
on folder - follows item number 201 on the microfilm. There is
no writing on the cards.]

DELIUS, FREDERICK   178B-225   (263)
To Jelka Delius
n.d. <30 September 1912>
[London]
PCS   pmk London.W Sep 30 12
           pmk Grez   1-10 12
           addressed: Grez

           There was a little swell on the sea but other/
           wise I had a good journey - ...

He was unexpectedly met by Beecham at Charing Cross and driven by
him in a taxi to the Hotel Cecil, 'where we spoke until 1-30 -',
after which he slept well.

Delius is en route for the Birmingham Festival of that year, as
Sea Drift was to be performed on 3 October. He plans to leave
Birmingham again on 4 October.

DELIUS, FREDERICK   178B-226   (266)
To Jelka Delius
2.10.1912
The Queens Hotel/Birmingham [letterhead]
ALS   One leaf folded
           20.2 x 12.7 cms.
           Envelope addressed: Grez
           pmk Birmingham Oct 2 12 7. pm

           Dearest Jelka -/I just have a little time so/I
           will write a letter - Beecham was/just the same
           as ever & we were to-/gether the whole time in
           London -/He gives the "Mass" on Dec 7th &/he
           wrote to engage Kraus for/2 Concerts - for the
           "Mass" on/Saturday afternoon & also/for his
           Sunday Concert -

He has heard Elgar's work 'the "Musik Makers"' [*The Music Makers*]
and finds it 'not very interesting', 'noisy', and 'The chorus
treated in the old way & very heavily orchestrated'. The Sibelius
Symphony interested Delius much more because Sibelius 'is
trying to do/Something new & has a fine feeling for nature & he is/
also unconventional' - but he finds him sometimes 'a bit sketchy
& ragged'. He has enjoyed meeting Sibelius and wants to hear the
work again. As regards 'the Matthew Passion', also performed at
the Festival, he found that he could not stand more than forty
minutes of it and has decided that he has finished with what he
calls the 'old music'. He is disappointed that Scriabin's
Prometheus has been taken out of the programme.

DELIUS, FREDERICK   178B-227   (267)
To Jelka Delius
n.d. [3 October 1912]
[Birmingham]
PCS   pmk Birmingham Oc 3 12
         pmk Grez   4-10 12
         addressed: Grez

         Just received your letter - Mrs Ouvré is doing/
         the "commande" - ...

         Bantocks work last night was really/very good - ...

Delius confirms that *Sea Drift* is to be performed that night and
that the 'Hall is fine'. He plans to leave Birmingham 'tomorrow
Friday for Balfours' [Balfour Gardiner's].

DELIUS, FREDERICK   178B-228   (269)
To Jelka Delius
n.d. [5 October 1912]
[Ashampstead, nr Reading]
PCS   pmk Reading 5 Oct 12
         pmk Grez   7-10 12
         addressed: Grez

         Your letter just received. - It is/lovely here at
         Ashamsptead [sic] -

         Seadrift went off very well ...

Unfortunately the words had been left out of the programme. Beecham
is giving the *Dance Rhapsody* (no. 1) in his Sunday Concert 'tomorrow
night' - so Delius plans to leave Balfour Gardiner's country house
in the morning and will stay at the Kensington Palace Hotel.

DELIUS, FREDERICK   178B-229   (270)
To Jelka Delius
n.d. <6 October 1912> [A pencilled '1912? 10.14' does not agree
      with 178B-228 above]
[Ashampstead, nr Reading]
PPCS   pmk illegible
        addressed: Grez
        photograph: an Elizabethan brick house and outhouses

        This is Balfours house./We leave for London this/
        afternoon ...

        Tonight *Dance/Rhapsody* -

Delius plans to do his shopping the next day and to leave on the
eleventh.

Another hand has written: 'Wish you were here. H.M.G.'

DELIUS, FREDERICK   178B-230   (272)
To Jelka Delius
8.10.12
Kensington, London
PCS   pmk Kensington 8 Oct 1[2]
        pmk Grez 8-10 12 [presumably the stamp had not been changed
                            overnight]
        addressed: Grez

        I shall leave on Friday morning at 9/from Charing X - ...

Beecham, who left for Paris 'yesterday', will probably meet Delius
on arrival, but one gathers that previous arrangements to meet Jelka
in Paris for a few days shopping still stand, and his particular
interest is to compare the price of furs in the two capitals, since
they are cheap in London.

Delius has just returned from visiting his mother at Datchett
(nr Windsor) and records that he felt they were like 'Aase & Per
Gynt today'.

DELIUS, FREDERICK   178B-231   (273)
To Jelka Delius
n.d. <late May 1913> ['1913' has been added in pencil]
Hôtel Oxford et Cambridge/13 Rue d'Alger/(Corner) Rue St. Honoré/Paris
      [letterhead]
ALS   One leaf folded of which one side is blank
        20.9 x 13.7 cms.

        Dearest Jelka - I am afraid/I have no better
        memory than/you but luckily you sent me/my
        shaving things & they arrived/just as I was
        getting up & in/time - ...

Delius has seen *Boris Godunov* ('Godounov') with Bakst's designs and has met many old friends of the musical world including Ravel, Schmitt, d'Humières and also Stravinsky and [Oscar] Klemperer.

He tells Jelka that the 'Princess' will take her to *Boris Godunov* on 3 June and to dinner afterwards.

> I go to-night to/the *Oiseau de feu** -

*More programme research is needed to date this letter precisely. While it definitely reads as if Delius is enjoying the Russian season in Paris while en route for Jena, it is strange that there is no mention of *The Rite of Spring*, to whose first performance on 29 May 1913 he intended to go with Stravinsky himself, being unable to attend the rehearsal on 28 May [Delius to Stravinsky: Grez 27 May 1913 (copy DT/LKC)].

DELIUS, FREDERICK   178B-232   (274)
To Jelka Delius
Saturday [31 May 1913]
Cöln-Bayenthal [letterhead of Walter Jagenberg Papier-Export]
PCS   pmk Cöln-Bayenthal   31.5.13
         pmk Grez   2-6 13
         addressed: Grez

> Dearest - I arrived safely after a fearfully/hot journey ...

He concludes:

> Shall write from/Jena - With love/Fred

DELIUS, FREDERICK   178B-233   (276)
To Jelka Delius
4th June 1913
Bieringers Hotel zum schwarzen Baeren/Jena [letterhead]
ALS   One single leaf
         28.7 x 22.3 cms.

> Dearest Jelka - your 2 letters just arrived - ...
> The Concert came off/very well - Stein did it
> really remarkably/well & so did the Orchestra* ...

Delius notes that Tischer (Tischer & Jagenberg) is enthusiastic about his new songs and two little orchestral pieces [see 178B-245/6 below].

He plans to return to Cologne on Saturday night - to hear Mahler's Eighth Symphony on the Sunday at the Nieder Rhenische Musikfest, leaving for Paris at 2.0 p.m., staying overnight in Paris and out to Grez on Monday again.

In a Summer Garden (1908) in revised version was given its first European performance on Tuesday 3 June 1913 at Jena by Stein.

DELIUS, FREDERICK   178B-234   (277)
To Jelka Delius
n.d. [6 June 1913]
[Jena]
PCS   pmk Jena 6.6.13
         pmk Grez 7-6 13
         addressed: Grez

         Your card just received/I am glad you enjoyed/
         yourself in Paris - ...

         Tomorrow I leave/for Weimar & shall visit/Frau
         Förster Nietzsche -/shall then travel Schlaf/Wagen
         to Cologne ...

Delius's plans then remain the same as outlined in the previous
postcard, but he intends to try to reach Grez late on Sunday night
instead of on Monday.

         ... I have heard/so much bad music/that I
         can hear no/more ...

Apart from a surfeit of German classics mentioned in the previous
postcard, the journey seems to have been very happy and successful
for the future of *In a Summer Garden*. His publisher is enthusiastic.
A contract with 'Sanders' is imminent.

DELIUS, FREDERICK   178B-235   (280)
To Jelka Delius
n.d. [9 July 1913]
[Kristiania]
PCS   pmk Kristiania 9.VII.13, overstamped 'centenary exhibition'
         pmk Grez 12-7 13
         addressed: Grez

         Dearest - I arrived last night/at 12-30
         The trip was very nice - I had a lovely cabin ...

He suggests the Bergen boat for Jelka when she comes to join him on
this holiday.

DELIUS, FREDERICK   178B-236   (281)
To Jelka Delius
n.d. [10 July 1913]
[Kristiania]
PCS   pmk Kristiania 10.VII.13
         pmk Grez 13-7 13
         addressed: Grez

         Dearest - your letter with enclo/sure just received -
         also the 2/packets - I am glad you are at/work again - ...

Delius outlines his walking tour plans and tells Jelka to be sure
to stop in Kristiania to see the Munch paintings in the National
Gallery. She must also see 'The Viking Queen Ship. Perfectly
marvellous'.

DELIUS, FREDERICK   178B-237   (282)
To Jelka Delius
10th [July] 13 [1913 has been added in pencil]
Hotel Westminster [Kristiania]
ALS   Two single leaves [torn from an account book]
           22 x 14 cms.

           Dearest - Enclosed both Contracts/which please
           send on -

This is a business letter.

DELIUS, FREDERICK   178B-238   (284)
To Jelka Delius
n.d. [12 July 1913]
[Gjeilo]
PPCS   pmk Gjeilo 12.VII.13
           pmk Grez 15-7 13
           addressed: Grez
           picture: Finse, Bergensbanen

           Left Kristiania 10th, 4 p.m. arrived/Kongsberg
           8.15. Nice old hotel & good/food ...

DELIUS, FREDERICK   178B-239   (285)
To Jelka Delius
n.d. [12? July 1913]
[Gjeilo]
PPCS   pmk Gjeilo 12[?] VII.13
           pmk Grez 15-7 13
           addressed: Grez
           picture: Haugastøl-Bergensbanen

           What I did on Sanders Contract was/very wise ...

DELIUS, FREDERICK   178B-240   (286)
To Jelka Delius
13/7/1913
Høifjeldsaerteren Oset [letterhead]
Gol
ALS   One single leaf
           29 x 22 cms.

           Dearest - I arrived here at 9.p.m. & like it
           immensely/The situation is beautiful - ...

DELIUS, FREDERICK   178B-241   (290)
To Jelka Delius
20th/7 1913
Tyin Hotel/Tyin/Jotunheimen [letterhead]
ALS   One single leaf
           29 x 22 cms.
           Envelope addressed: Grez [also carries hotel letterhead]
           pmk Øie i Valdres 21 VII 13

194

Dearest Jelka - When I left Oset Hojfieldsaeter [sic] -/
which is very good indeed & beautifully situated -
3-50/per day - I drove over a fearfully bad road
across/the Fjeldvidder ...

DELIUS, FREDERICK   178B-242   (291)
To Jelka Delius
n.d. [21 July 1913]
[Tyin: posted in Øie i Valdres]
PPCS   pmk Øie 21.VII.13
          pmk Grez 23-7 13
          addressed: Grez
          picture: Tyin, Jotunheimen

          Dearest - Dont forget before/leaving to get Salomon/
          to arrange the vines ...

He may move on 'into Gjendin tomorrow or/if the weather is not fine
down/to Maristuen - ...'.

DELIUS, FREDERICK   178B-243   (292)
To Jelka Delius
n.d. [July 1913]
[Maristuen]
PPCS   pmk Maristuen [Norway] date illegible
          pmk Grez faint, but definitely 1913 and the seventh month
          [several pencilled attempts to suggest a date as 29.7.1910
          have been added]
          picture: Hoifjeldsaeteren Oset, Gol. Hollingdal

          I am now at Maristuen ...

[Misplaced in the year 1910 on the microfilm and there numbered 201.]

DELIUS, FREDERICK   178B-244   (293)
To Jelka Delius
24/7/13
[Maristuen]
PPCS   pmk Maristuen [date illegible]
          pmk Grez 28-7 13
          addressed: Grez
          re-addressed: Poste Restante/Rotterdam Hollande
          picture: Maristuens Turisthotel, Filefjeld

          I leave here tomorrow at/11.am ... & next day Saturday
          at/6.am for Flaam ...

Delius is going to meet Jelka at Bergen, and, after a few days they
will go to Lofoten ...

Jelka's postcard from Grez dated 24 July 1913 [178A-50] shows that
she was due in Bergen on 1 August.

DELIUS, FREDERICK   178B-245   (296)
To Jelka Delius
n.d. [22 October 1913]
[Leipzig]
PCS   pmk Leipzig 22.10.13.
        pmk Grez 24-10 13
        addressed: Grez

              *
        Your card just arrived. I/shall leave here on
        Friday ...

Delius reports that at the final rehearsal of his Two Pieces for
Small Orchestra, generally referred to in the correspondence of
this time as the 'two mood pictures', 'Nikisch played the 1st
piece (Spring)/much too slow - but very expressively/the 2nd He
played most beautifully -/perfect -'.

By 'Spring' Delius means *On Hearing the First Cuckoo in Spring* and
'the 2nd' is *Summer Night on the River*. Nikisch gave their first
performance at the Gewandhaus on 23 October 1913.

*This card has not survived in this archive.

DELIUS, FREDERICK   178B-246   (297)
To Jelka Delius
n.d. Friday [24 October 1913]
Hotel Hauffe/Leipzig [illustrated letterhead advertising 'Fliessendes
        Kaltes und Warmes Wasser und Post-Telephon in allen Zimmern']
PCS   pmk Leipzig 24.10.13
        pmk Grez illegible
        addressed: Madam Jelka Delius/Hotel Oxford & Cambridge/
                    13 Rue d'Alger/Paris

        I leave at 1. arrive Cologne at 10 - ...

Delius will overnight at Cologne and join Jelka at the Paris hotel
soon after 5.30. He reports that the two pieces went well and it
was a 'beautiful performance'. The audience appeared to like
On Hearing the First Cuckoo in Spring despite Nikisch's slow tempo -
and Delius sums up:-

        ... the public seemed to/like it the best -
        altho I like the/2nd best - love - Fred

DELIUS, FREDERICK   178B-247   (299)
To Jelka Delius
25 <November> 1913 [a pencilled editing 25.<u>10</u>.1913 is
        incorrect on internal evidence]
Hotel Residenz/Ludwig Domansky/Wien, I. [letterhead]
ALS   One leaf folded
        22.5 x 14.4 cms.

Dearest - You will have seen by the/telegramm [sic]
that must be lying in Grez/that the Concert is
postponed until/26th January - Charmant! to have/
come all this fearful way for/nothing - ...

The reason for the postponement of the first performance of *An Arabesk*
(Eine Arabeske) was that the orchestral parts of another composer's
work were so badly copied that they could not be read, and 'Schrecker'
[Schreker, the conductor] told Delius that the parts of his work
were almost as badly copied.

DELIUS, FREDERICK   178B-248   (300)
To Jelka Delius
n.d. <25 & 26 November 1913> concluded on a 'Wednesday morning'
        [found edited as for 178B-247]
[Vienna]
PCS   pmk Austria illegible
         pmk Grez imperfect:[?]-12 13
         addressed: Grez

         Your letter just to hand - I am glad/you did not
         send M. la R. to Fliegel./Send it to Hertzka as
         he will have/it performed in Leipzig - in Feb.
         March/& will also edit it - ...

A postscript on the address side begins:

         Me Gutheil-Schoder sings/my songs very well
         indeed ...

DELIUS, FREDERICK   178B-249   (302)
To Jelka Delius
27 <November> 1913 [27.10.1913 added in pencil, the tenth month
        being incorrect on internal evidence as for 178B-247
        and 178B-248 above]
Hotel Residenz/Wien, I. [letterhead as above]
ALS   One single leaf and one leaf folded
         22.5 x 14.4 cms.

         Dearest - Your letter arrived yesterday/Of course
         it is a horrible nuisance to/have come so far for
         no concert, but it/has not been for nothing - I *
         have come/at last to an arrangement with/Hertzka
         after a fearful pitched/battle - ...

The arrangement included the final transference of his works from
Harmonie Verlag to Universal Edition, the re-engraving of the Piano
Concerto and the separate publication of the Entr'acte from
A *Village Romeo and Juliet*, or so Delius hoped.

*of Universal Edition.

Delius has been well entertained in Vienna: he has seen the opera
Die Königin en Saba and has visited the Royal Library while people
met include Schreker, d'Albert, Loewe, Gregor, Nedbal, Roger
Quilter and Dr Simon of the *Frankfurter Zeitung*.

He hopes to hear a rehearsal of *An Arabesk* (Nedbal's orchestra is
suggested), and is busy correcting the parts.

DELIUS, FREDERICK   178B-250   (304)
To Jelka Delius
n.d. [23 June 1914]
4, Pembroke Villas, Kensington, W. [Norman O'Neill's letterhead]
ALS   Two folded leaves
         15.2 x 11.5 cms.

         Dearest - I had a fairly smooth/passage - the
         sandwiches/were very welcome at Folk-/stone -
         Beecham met me at/the station ...

Delius reports that the previous afternoon he attended the dress
rehearsal of Richard Strauss's *Joseph* and in the evening *Prince
Igor* by Borodin at Drury Lane, after which he had supper with
Beecham at his house and Lady Cunard joined them later.

Delius is attending Sir Joseph Beecham's 'Grand Season of Russian
Opera, English Opera and Russian Ballet'. *La Légende de Joseph*
(ballet) was given its first English performance on 23 June 1914
and *Prince Igor* (with Chaliapin) was given in the evening of the
22nd.

DELIUS, FREDERICK   178B-251   (307)
To Jelka Delius
n.d. <26 June 1914, Friday a.m.>
Ashampstead Green, Pangbourne, Berks.   [Balfour Gardiner's letterhead]
ALS   One leaf folded
         17.8 x 11.4 cms.

         Dearest - I am here - arrived/on Wednesday
         afternoon -/On Tuesday I went to the Première/of
         Joseph Everybody was there - ...

Delius sat in the royal box at Drury Lane with Lady Cunard and he
met 'Chaliapine'. He says 'I shall send him Niels when edited'
[*Fennimore and Gerda*].

DELIUS, FREDERICK   178B-252   (309)
To Jelka Delius
n.d. <27, 28 or 29 June 1914>
Ashampstead Green, Pangbourne, Berks.
ALS   One leaf folded
         17.8 x 11.4 cms.

         Dearest -/I hope you sent off the parts -/I go
         on Wednesday/to "The Cottage" 8a/Hobart Place -
         to Beecham. ...

Delius has attended the reception and supper at the French Embassy
after the London première of Rimsky-Korsakov's *Nuit de Mai*, 26
June 1914. We know from *The Times* report of the evening that a
concert of French music was given by Beecham and his orchestra and
that Debussy's setting of Rossetti's poem *The Blessed Damozel* was
performed. Delius also mentions 'Beecham did the Entracte [sic]
of R & J. <u>very well</u>'. He also says that he met 'George Moor' [sic]
at the Embassy and that 'He loved R & J. [*A Village Romeo and
Juliet*]. In 178B-251 above he is expecting Beecham to perform
'The Dance/Rhapsody' along with the Debussy work.

[For a full discussion of this letter see RLD/*SIM* 12.]

DELIUS, FREDERICK   178B-253   (310)
To Jelka Delius
n.d. <27 or 28 June 1914>
[Portsmouth]
PCS   pmk Portsmouth 28 Ju 14
          addressed: Grez 29-6 14

          I wired for you to send me the/Orchestral parts
          of the 2nd Act/of *Koanga* - send them by/post -
          The Concert is on the 8th/afternoon - Are you
          coming?/Love from Balfour &/your Fred

DELIUS, FREDERICK   178B-254   (313)
To Jelka Delius
n.d. <2 July 1914>
The Cottage, 8a Hobart Place, S.W. [Beecham's letterhead: Telephone/
          Gerrard 366]
ALS   Two single leaves
          25 x 19.6 cms.

          Dearest - I received all your letters/& am
          glad all things are going on so/well in Grez.
          Here it is tropical/88 in the shade fahrenheit.
          I came/here yesterday & am very comfortable. ...

Delius has just come from 'a grand reception at Grosvenor House'
(the Duke of Westminster), where there was a French exhibition of
paintings. Rodin was there and also George Moore. 'Tonight' he
is going to Rimsky-Korsakov's *Le Coq d'Or*.

DELIUS, FREDERICK   178B-255   (314)
To Jelka Delius
n.d. <3 or 4? July 1914>
8a Hobart Place
ALS   Two leaves folded
          17.8 x 11.4 cms.

          Dearest - The Concert is/fixed & advertised - ...

The concert is the all-Delius concert given by Beecham at the Duke's Hall, Royal Academy of Music, 8 July. Delius outlines the projected programme and describes the evening at *Le Coq d'Or* and the account given to him by Nancy Cunard of the midnight river party afterwards at which Sir Denis Anson and one of Beecham's orchestra members were drowned.

[See RLD/*SIM* 12.]

DELIUS, FREDERICK   178B-256   (317)
To Jelka Delius
n.d. <8 July 1914>
The Cottage, 8a Hobart Place, S.W. [letterhead]
ALS   One single leaf
         25 x 19.7 cms.

         Dearest -/The Concert is just over - I never heard/
         Beecham play my things so wonderfully/and indeed,
         I am sure, my music/has never been played as well
         by any/one - ...

Delius enclosed a programme but it has not survived.

[See *The Times* review dated 9 July entitled 'The Beauty of Delius's Music' quoted in RLD/*SIM* 12.]

DELIUS, FREDERICK   178B-257   (318)
To Jelka Delius
n.d. <9 July 1914>
[London. Kensington]
PCS   pmk London indistinct: Ke[nsington] 9 [Jul 14]
         pmk Grez 10-7 14
         addressed: Grez

         I have got off the dinner at the/Embassy.

He concludes 'leave tomorrow/<u>Friday</u>!!

[In 178B-256 above Delius has noted an invitation to lunch at the French Embassy on Friday and has said that if he cannot get out of it he will come home on Saturday.]

DELIUS, FREDERICK   178B-258   (319)
To Jelka Delius
n.d. <4 December 1914> [a pencilled '5.12.1914' could have been
         the receiving date]
Midland/Hotel/Manchester. [letterhead]
ALS   One leaf folded of which one side is blank
         17.2 x 13.6 cms.
         The envelope has not survived but the contents indicate
         that Jelka is in the London region.

            Dearest Jelka -/The Concert went off/very well
            & my piece* was/again very successfull [sic]- /We
            shall be back in/London on Saturday/afternoon so
            I shall/probably fetch you./I hope you went to see/
            the "Kinema" of the South/pole Expedition - ...

Delius notes that Beecham is lecturing at the Manchester Royal
College of Music 'tonight' and he concludes with a postscript:

            We arrive in London at 4/so I will fetch you
            to/go to Watford ...

*The concert was a Hallé concert on 3 December 1914 at which May
and Beatrice Harrison played the Brahms Double Concerto and the second
half of the evening began with two extracts from *A Village Romeo and
Juliet*: (a) 'Village Fair and Dance' leading to (b) Intermezzo -
'The Walk to the Paradise Garden'. See RLD/*SIM*, pp. 121-22.

DELIUS, FREDERICK   178B-259   (320)
To Jelka Delius
n.d. <24 February 1915>
Midland/Hotel/Manchester. [letterhead]
ALS   One leaf folded of which two sides are blank
        17.9 x 13.6 cms.

            Dearest -/Beecham will come &/dine [?] on
            Sunday next - The Sonata* comes off/to night ...

            ... The Competition is on/Friday next (afternoon)
            & 2nd Act *R & J*/tomorrow night with/2 soloists - ...

The competition was that organised by Delius and Beecham to take
place at the Royal Manchester College of Music on 26 February 1915
for the baritone part in *Sea Drift*. The concert 'tomorrow night'
was the eighteenth Hallé concert of the season, Thursday evening,
25 February 1915. [See RLD/*SIM* 12, pp. 122-23.]

*Delius's First Violin Sonata, 1905-14, first performed at the
Houldsworth Hall, Manchester on Wednesday 24 February 1915 by
Arthur Catterall and R.J. Forbes in aid of the Sustentation Fund
of the Royal Manchester College of Music.

DELIUS, FREDERICK   178B-260   (321)
To Jelka Delius
n.d. <early March? 1915, possibly Thursday, 11 March>
Regent House, Victoria Park, Manchester. [letterhead]
ALS   One leaf folded of which two sides are blank
        15 x 12 cms.

            Dearest -/I am very comfortable/here & they
            expect/you next Wednesday/I return to London
            tomorrow Friday - ...

No musical event is mentioned, but since it is clear that Jelka is
expected in the following week, March 1915 would seem more likely
than the added pencilled date 'December 1914', especially as we
have accounted for the December concert and we know Jelka was not
there. This conjecture is reinforced by the Delius/Heseltine
correspondence in which we learn that he travelled to Manchester
for rehearsals a week ahead of the *Sea Drift* performance given in
aid of the Hallé Pension Fund on 18 March 1915 (British Library,
Add. MSS 52,547). See RLD/*SIM* 12, pp. 122-24.

DELIUS, FREDERICK   178B-261   (322)
To Jelka Delius   *
n.d. <7 July 1917>
Villa Javin/Pension de Famille/Tessé-la-Madeleine/Station de
        Bagnoles (Orne) [letterhead]
ALS   One leaf folded of which one side is blank
        18 x 13.5 cms.

        Dearest -/I arrived/here half an hour ago -
        Everything/crammed with people - ...

Delius notes that he will not be able to follow Dr Bas' instructions
to the letter, as the baths are closed on Sundays.

*See Jelka Delius to Marie Clews 23.7.17: 'I must tell you that
Fred is gone since the 6th ...' [copy DT/LKC].

DELIUS, FREDERICK   178B-262   (324)
To Jelka Delius
n.d. <9 July 1917>
Villa Javin/Tessé-la-Madeleine [letterhead as above]
ALS   One leaf folded
        18 x 13.5 cms.

        Dearest - I have/just taken my first bath - I
        con/sulted a doctor Rabier yesterday/he is
        homeopath - ...

DELIUS, FREDERICK   178B-263   (327)
To Jelka Delius
13th/7/17
Villa Javin/Tessé-la-Madeleine [letterhead]
Carte-lettre (blue)
        pmk Tessé-la-Madeleine Orne 14-7 17
        pmk Grez illegible
        addressed: Grez

        Dearest - I have received all your letters/
        the last dated the 11th ...

        ... I took my 5th bath to-day ...

Delius is taking a course of twenty-one baths at a hydropathic
institution and the initial effect seems to have aggravated a
weakness in his legs and numbness in his right hand.

DELIUS, FREDERICK   178B-264   (328)
To Jelka Delius
n.d. <Sunday? 15 July 1917> [see JD to FD 17.7.1917, 178A-66 (331)]
Villa Javin/Tessé-la-Madeleine [letterhead]
ALS   One leaf folded
         18 x 13.5 cms.

         Dear Love - I just re/ceived your wire: you
         will now/have my 2nd letter - ...

DELIUS, FREDERICK   178B-265   (330)
To Jelka Delius
n.d. [16 July 1917]
Villa Javin/Tessé-la-Madeleine [letterhead]
Carte-lettre (blue)
         pmk Tessé-la-Madeleine Orne 16-7 17
         pmk Grez illegible
         addressed: Grez

         Dearest - I hope you received all my 4 letters/
         Write to Lily & ask her what Ernest died/of ...

DELIUS, FREDERICK   178B-266   (332)
To Jelka Delius
n.d. [18 July 1917]
Villa Javin/Tessé-la-Madeleine [letterhead]
Carte-lettre (blue)
         pmk Tessé-la-Madeleine 18-7 17
         pmk Grez illegible
         addressed: Grez

         Dearest - Did not the receipt from Beecham's/
         letter come back? You forgot to pack my fla/
         nnel shirt - Bring it to Brittany ...

         ... Should/I write to Dr Bas how I am & about
         the/hair stuff? ...

DELIUS, FREDERICK   178B-267   (334)
To Jelka Delius
n.d. [July 1917]
Villa Javin/Tessé-la-Madeleine [letterhead]
ALS   One leaf folded
         18 x 13.5 cms.

Dearest - I have re/ceived all your letters &
papers./I am keeping you an article about/the
"Ruth Kruger case" in New York. ...

Delius asks for Dr Bas's address.

DELIUS, FREDERICK   178B-268   (338)
To Jelka Delius
n.d. [July 1917]
Villa Javin/Tessé-la-Madeleine [letterhead]
ALS   One leaf folded
        18 x 13.5 cms.

        Dearest - Your 2 letters &/Byres Moirs [sic]
        arrived - I wrote at/once to him - We are going
        to 'Val André ...

DELIUS, FREDERICK   178B-269   (339)
To Jelka Delius
n.d. [24 July 1917]
Villa Javin/Tessé-la-Madeleine [letterhead]
Carte-lettre (blue)
        pmk Tessé-la-Madeleine 24-[7 17]

        Dearest - I have already taken 12 baths/The
        effect upon me is marvellous &/I can walk
        already quite well again./I therefore
        shall continue & not write/to Dr Bas until
        afterwards - ...

DELIUS, FREDERICK   178B-270   (340)
To Jelka Delius
n.d. [24 July 1917]
Villa Javin/Tessé-la-Madeleine [letterhead]
Carte-lettre (brown)
        pmk Briouze   24-7 17

        Dearest - I have looked up the trains/in the
        latest guides ...

Delius has walked ten kilometres that afternoon and is only a little
tired.

DELIUS, FREDERICK   178B-271   (341)
To Jelka Delius
n.d. <25 July 1917?>
Villa Javin/Tessé-la-Madeleine [letterhead]
ALS   One leaf folded
        18 x 13.5 cms.

Dearest - Your letter/enclosing Marie's just received -
How/nice about the sugar - Please bring/1 copy of my
Sonata for Violin -/It is in my music cupboard on the/
right -, as I want to send it with a/dedication to
May Harrison - Our/room is engaged at Val-André/Hotel
de la Plage for Thursday/August 2nd - ...

DELIUS, FREDERICK   178B-272   (343)
To Jelka Delius
n.d. [28 July 1917]
[Villa Javin, Tessé-la-Madeleine]
Carte-lettre (brown)
        pmk Briouze a Couterne 28-7 17
        pmk Grez illegible
        addressed: Grez

        Dearest - Dont bother to get/the Urodonal & Tea
        as you/will not have enough time ...

In 178B-270(340) above Delius has shown anxiety because Beecham
has not paid some money into his account. He now reports that
Beecham has paid in 150 pounds, and adds 'so we are rich' and
suggests that Jelka should take a first-class carriage and be
comfortable.

For a discussion of the letters of 1917 and those of 1918 and 1919 to
follow, see RLD/*SIM* 13.

DELIUS, FREDERICK   178B-273   (344)
To Jelka Delius
n.d. <Thursday, 31 January 1918>
Sanatorium Malmaison/4 Rue Bergère/Rueil [Paris]
ALS   One leaf folded
        15 x 12.3 cms.

        Dearest -/How terribly I miss you:/come out
        as soon as you/can -

Delius begins some treatment 'tomorrow' and suggests that they take
a room in Rueil so that 'they can be together in the afternoons &
evenings ...'.

Postscript:

        Remember me kindly to/Madame Mersey.

DELIUS, FREDERICK   178B-274   (347)
To Jelka Delius
July 22 <1919>
Trevor Lodge/Sennen Cornwall
ALS   One single ruled leaf
        24.8 x 19.8 cms.

        Dearest Jelka - On getting back home I found/
        enclosed letter from Jeanne & also a very nice &
        long/letter from Garanger [sic][1] which I will keep
        for you. Madame/Muse [?][2] is also in Paris &
        both are longing to hear/from us ...

Delius has seen Jelka onto the train for London. From there Jelka
is going to Grez via Paris to describe for the War Commission the
state of their house after its use by the French Army.

1. Grainger?

2. Compare also 178B-273 and the footnote to 178A-72.

DELIUS, FREDERICK   178B-275   (348)
To Jelka Delius
23 July 19
Trevor Lodge/Sennen [Cornwall]
ALS   One single leaf of which one side is blank
        24 x 20 cms.

        Dearest - I received your card this/morning &
        also a letter to you from Mrs Schou/which I will
        keep for you as it is long: she/enclosed a
        cutting which will astonish you/& please you. Just
        fancy *Fennimore & Gerda*/to be given in September
        in Frankfurt!!/what a surprise*. ...

*See FD to PG, 17 December 1919, 95-25.

DELIUS, FREDERICK   178B-276   (351)
To Jelka Delius
n.d. [31 July 1919]
[London]
PCS   pmk London W.C. 31 Jul 19
        pmk Grez omitted
        addressed: Grez

        Just received letter. delighted/everything goes
        well. I wired/twice last time saying we/could
        travel Tuesday ...

Delius is planning a Norwegian holiday. Jelka met him in London.
A comparison of this correspondence with that of Delius to
Heseltine (British Library Add. MSS 52,547) suggests they then
travelled together on 5 August.

DELIUS, FREDERICK   178B-277   (352)
To Jelka Delius
n.d. <February 1920: before 21 February> ['Febr. March 1920' -
    added in pencil by Jelka]
4 Pembroke Villas, Kensington, W. [letterhead]
ALS   One leaf folded of which one side is blank
        16.5 x 13.5 cms.

        Dearest Jelka -/Just a few words to tell/you
        that everything is alright -/I had 2 rehearsals
        today -/one in the morning with Orchestra/& one
        at Wood's house at 6 in/the afternoon until 8. ...

        ... W. gives himself endless trouble ...

Delius says that if he has to stay longer for *A Village Romeo and
Juliet* he will probably stay with the Harrisons. He has not heard
the dates yet. Jelka is in Grez with sciatica and unable to come
over for this concert, which is the première of the Double Concerto
on 21 February 1920, London, Queen's Hall, May and Beatrice Harrison,
conductor Sir Henry Wood.

DELIUS, FREDERICK   178B-278   (353)
To Jelka Delius
n.d. <22? February 1920>
4 Pembroke Villas/Kensington W
ALS   One single leaf
        22.3 x 18 cms.

        Dearest Jelka -/I received your card, letter
        & also/Tischer's - ...

        ... The Concerto went wonderfully well -/The
        girls played superbly & Wood/surpassed himself -
        It was enthusias/tically received - The house was
        crowded -/the best of the season - ...

Delius encloses an interview article from the *Daily Mail*, but this
has not survived in this archive.

He is to 'sup with Mrs Woodhouse' (Violet Woodhouse, the harpsi-
chordist). Zogheb is enthusiastic over the Double Concerto and
the Violin Concerto. Beecham's revised performance of *A Village
Romeo and Juliet* is scheduled for early March and Delius is to
attend a choral rehearsal of *The Song of the High Hills*. Delius's
handwriting is uneven in strength and we know from Derek Hudson's
book, *Norman O'Neill: A Life of Music* (pp. 69-70), that he was,
at this time, showing the first signs of paralysis. However, the
composer's mood is buoyant and he says that 'Things seem to be
going well here at last!!'

DELIUS, FREDERICK   178B-279   (356)
To Jelka Delius
n.d. <27 February 1920> ['1920.2.3' added in pencil]
4, Pembroke Villas, Kensington, W. [letterhead]
ALS   One single leaf of which one side is blank
        16.5 x 13 cms.

        Dearest - I enclose a few/criticisms for you
        to read -/*The Song of the H.H.* w as wonder/fully
        received although the per/formance was not
        perfect. The/Choir was splendid. Coates/had
        not absorbed the work enough./However it was a
        great success. ...

        ... I go to/night to Lady Cunards box/& will
        write you all about the/*Village R.* ...

The Song of the High Hills was first performed 26 February 1920,
London, Queen's Hall, Royal Philharmonic Society, Philharmonic
Choir, conductor Albert Coates.

Delius is debating whether to stay on in England for the revised
performance of *A Village Romeo and Juliet* or whether to come back
for it. The date appears still to be uncertain, although it is
expected to be the first week of March. See 178B-280.

DELIUS, FREDERICK   178B-280   (357)
To Jelka Delius
n.d. [28 February 1920]
4, Pembroke Villas, Kensington, W. [letterhead]
ALS   One single leaf of which one side is blank
        16.5 x 13 cms.

        Dearest -/Enclosed 2 more criticisms -/It appears
        the Song of the H.H./was a great success - I do
        hope/you are better now -/I went to *Tristan* last
        night & saw Lady C./& Beecham - *The Village Romeo*/
        comes off on the 17th March - I dont/think I shall
        stay. ...

DELIUS, FREDERICK   178B-281   (359)
To Jelka Delius
n.d. <Week beginning 2 March 1920>
4, Pembroke Villas, Kensington, W. [letterhead]
ALS   One leaf folded
        16.5 x 13 cms.

        Dearest Jelka/I received your 2 cards &/letter
        at the same time - Thank/goodness the strike is
        over - ...

Delius notes that there are to be three performances of *A Village
Romeo and Juliet* (17, 23 and 29 March), and so he proposes to stay and
go out 'on Saturday' to Balfour Gardiner's house for a few days.

DELIUS, FREDERICK   178B-282   (360)
To Jelka Delius
9/3/20
Ashampstead Green/Pangbourne/Berks
ALS   One single leaf
          22.7 x 17.4 cms.

          Dearest Jelka/Your letter just arrived - I/
          wired to Berlin saying nothing/had arrived -
          Please write &/ask them to keep the shares if/
          not sent off. ...

Delius proposes to stay at Ashampstead Green with Balfour Gardiner
until Monday, 15 March; then, after one night at the O'Neills to
collect his trunk, to the Rubens Hotel and back to Paris the following Sunday, out to Grez the next day.

DELIUS, FREDERICK   178B-283   (361)
To Jelka Delius
n.d. [March 1920]

ALS   One leaf folded
          17.7 x 11.4 cms.

          Dearest Jelka -/I received your letter/with 2   *
          enclosures. I am/so glad you are getting/better -
          The Opera comes/off on the 19th, so I shall/leave
          London on Sunday/the 21st & arrive in Grez/on the
          22nd at 1 pm. ...

          ... They are giving *The/Song of the H.H.* again on
          the 2nd June - ...

*This letter is written in answer to Jelka's letter dated 29 February
1920, presumably delayed by the rail strike in France, of which
mention has been made.

Despite Delius's predictions in 178B-281, all the dates for *A Village
Romeo and Juliet* were changed and it was given at Covent Garden on
19 and 24 March and 10 April 1920. See D. Redwood, p. 27.

DELIUS, FREDERICK   178B-284   (362)
To Jelka Delius
n.d. [17 March 1920]
[London]
PCS   pmk London.W.C.   17 Mar 1920
          pmk Grez illegible
          addressed: Grez

          Card just received/am over head & ears/in
          rehearsals - Am/going Hotel Rubens/to day - ...

209

DELIUS, FREDERICK   178B-285   (363)
To Jelka Delius
Sept. 4th 1920
Grand Hotel Imatz/Hendaye/Basses-Pyrénées
     [letterhead]
ALS   Two leaves folded of which three sides are blank
       21.7 x 13.5 cms.

       Dearest - Here I am -/The journey was not too/
       bad ...

DELIUS, FREDERICK   178B-286   (364)
To Jelka Delius
n.d. [4 September 1920]
[Hendaye]
PPCS   pmk Hendaye Basses-Pyrénées 4 9 20
       pmk Grez illegible
       addressed: Grez
       picture: Hendaye - vue genérale de Notre-dame de la
              Guadeloupe

       Please bring 2/silk singlets &/three silk
       drawers/They are just/the thing for/here.
       Fred

DELIUS, FREDERICK   178B-287   (365)
To Jelka Delius
5/9/20
Grand Hotel Imatz/Hendaye/Basses-Pyrénées
     [letterhead]
ALS   One leaf folded of which two sides are blank
       21.7 x 13.5 cms.

       Dearest./Please bring my brown/waistcoat - The
       food here/is not first rate & badly/served -
       always cold plates. ...

DELIUS, FREDERICK   178B-288   (366)
To Jelka Delius
7th/9/20
Hotel Imatz/Hendaye
ALS   One single ruled leaf of which one side is
       blank
       28 x 21 cms.

Dearest -/Your letter & those of Dean[*] & V.[?] G.
arrived/last night - I am so glad it only comes off/
in March - Why not go at once from here to Spain - ...

*Basil Dean, who had commissioned incidental music for a forthcoming
production of *Hassan or the Golden Journey to Samarkand* by Elroy
Flecker. See D. Redwood, Ch. 3.

DELIUS, FREDERICK   178B-289   (367)
To Jelka Delius
Tuesday <7 September? 1920>
Hotel Imatz, Hendaye.
ALS   One ruled leaf folded of which two sides are blank
       21 x 13.4 cms.

       Dearest/I have engaged a room/for Monday at Hotel
       de/la Plage ...

DELIUS, FREDERICK   178B-290   (368)
To Jelka Delius
Wednesday <8 September? 1920>
Hotel Imatz [Hendaye]
ALS   One single ruled leaf of which one side is blank
       28 x 21 cms.

       Dearest - Your 2 letters with enclosures -/arrived, -
       The registered one I only got today/tho' it came
       yesterday & no one told me -/Enclosed the key - ...

Jelka will be met at Hendaye on Monday morning by the bus of the
Hotel de la Plage and call for Delius and his things at his hotel
en route.

DELIUS, FREDERICK   178B-291   (369)
To Jelka Delius
n.d. [9 September 1920]
[Hendaye]
Carte-lettre
       pmk Hendaye 9.9.20
       pmk Grez 11.[9].20
       addressed: Grez

       Dearest - If you have/time look at W./Rogers'
       Contracts - I/am sure I have 4th in the/shilling -
       just double what/he counts - ...

DELIUS, FREDERICK   178B-292   (370)
To Jelka Delius
n.d. [18.11.1920 - added in pencil]
Carlton Hotel/Frankfurt a.m. [letterhead]
ALS   One leaf folded of which two sides are blank
         18 x 14 cms.

         Dearest - I could go no farther/than Mainz no
         connection -/so I stayed at the Central Hotel/
         near the station - ...

Delius urges Jelka to follow as soon as possible. He has a lovely
suite in the hotel.

DELIUS, FREDERICK   178B-293   (371)
To Jelka Delius
20/9/21
84 Fellows Rd [London NW3]
ALS   One single leaf of which one side is blank
         24.5 x 20 cms.

         Dearest -/Your letters & card received - I/
         enclose a few cuttings - I saw a/lot of old
         friends & it was/great fun - ...

DELIUS, FREDERICK   178B-294   (372)
To Jelka Delius
Tuesday - [1921.25.10 - added in pencil]
12 Park Avenue [Delius's autograph on the letterhead of
         Bradford Liberal Club, Bradford, Yorks.]
ALS   One single leaf
         18.5 x 11.5 cms.

         Dearest - Altho' when/I left Paris & the *Daily*/
         Mail prophesied a very/rough passage, I had/a
         very good one: ...

ELLA GRAINGER'S TYPESCRIPT COPIES

WITH PERCY GRAINGER'S LONGHAND COMMENTS IN RED INK

Numbered in ink by Percy Grainger. The revised Grainger Museum
numbers of the corresponding originals are placed to the right
in square brackets.

Cover Title
[P.G.'s holograph]   GM91-1 to 13(T)/GRAINGER MUSEUM/Typed copies
                     of/Rose Grainger's &-Perey-Grainger's [deleted]
                     letters/to//Frederick Delius & (Mrs) Jelka Delius.

                     Notes in red ink by/Percy Grainger.

Title Page
[P.G.'s holograph]   GRAINGER MUSEUM/copies of/Rose Grainger's letters
                     to/Fred Delius & Jelka Delius/(copied by Ella
                     Grainger) GM91-1 to [13](T)

Percy Grainger's Comments in red ink written as marginalia

They will be listed here as PG/FN1 to PG/FN9 (Percy Grainger Foot-
notes 1-9).

PG/FN1   *Evelyn Suart played Delius Concerto at Balfour Gardiner's*
          concert, March 18, 1912? [P.G.'s query]

          GM91-3(T) 19.3.13   [91-6]
          'We enjoyed yr Concerto last night, but I think it
          required a Man's power in the loud parts.'

PG/FN2   *Uncle Jim (James Aldridge, Richmond Park, Adelaide, S.A.)*
          & Aunty Sarah (his wife)   [91-2]

PG/FN3   *Dagny Sorensen (now Mrs Oscar Petersen) & (Dagny Wang?)*

          GM91-5(T) Sept. 23rd [1912]   [91-2]
          'My brother & wife are over from Australia & we have 2
          Norwegians in our house ...'

PG/FN4   *First performance, Rubio (cellist) present, Oct. 19.1912*

          GM91-5(T) Sept. 23rd [1912]   [91-2]
          'Percy will be conducting *Green Bushes* at Q. Hall Sym.
          Con. Oct. 19th.'

PG/FN5   *After my shammed sickness, on putting off Berlin piano*
          recital because I didnt like the ugly faces of folk in
          the Berlin Hotel & because I was scared stiff

GM91-6(T) Oct. 18 [1912]   [91-3]
'I am glad to tell you that after a rest in the country,
where Percy got every care, fresh air, & sunshine, he is
now almost quite strong again.'

PG/FN6   *These were the splendid ones of P.G. & Rocco Resta,
            P.G. & Rose G., & P.G. alone with saxophone, with
            background of a tree, taken just near the bandleader's
            (R. Resta's) quarters, F<u>t</u> Hamilton, N.Y.*

GM91-10(T) July 29th 1917   [91-11]
'Percy was photographed to-day by the assistant Band Leader,
if it turns out a success I will send you one.' (postscript)

PG/FN7   *N. York.   This was the concert at which mother & I
            munched biscuits, greatly disgusting x x x x x*

GM91-12(T) Dec. 13th 1918   [91-13]
'... the great success of your *Life's Dance* at last
night's Philh. Concert.'

PG/FN8   *Kinsey's 1st Chicago Musical College master class*

GM91-12(T) Dec. 13th 1918   [91-13]
'He has such splendid offers for next Spring & Summer
but cannot accept them yet, not knowing when he will be
free to do so.'

PG/FN9   *Norman Aldridge (Uncle Charlie's son)*

GM91-12(T) Dec. 13th 1918   [91-13]
'One of my 4 fighting nephews ... has been awarded (by
Haig) the Military Cross ...'

Cover Title
[P.G.'s holograph]   GM93-1 to 29(T) Grainger Museum/Typed copies
                     of/Percy Grainger's letters to/Frederick
                     Delius & (Mrs) Jelka Delius

                     Notes in red ink by/Percy Grainger

Title Page   GRAINGER MUSEUM/copies of/Percy Grainger's
                     letters to/Fred Delius & Jelka Delius/(copied
                     by Ella Grainger)

Percy Grainger's Comments in red ink written as marginalia

They will be listed here as PG/FN10 to PG/FN23.

PG/FN10   *First performance of any truly orchestral (as distinguished
           from string orchestra) work of mine: English Dance given
           by Beecham at London Paladium, Feb 18, 1912*

           GM93-3(T) 15 Feb 1912 [wrongly dated 16 by PG]   [93-4]
           'As for Beecham, he is a <u>genius</u> from top to toe
           in my *English Dance* just as he is in your adorable
           things. He would do it <u>perfectly</u> if only the orchestral
           parts were not so badly copied.'

PG/FN11   *This request led Delius to compose his 2 pieces for
           small orchestra: "On hearing the first Cuckoo in spring"
           & "Summer Night on the River".*

           GM93-8(T) 5.3.13   [93-7]
           'I <u>do</u> wish you had in print some piece for not <u>too big</u>
           orchestra (4 horns, 2 trumpets, no strange woodwind, nor
           too many strings required) & not too wildly hard, that
           orchestras such as those at Bournemouth[,] Belfast etc.,
           could perform it, a piece that could be performed with
           an hours or 3/4 hours rehearsal & then form part of
           general repertory.'

PG/FN12   *"Cuckoo" & "Summer Night"*
           GM93-10(T) 25.1.1914   [93-11]
           'I hear Mengelberg did your 2 new pieces for small orch.'

PG/FN13   *by Stock?*
           GM93-10(T) 25.1.1914   [93-11]
           'I see your & my pieces were done together in Chicago
           with much success the other day.'

PG/FN14   *Torquay Festival, Ap. 16, 1914, conducted by Basil
           Cameron with Beecham as guest conductor. I played
           Delius Concerto there (Beecham conducting) & conducted
           my Colonial Song (1st perf., or did I do it in
           Bournemouth before?) & Molly* with mother & Miss Du
           Cane playing resonophone parts.*
           *[Molly on the Shore 'Molly' is substituted instead
              of 'Shepherd's-Hey-(1st-perf.?}' deleted.]

           GM93-14(T) 26.4.14   [93-14]
           'Torquay was <u>delicious</u> ...'

PG/FN15   *Balfour Gardiner's then London house*

           GM93-15(T) 6 May 14   [93-15]
           The address: 7 Pembroke Villas, where Grainger is
           staying.

PG/FN16   *First London performance of "Shepherd's Hey" for full*
           orchestra; also Colonial Song

           GM93-17(T) Aug. 10.1914   [93-17]
           'Am conducting at Wood's "proms" on Aug. 18.'

PG/FN17   *Irish Tune from C? Derry (strings & horns), Shepherds*
           Hey (full orchestra). I took part in this latter piece
           & the resultant success did much to decide me to stay
           in USA

           GM93-18(T) Nov. 11 1914   [93-19]
           'Damrosch is doing 3 of my orchestral things in Dec ...'

PG/FN18   *Cuckoo & Summer Night*

           GM93-20(T) June 19, 1915   [93-21]
           'If you could happen to spare me scores of ... the 2
           Stimmungsbilder ...'

PG/FN19   *In N.Y. "Musical Quarterly" (G. Schirmer)*

           GM93-21(T) Aug. 18.1915 postscript   [93-22]
           'If you have no use for my "Impress of Personality"
           article after seeing it, you might let me have it back,
           but if you want to keep it, please just do so.'

PG/FN20   *a Kinsman of Robert Louis Stevenson*

           GM93-23(T) Dec. 7. 1915   [93-24]
           'We have had such happiness in meeting the Osbornes [sic]
           & hearing about you & your dear wife from them.'
           [Lloyd Osbourne and his wife, stepson and daughter-in-
           law of Robert Louis Stevenson.]

PG/FN21   *"In a Nutshell" Suite*

           GM93-24(T) Sept. 14. 1916   [93-25]
           'Bringing out a new orchestral Suite (4 movements) 10
           new piano pieces, 4 pieces for 2 pianos, & 2 other trifles
           is no light matter when one designs all ones own covers &
           has a vast pianistic winter ahead.'

PG/FN22   *Eating biscuits as above referred to in R.G.'s letter to*
           Deliuses

           GM93-27(T) Dec. 15, 1918   [93-29]
           'Stransky and the New York Philharmonic gave your *Life's*
           Dance last Thursday and mother and I were there.'

PG/FN23   *That was the time mother (worn out by the walk from the*
           Brooklyn Academy of Music to the Subway) had to rest
           sitting on the subway stairs.

GM93-28(T) Nov. 3, 1921   [93-30]
'Also I shall be playing your piano concerto (with New
York Symphony orchestra) in Brooklyn, Jan. 7, ...'

A further set of unbound, unannotated carbon copies of these typed
transcripts was received from Adelaide in 1976.

RELATED DOCUMENTS FOUND WITH THE LETTERS OF PERCY AND ROSE GRAINGER

AND FREDERICK AND JELKA DELIUS

I   CORRESPONDENCE CONCERNING THE DELIUS PIANO CONCERTO:

   (i)   TLS 17 May 1915 from Universal Editions, Vienna

  (ii)   TLS 1 July 1915 from Universal Editions, Vienna

 (iii)   TLS 17 May 1915 [copy only] from Universal Editions,
       Vienna, enclosed in (ii) above
       Envelope addressed: Percy Grainger
                        c/o Concert Direction,
                        Antonia Sawyer
       Subject: performing rights

  (iv)   TLS 7 July 1915 from Breitkopf and Härtel, New York
       Subject: the loan of the Delius Piano Concerto
                material for one year and purporting to
                enclose a bill for 25 pounds sterling [no
                bill found in cataloguing: see (vi) below]

   (v)   TLS 20 July 1915: a chaser for (iv) above
       Envelope addressed: The Southern, 680 Madison Avenue,
                       New York City

  (vi)   Receipt for item mentioned in (iv) above dated
       'August 2nd 1915, New York'

II   TYPESCRIPT headed:
                     TO MY FELLOW-COMPOSERS, MAY 1924
               S.S. Tahiti, San Francisco-Australia, May 25

[five pages of quarto single spacing, 5400 words]

Opening Sentence:

      'Most of you know that for over 20 years it has been
      the dream of my artistic life to give concerts of
      Anglosaxon and Scandinavian modern music on a big
      scale, & that my beloved mother shared that dream &
      fought hard to help me earn the money with which to
      realise it.'

Synopsis:

Grainger discusses the value of the Bridgeport and New York
concerts which he has recently conducted and sponsored in
the light of a first venture towards realising his dream, and
with special reference both to his own growing experience as
a conductor and his opinion of *The Song of the High Hills* and
North Country Sketches by Delius. Of the former he sums up:-

> 'Here is one of the few great works of all
> time ... and that rare thing an Anglo-Saxon
> work of "SIZE" ...'

He compares it illuminatingly with the earlier 'inexperienced-
ness' of *Appalachia* and the 'less perfect in orchestration'
North Country Sketches. He contrasts Delius's belief in 'Pure
colors' with his own liking for a mixed palette and attributes
much of the success of *The Song of the High Hills* to a contra-
diction of Delius's avowed beliefs in that he uses 'an unusual
amount of doubling' 'thereby obliterating the color impression
and heightening concentration upon more purely intervalic
appeals ...'

He considers it the best introduction to Delius for the
uninitiated audience and 'to show the highest flights of
British music' and for a conductor 'no score ... holds finer
thrills' '... or offers him finer chances of passion, calm
and wide-flung transitions'.

As regards his own music in the Bridgewater-New York programmes, he is well satisfied at last with *The Marching
Song of Democracy*:-

> 'It sounds as I wanted it to, as I still want
> it to. It is hard to do, but not too hard, and
> the "nonsense syllables" seem to me wholly
> successful. I do not think that the audience
> cares much for this work, or that other musicians
> prize it very highly - not even "Graingerites".
> But I like it, and naturally care more for my own
> opinion than the whole world's.'

Of his own *Colonial Song* he regrets that neither Balfour
Gardiner nor English critics generally find it satisfactory
and adds

> 'their indifference to the Australian side
> of an Australian composer ... went far to
> make me feel "not at home" in England.'

He thinks it one of his very best smaller pieces and is happy
over its popularity in America and that it 'went splendidly'
at the concerts.

The 'a capella' items in the concerts, the Grieg *Psalms* and
the Rachmaninoff *Songs of the Church*, were excellently
performed under Mr Kasschau [the successor of Grainger's friend
Dr Mees] and well received while 'the public response to the
Delius works was, in Grainger's view 'all that could be
expected' since 'Delius is the Bách of his era, or the musical
Walt Whitman of his era ...'

On reflection he finds the whole experience worth the
'$5000 (about 1000 pounds)' it cost him because he has proved
his ability to handle 'a big scheme' and may become 'the ACTIVE
FORCE in modern music I have always longed to be'.

More works he hopes to produce are:-
Grieg's *Symphonic Dances*, Cyril Scott's *Aubade* and Herman
Sandby's *Haustemning* (sea-mood) for orchestra. He hopes
to introduce Roger Quilter and his 'lovely songs' to America
and Balfour Gardiner's piano piece *Michaelchurch*: 'fit to
rank beside the best Schumann *Novelette* or Brahms *Rhapsody*'.

American works, owing to his 'whole year in Europe [1922-23]
and ... unusually busy concert season' [1923-24] since his
return, he has not heard much lately, but pieces he praises
highly are:-
David Guion's *Sheep and Goat Walkin' to the Pasture* and
Turkey in the Straw for piano; Nathaniel Dett's *Zion
Hallelujah* for voice and piano; and Howard Brockway's
Lonesome Tunes and *Kentucky Mountain Tunes* which, with
Quilter's, he feels are 'the most important and perfect songs
in the English language'.

Concluding Paragraph:

> 'We live in an age of crazes, isms, rushings
> after "the latest". I am the last to say, or
> feel, anything against such activities. Anything
> is better than stagnation, deafness to the new.
> But while I revere Schönberg, Hindemith, Stravinsky,
> etc, I am particularly desirous of presenting to
> the musical world works that especially abound in
> harmoniousness calm, balance, melodiousness; - -
> qualities I see in abundance in the particular
> works I care to produce of Grieg, Delius, Cyril
> Scott, Sandby, Balfour Gardiner, Roger Quilter,
> Natalie Curtis, Guion, Dett, and others.

> Percy Grainger'

III DIPLOMA AWARDED TO FREDERICK DELIUS BY THE LEIPZIG
CONSERVATORIUM

Headed, KÖNIGLICHES CONSERVATORIUM DER MUSIK ZU LEIPZIG,
it is awarded to Fritz Delius, as the composer was then known,
and describes him as of Bradford, England. It is dated 17th
January 1889, by which time Delius had been resident in
Paris for some nine months. Originally unwilling to grant
a diploma to a student of only eighteen months standing,
the authorities had been persuaded by the composer's friend,
Christian Sinding, who was still resident in Leipzig and a
much respected mature student. Delius received the Diploma
in Paris on 31 March 1889 according to the postmark on the
envelope. It was forwarded from his uncle's home in the Rue
Cambon to his lodgings in Ville d'Avray. A translation by
Pamela Maclean of Melbourne University follows here:-

DIPLOMA OF THE ROYAL CONSERVATORIUM OF MUSIC, LEIPZIG,
AWARDED TO FRITZ DELIUS OF BRADFORD, ENGLAND,
17 JANUARY, 1889.

Photograph by courtesy of the Grainger Museum Board,
University of Melbourne.

Royal Conservatorium of Music, Leipzig.

Mr Fritz Delius of Bradford (England), was born at the above mentioned place on the 29 January 1862, he was accepted as a student at the Royal Conservatorium of Music in Leipzig on the 30 August 1886 (sub. no. 4486) and at Easter 1888 he was honourably discharged from the above mentioned place. In this period he undertook study in the Theory of Music and Composition, in Practical Piano, in Practical Violin, as well as in the History and Aesthetics of Music performance and, assisted by a strong capacity [for this work], he has made 'substantial and most respectable' progress. Mr Delius has a very advanced and excellent knowledge of the Theory of Music; in Practical Composition 'he is on the way through solid practice to a most valuable development'; he has 'some knowledge' in the History and Aesthetics of Music.

Mr Delius's moral demeanour at the Conservatorium has been 'exemplary' (1).

The unanimous conclusion above is based on the particular assessments by the relevant teachers at the institute as well as on personal knowledge.

Directorial-diploma conferred on Mr Fritz Delius of Bradford and completed to-day in good faith.

Leipzig, 17th January 1889.

Particular results have been awarded personally by the following undersigned teachers from the institute. [Signatures follow.]

IV   HESELTINE, PHILIP [PETER WARLOCK]
      To Percy Grainger
      November 18th 1923
      125 Cheyne Walk, Chelsea, London SW10
      ALS   Envelope addressed: White Plains [New York]

He thanks Grainger for sending a copy of his arrangement of the Delius *Dance Rhapsody** for two pianos. Lanes are sending Grainger a copy of Heseltine's newly published biography of Delius, and he encloses a printed brochure of all his publications to date.

*Grainger's arrangement was made in 1922; published 1923 UE7142.

V   BUCKLEY JONES, EDITH
      To Jelka Delius
      Jan 3rd 1931
      ALS

This answers Jelka's letter of sympathy on the death of Mrs Buckley Jones's son, Philip Heseltine.

VI A RED, LEATHER-BOUND POCKET NOTEBOOK   179A-i
    A Travel Notebook in Delius's Hand
    15.3 x 8.5 cms.

Fly leaf (i) FRITZ DELIUS/MARCH 26th/86/DANVILLE VA.
Folios 1-46 and end papers (i) [as above] and (ii).

As well as memoranda concerning reading, music, train times,
hotels and miscellanea it records two walking tours in
Norway, that of 1887 on his own and that of 1889 with Grieg
and Sinding, a visit to Jersey [1890], and his visit to
Norway in 1891 when he stayed with the poet Bjørnson and
Hjalmar Johnsen. [Folio 45 evidence of two other hands.]

VII RELATED PAPERS IN JELKA DELIUS'S HAND FOUND WITH HER
     LETTERS TO FREDERICK DELIUS

     (1) Jelka Delius to 'Leni' in German dated 4.1.1911
          from Weisser Hirsch bei Dresden, Villa
          Hohenzollern. [See 178-JD/Leni(i) 4 January
          1911, microfilm 1 item 39, with the letters of
          Jelka Delius to Frederick Delius.]

     (2) Undated notes <1896-8?> for a biographical   179B-i
          sketch, written on both sides of a single
          leaf 20 x 13.2 cms with many deletions
          [microfilm 1 item 81].

          Born at Bradford/England/1863/commenced the
          serious study/of music alone at the age of/21
          on a plantation in/Florida, completed his/
          studies two years later/at the Leipsic conserva/
          tory and/Paris where he still/resides./

          Written 2 opera's [sic] and is completing/the
          third one; this last is a/negro subject[1].

          Incidental music to/a comedy by Gunnar/Heiberg,
          which was given/in October 97 at Christia-/nia
          and caused a good/deal of controversy/an
          ouverture played/in Elberfeld (Germany) also
          97/a Symphonic poem/after a play by Ibsen/"Paa
          vidderne" played/at Monte Carlo at the/Monte
          Carlo Symphony/Concerts 94[2].

          He has also written 3/orchestral Suites and/a
          Concerto for Piano/and about 40 songs,/amongst
          which a Cyclus/of songs by Friedrich/Nietzsche,
          just completed./[3] A légende for violin/and
          orchestra[4]./American Rhapsody/for Orchestra[5].

     1. *Irmelin*, 1890-2,
         The Magic Fountain, 1893-4,
         Koanga ['negro subject'], 1895-7.

                              222

2. Philip Heseltine and all writers until
   Dr Lionel Carley in his *Delius. The Paris
   Years* (Triad Press, 1974) placed this as
   1893. Dr Carley, quoting *Figaro*, established
   1894.

3. 1898 according to Philip Heseltine

4. 1895

5. 1896

(3) Undated memorandum on a single leaf   179B-ii
    20 x 12.5 cms [filmed after the letters
    of Jelka Delius to Frederick Delius as
    item 82 of microfilm 1]. Written in German,
    it begins:

    Influenza Ende Juni. 1909
    [See Black Forest Walking Tour letters
    of 1909: Delius to Jelka, catalogue
    numbers 178B-189 to 178B-202.]

    and continues to outline the first serious
    breakdown in health suffered by Delius then
    and in February 1910. Jelka wonders what is
    best to be done for treatment. [See Zürich
    and Mammern letters of 1910, catalogue
    numbers 178B-206 to 178B-224.]

(4) A Black-Covered Exercise Book   179B-iii
    20 x 16 cms.

    A label shows that it was bought in Frankfurt
    A.M.
    Folios 1-9(a) are written by Jelka Delius.
    Folios 10 and 11(a) are blank.
    Folios 11(b) and 12 are again in Jelka Delius's
    hand.
    The rest are blank.

    The jottings:

    (i) the record of a conversation between
        Percy Grainger and Frederick Delius on
        the subject of musical influences in the
        work of Ravel and himself dated 19.2.23;

    (ii) dated 5.2.23 records Delius's outraged
         feelings at a Bad Oeynhausen spa hotel
         when the band started to play, and a dream
         he has had of walking over moors in Norway;

    (iii) dated 31.3.27,) are dictations concern-
) ing his life from his
    (iv) dated 1.4.27, and) first meeting with Grieg
) in Leipzig 1887 to his
    (v) dated 1927.8.4   ) moving to Grez in 1897.

Highlights described are the private
performance of *Florida* in 1888, the
Jotunheim trip of 1889, a holiday in
Jersey 1890 and details of his winter
in Croissy 1889-90, such as the landlady's
'pot au feu', the old gardener and skating
on the frozen Seine.

(5) Dictated memoir on verso (concluded recto)
of a typed addressed envelope directed to
Frederick Delius from Geneva pmk 31-11-1927
[microfilm 1 item 81].

From Dale we went to Skien/over inland
lakes and by/[k]erriol [sic], where we
spent the/night. Holter left for Xania/
and I stayed alone to/see the Exhibition./
Going from there back/to Fredricksvaern
[sic] where I stayed till/the beginning
of November associat-/ing a great deal/
with the painter Hjal-/mar Johnson. I
left/on Nov 4th for Paris/via Sweden and
Copen-/hagen for Paris. In/Copenhagen
I stayed/at the Phenix Hotel and/met
Helge Rode with/*whom I spent the evening.*

* ... * written on recto of envelope.

Note: Since these letters show Delius in Copenhagen
in 1896 and 1899 yet back in Paris by November, we
must assume another year, possibly 1891. We know from
the Grieg and Holter letters in the Archive of the
Delius Trust that Delius stayed in Norway late into
the Autumn to hear his overture *Paa Vidderne* performed
under Iver Holter's baton in Christiania [Oslo] on 10
October 1891; and that he spent much time in
Fredriksvaern [Stavern] which was the home of the
marine painter, Hjalmar Johnsen. See Rachel Lowe,
'Frederick Delius and Norway' in *A Delius Companion*
edited by C. Redwood (London: John Calder, 1976),
pp. 167-185; and L(K)C & RT/DALP, p. 22.

Grainger to Introduce Delius Concerto at Philharmonic.

At the next Philharmonic concert Percy Grainger will introduce the Delius piano concerto to America. Grainger is said to consider Delius the greatest of all living composers and the concerto one of the most musically significant works in this work produced in many years.

In a recent letter to his young Australian interpreter Delius wrote from London:

"I should like no one better than you, dear friend, to play my Concerto in America, and in confiding it to you, I feel that your own genius will light it up from beginning to end.

"In your hands its destiny is safe and it will be of great interest to me to learn how the Americans like it. Again I repeat that it is a great joy and satisfaction to me to know that it will be you to introduce my work to America."

Grainger made a sensation when he played the Delius Concerto at the Torquay (England) Festival three years ago, and since then this original and appealing composition has become a great and ever-increasing favorite.

Publication Office
437-439 Fifth Ave.
New York.

The Attached Clipping Appeared in the

MUSICAL COURIER
Weekly Review OF THE World's Music

Issue of _____

Delius Accepts Grainger's Invitation to Visit United States

In spite of delicate health, Frederick Delius, the great English composer (who is a great sufferer from nervous rheumatism) is planning to journey especially from Italy to America in order to hear two of his largest and most important works presented for the first time to American audiences under the baton of his friend and fellow composer, Percy Grainger, at Bridgeport, Conn., on April 28, and at Carnegie Hall, New York City, on April 30. In this connection Percy Grainger recently received the following letter from Delius:

Villa Raggio, San Ambrogio,
Rapallo, Italy.
January 23, 1924.

Dear Percy:

We are sitting in the sunshine on the terrace of our villa overlooking the lovely bay of Rapallo and talking of you; and we were wondering whether ever any other composer had met with a colleague and friend like you, so devoted and interested in his friend's work, and understanding it through his own genius. I am awfully pleased that you have done the two-piano arrangement of The Song of the High Hills, and am most eager to hear it or see it. Your arrangement of my Dance Rhapsody is so wonderfully good; I am very keen, therefore, to hear the effect of this one.

It is simply splendid that you are really giving the two concerts with chorus and orchestra, and a finer consecration than this of April 30 (as the anniversary of the death of your dear mother) could not be imagined. We shall come, of course. It will be so charming to stay with you and hear all this music and hear you conducting again. We shall probably come straight from Italy and in time for the rehearsals. It is too good a thing to miss!

Ever your loving friend,
(Signed) FREDERICK DELIUS.

TWO NEWSCLIPPINGS FROM PERCY GRAINGER'S COLLECTION:

The Musical Leader (Chicago), 18/11/1915

Musical Courier (N.Y. City), 17/4/1924

Photograph by courtesy of the Grainger Museum Board,
University of Melbourne.

NEWSCLIPPINGS FROM PERCY GRAINGER'S COLLECTION

Concerning Matters Discussed in the Letters

DATE	JOURNAL	TITLE AND/OR CONTENT	AUTHOR
		1912	
23/12/1912	The Standard (London)	The Beecham Orchestra Congratulations from Dr. Strauss [Concert in the Blüthner Hall Dec. 21 concluding a month's tour.] [Richard Strauss 'warmly applauded the performance of a Delius piece and Grainger's Mock Morris ...']	Berlin correspondent 22 December
		1915	
? 1915	Musical Courier (N.Y. City)	Nov. 26 1915, Carnegie Hall, New York New York Philharmonic, cond. Josef Stransky Advance Publicity The Genius of Frederick Delius [one and a half columns]	
18/11/1915	The Musical Leader (Chicago)	Grainger to introduce Delius Concerto at Philharmonic [quotes a eulogistic paragraph from Delius to Grainger authorising him to introduce the concerto to America]	Percy Grainger

DATE	JOURNAL	TITLE AND/OR CONTENT	AUTHOR
21/11/1915	The Citizen (Brooklyn, N.Y.)	Best of Music/for B'klynites/Philharmonic Society Be-/gins Here Today./ [advertises the afternoon's opening of season concert and Friday afternoon, Nov. 26 in Carnegie Hall 'first performance in America of the new piano concerto of Frederick Delius, one of the foremost English composers ... solo ... Percy Grainger ...']	
21/11/1915	The New York Call	The Philharmonic Concert	
		Reviews	
27/11/1915	German Herold (N.Y. City)	Philharmonische Gesellschaft	
27/11/1915	The Evening World (N.Y. City)	Begins: 'Mr Stransky at the Philharmonic/ Society's concert in Carnegie Hall/yesterday afternoon ...'	
27/11/1915	Deutsches Journal (N.Y. City)	Matinee der Philharmoniker	Dr Heinrich Müller
27/11/1915	New York Evening Post	Music and Drama/Grainger Plays Delius	
27/11/1915	New York Evening Globe	Concerts Yesterday 'Percy Grainger was soloist yester-/day at the fourth Friday afternoon concert of the Philharmonic Society in Carnegie Hall ...'	
27/11/1915	New York Evening Sun	Begins: 'Way down on the Suwanee River or somewhere in a Florida orange grove ...' and continues with such remarks as 'a bully bit of piano literature'	

DATE	JOURNAL	TITLE AND/OR CONTENT	AUTHOR
27/11/1915	*The New York Times*	Philharmonic Concert Percy Grainger, Soloist, Plays/Delius's Piano Concerto.	
27/11/1915	*The Sun* (N.Y. City)	Delius Concerto/at Philharmonic Composition Based on Negro/Melody Is Played by/Percy Grainger.	
27/11/1915	*New York Tribune*	Glittering Pianoforte/Music by Mr. Grainger A Novelty at a Concert of the/Philharmonic Society./	H.E. Krehbiel
27/11/1915	*The Herald* (N.Y. City)	Philharmonic/and Mr Grainger/in New Concerto. Pianist and Orchestra Play for First/Time Here Music of Frederick/Delius Written in 1897.	
28/11/1915	*Staatszeitung* (N.Y. City)	Philharmonisches Konzert	
28/11/1915	*Revue* (N.Y. City)	Concerte der/vergangenen Woche Philharmonische Gesellschaft	
10/12/1915	*Town & Country* (New York)	'... Last week it was the [Delius] concerto in C minor for piano and orchestra played by Percy Grainger and the Philharmonic Orchestra with great success ...'	

DATE	JOURNAL	TITLE AND/OR CONTENT	AUTHOR
		Nov. 28 1915, Aeolian Hall, New York New York Symphony, cond. Walter Damrosch <u>Publicity</u>	
27/11/1915	*New York Commercial* [*Advertiser*?]	Notes of the Music World	
27/11/1915	*New York Evening Post*	New York Symphony Orchestra	
27/11/1915	*Review* (N.Y. City)	Julia Culp Soloist/with Mr. Damrosch/Tomorrow Afternoon [A second paragraph advertises 'Two Mood Pictures by Delius ...'.]	
28/11/1915	*New York Tribune*	Impressions Made by the/First Quarter of the Season The Onrush of Concert Givers of All Sorts - Notes on/Some Novelties. [The last paragraph advertises the Delius items for the afternoon's concert at the Aeolian Hall.]	E.H. Krehbiel
		<u>Reviews</u>	
29/11/1915	*The Sun* (N.Y. City)	Symphony Society/Gives Delius Music Two Pieces Heard Here for/First Time at Afternoon/Concert. [*Summer Night on the River* and *On Hearing the First Cuckoo in Spring*. Grainger's excellent programme notes.]	
29/11/1915	*New York Evening Post*	Sunday Concerts	
29/11/1915	*The New York Times*	Notable Concerts/Crowd City Halls	

DATE	JOURNAL	TITLE AND/OR CONTENT	AUTHOR
2/12/1915	*The Nation* (N.Y. City)	Nov. 26 and 28 in Retrospect Cutting from the week's music column concerning 1) the Delius Piano Concerto: N.Y. Phil.; pianist Grainger; cond. Josef Stransky. *Summer Night on the River* and *On Hearing the First Cuckoo in Spring*; N.Y. Symph., cond. Walter Damrosch. 2) Folksongs and Dances. Article on *Sixty Folksongs of France* pub. Oliver Ditson Coy. ed. Julien Tiersot - surveys the European folksong renaissance in general and claims that Percy Grainger is doing for English folksong what Grieg did for Norway. [See PG/FD 2 December 1915, GM93-23.]	Henry T. Finck

1923

DATE	JOURNAL	TITLE AND/OR CONTENT	AUTHOR
28/11/1923	*Manitoba Free Press* (Winnipeg)	With the Pianists Wordless Song Attempt/Upheld by Grainger [Grainger's comments on modern music, especially Delius, during his stay as assisting artist with the Winnipeg Male Voice Choir.]	

1924

DATE	JOURNAL	TITLE AND/OR CONTENT	AUTHOR
		The Concerts of the Bridgeport Oratorio Society, Bridgeport, Conn., April 28 and Carnegie Hall, New York, April 30. Orchestra: Selected from New York Philharmonic; Cond. Frank Kasschau and Percy Grainger Publicity Notices in Advance and Retrospect	
10/4/1924	*Musical Courier* (N.Y. City)	Grainger's Choral and Orchestral Concerts	
17/4/1924	*Musical Courier* (N.Y. City)	Delius Accepts Grainger's Invitation to Visit/ United States	
18/4/1924	*The Musical Leader* (Chicago)	Delius Coming to United States [Includes photograph of PG and FD in Frankfurt and prints a letter from Delius to Grainger dated 23 January 1924 from Rapallo, Italy, written for publication.]	
25/4/1924	*The Musical Leader* (Chicago)	Grainger's Tribute to the/Late Dr. Arthur Mees [former conductor of the Bridgeport Oratorio Society]	
2/5/1924	*The Musical Leader* (Chicago)	Delius's Visit Postponed [a 'severe attack of nervous rheumatism from which he is a great sufferer']	
8/5/1924	*Musical Courier* (N.Y. City)	Grainger's Tribute to the late Dr Mees	

DATE	JOURNAL	TITLE AND/OR CONTENT	AUTHOR
		Reviews	
1/5/1924	*New York Evening Post*	Delius and Grainger Novelties in Carnegie Hall Concert	Henry T. Finck
1/5/1924	*The Sun* (N.Y. City)	Bridgeport Choir Makes Debut Grainger and Kasschau Conduct Oratorio Society's Concert in Carnegie Hall	W.J. Henderson
1/5/1924	*The Evening World* (N.Y. City)	Realm of Music	Frank H. Warren
1/5/1924	*The World* (N.Y. City)	Music/The Grainger Concert	Deems Taylor
1/5/1924	*New York Herald Tribune*	Grainger Gives/Delius Works/N.Y. Premiere Leads Orchestra of 94 and/Bridgeport Oratorio So/ciety Chorus of 200 in/ Program at Carnegie Hall	F.D. Perkins
1/5/1924	*The New York Times*	Music/Voices of Bridgeport	Olin Downes

1926

DATE	JOURNAL	TITLE AND/OR CONTENT	AUTHOR
		April 30 1926, Los Angeles Concert	
		Reviews	
1/5/1926	*Evening Herald* (Los Angeles)	Gra[i]nger Is Star Of/Oratorio Program	Carl Bronson

DATE	JOURNAL	TITLE AND/OR CONTENT	AUTHOR
1/5/1926	*Los Angeles Evening Express*	Unique Choral/Concert Stirs. Ovation for Grainger, John/Smallman and Oratorio/Society [Grainger·conducts his *Fadir og Dotir* and Delius's *The Song of the High Hills*]	B.D.U.
		1934	
17/6/1934	*The New York Times*	Frederick Delius/Late Composer Not a Nationalist-Poetic/Content of His Work	Olin Downes
17/6/1934	*The Sunday Times* (London)	Delius/The End of a Chapter in Music	Ernest Newman

NOTES